ARTHUR ALLOM DEL DALZIEL SC

JAPANESE LADY.

JAPAN:

AN ACCOUNT,

GEOGRAPHICAL AND HISTORICAL,

FROM

THE EARLIEST PERIOD AT WHICH THE ISLANDS COMPOSING THIS EMPIRE WERE KNOWN TO EUROPEANS,

DOWN TO THE PRESENT TIME,

AND THE

Expedition Fitted Out in the United States, etc.

BY

CHARLES MAC FARLANE, ESQ.,

AUTHOR OF "BRITISH INDIA," "LIFE OF WELLINGTON," ETC., ETC.

With Numerous Illustrations.

NEW-YORK:

GEORGE P. PUTNAM & CO., 10 PARK PLACE.

MDCCCLII.

E. O. JENKINS, STEREOTYPER AND PRINTER,
114 Nassau Street

TO

THE HONORABLE BROWNLOW C. BERTIE,

OF THE 2d LIFE GUARDS.

MY DEAR SIR,

I inscribe this volume to you for two good and valid reasons,—1st. You take a greater interest in the country and people, of which the work treats, than any one in England with whom I have the pleasure of being acquainted. 2nd. You have, in the kindest and readiest manner, rendered very valuable assistance while I have been engaged in the compilation.

I am, my dear Sir,

With all respect and thankfulness,

Your devoted Servant,

CHARLES MAC FARLANE.

CANTERBURY, *July* 1, 1852.

CONTENTS.

BOOK VIII.

BOOK IX.

BOOK X.

BOOK XI.

LIST OF ILLUSTRATIONS.

PREFACE.

It appears to me erroneous to say—though it very commonly *is* said—that we know next to nothing of Japan and the Japanese. We possess, in books, old and new—but mostly old and voluminous—the means of knowing quite as much of them as we know of any other Eastern nation.

I have now before me (chiefly through acts of kindness presently to be acknowledged) what might almost be called a Japanese library, or a library about Japan, and its interesting inhabitants. These books are in Latin, Portuguese, Spanish, Italian, French, Dutch, German, and English. These books vary in date from 1560 to 1838. The contributions furnished by the Dutch, or by the German medical officers in their service, are, perhaps, the best as well as the most voluminous. It is therefore very unfair to state (and this too is frequently done) that the Dutch, in order to preserve their commercial monopoly, invariably endeavored to keep the rest of the world in ignorance as to the extra-ordinary empire of Japan.

Taking all these works as a fund of information, we may safely be said to know more of the Japanese than we knew of the Turks a hundred years ago. This arises out of the sociable disposition and habits of the Japanese, the great freedom enjoyed by the gentler sex in their country, and various other causes which will be made apparent in the course of this work.

My attention was first drawn to these subjects twenty years since, by a dear and excellent old friend—the late James Drummond, Esq., Commissary-General, Commissioner for settling English claims at Paris, after our crowning victory at Waterloo, &c. In early life Mr. Drummond was engaged in trade, and, passing for a Dutchman, he resided several years in Japan. Our acquaintance commenced at Brighton, where, in a well-stored, choice library, he had collected every work that had, up to that period, been published about the country. Besides lending me all these books, he gave me, in many a pleasant fireside conversation, a great deal of information derived from his own observation and experience. Of all this I took notes and memoranda, with the intention of producing some such work as the present; but I was called away from the subject by other literary occupations, and have never seriously returned to it until the American movement rendered it one of the foremost and most interesting topics of the day.

My dear old friend, with strong literary tastes, was well mated. Mrs. Drummond was a grand-niece of Smollett, and as fond of books and of quiet, unpretending literary society as was her husband. He died, at Tunbridge Wells, full of years and honored by the respect of all who knew him, in the year 1844: his lady died within a week after him, and was buried in the same grave with him. The expression of my praise or gratitude cannot reach their ears, but I feel a melancholy pleasure in thus recording them.

In compiling this volume, I have carefully consulted all the best authorities. These I have named in my foot notes and Appendix, so that those who wish to follow up the study may find therein a tolerably complete Index.

I have purposely avoided minutiæ, my present purpose being to give a broad, general view of the subject. I trust (but I may be mistaken) that I am too old a traveller, and too constant a reader of the voyages and travels of others, to be a *gobe-mouche*, or a credulous recipient of every tale that is told in such books. In using the facts collected by others, from the middle of the sixteenth century down to our own day, wherever there is anything which startles belief, or which is not confirmed and supported by several authorities, I have spoken of it doubtingly.

I cannot conclude this brief preface without some further expressions of gratitude. I have been indebted to my very old, learned, most ingenious, invaluable friend, Edwin Norris, Esq., of the Foreign Office and Royal Asiatic Society, for many hints and much information. To the Royal Asiatic Society I have been indebted for the use of many books and other materials. I am under the same obligation to Sir James Weir Hogg, to Professor Horace Hayman Wilson, and to the gentlemen employed in the Library of the East India House. My thanks to the Hon. Brownlow Bertie, for services of the like nature, appear on another page.

C. M. F.

THE

EMPIRE OF JAPAN.

FIRANDO OR FIAANGO.

BOOK I.

EUROPEAN INTERCOURSE.

In the year 1542, a Portuguese ship, bound for Macao in China, was driven from her course, and forced by a storm upon one of the islands of Japan, which were as yet unknown to the European world.* After great dangers and sufferings, she came safely to anchor in the harbor of Bungo, on the island of Kiusjú. Though vigilant and circumspect, the native government was not then adverse to intercourse with foreign nations: the Portuguese were received with courtesy and kindness, and freely allowed to traffic with the inhabitants. They were much struck with the beatuy, fertility, and high state of cultivation and populousness of the empire, and by the evident abundance of gold, silver, and copper. The honor of the first discovery of Japan, by the way of the Indies, is thus unquestionably due to the Portuguese, though it happened accidentally.

The first two of them who set foot on shore on this *terra incognita* were named Antonio Mota and Francesco Zeimoto. The Japanese have preserved portraits of them, which are said to be very curious and characteristic specimens of native art. It is quite evident that their memory must have been cherished with affection, and that the first impression they made on the Japanese must have been highly favorable to their own nation.

From this time, by an arrangement with the prince or viceroy of Bungo, a Portuguese ship, laden with woollen cloths, furs, manufactured silks, taffetas, and other commodities in request, was sent once a year to the same island. In 1549, only seven years after the discovery, a young Japanese fled to the Portuguese settlement at Goa, on the Malabar coast, and there meeting with some mis-

* Strictly, we ought to say, with the exception of the brief mention of the country made by the old Venetian traveller, Marco Polo. But the correctness of that illustrious Venetian was very much doubted in the sixteenth and seventeenth centuries. Modern research has fully established his reputation as a traveller and accurate observer.

sionaries of the Church of Rome, he was converted to the Christian faith, and baptized. Like many of the Japanese, he was shrewd, intelligent, and enterprising. He showed the Portuguese merchants the great gains they might make by extending their commerce in Japan, and by supplying other provinces with their manufactures; and he discoursed with the Jesuits as to the facility or possibility of Christianizing his countrymen. The Portuguese proceeded at once to act upon these double considerations, and to devise means for erecting a factory in Japan. The young Japanese was sent back to his native country on board a ship loaded with goods and presents, and some Jesuit fathers went with him to undertake the labors of spiritual conversion. In the latter number was Father Francisco Xavier, a joint founder, with Loyola, of the order of Jesuits, and who was subsequently canonized by his church. This high-born Spaniard had all the accomplishments and qualities most calculated to command success as a missionary among a people like the Japanese; and his zeal and courage were never surpassed by mortal man. Some of his friends at Goa endeavored to turn him from his project, by representing the great length of the voyage—good thirteen hundred leagues—the great risk of falling among Malay pirates, who pitilessly massacred all the prisoners they took; the dangers of the rocky coasts of Japan, which had not been surveyed by any mariner; the dangers of whirlpools which were known to exist there; and the perils of those tremendous hurricanes called typhons, which prevail at certain seasons on the ocean between Japan and China. But the ardent propagandist said it were a shame that he should be afraid to venture for the sake of religion where sailors and merchants went for the mere love of worldly gain; that missionaries ought to have as much courage as they; and that he felt it was the will of God that he should go.* He went, and truly wondrous was the success which attended him.

The Portuguese,—mariners, merchants, padres and all,—were received with open arms, not only at Bungo, but at whatsoever other part of the empire they chose to repair unto. The local governments and the minor princes, who then enjoyed a considerable degree of independence, vied with each other in inviting them to their ports and towns. They went wherever they pleased, from one extremity of the empire to the other, and by land as well as by sea. The merchants found a ready and a most profitable market for their goods; the missionaries, an intellectual, tolerant people, very willing to listen to the lessons which they had to teach them. There was no *one* established, dominant religion in the country; the most ancient faith was split into sects; and there were at least three other religions imported from foreign countries, and tolerated in the most perfect manner. Moreover, a faith, said to be of Brahminical origin, and which had been imported from India, was, at the time, widely spread among the people.† This faith bore so near a resemblance to the doctrines intro-

---

* Père Bouhours, "Vie de Saint François Xavier, Apôtre des Indes et du Japan."

Other interesting notices of the first proceedings of the Christian missionaries in Japan will be found in the following works:—Padre G. Marini, "Delle Missioni del Giapone, etc." 4to. Roma, 1663; F. Luigi Frois, "Avvisi Nuovi del Giapone, etc." Venezia, 1586; and C. W. King, "Claims of Japan and Malaysia upon Christendom, exhibited in Notes of Voyages made in 1837." 2 vols. 8vo. New York, 1839.

† At one time it appears to have been universal.

duced by the Portuguese, that it must have greatly favored their reception. It appears to have comprised the *existence, death, and resurrection of a Saviour born of avirgin,* with almost every other essential dogma of Christianity, including the belief in the Trinity. If this be a true statement and correct description, and if we then add to it the tradition, that this form of religion was introduced under the reign of the Chinese emperor Mimti, who ascended the throne in about the fiftieth year of the Christian era, can we avoid admitting the conclusion, that some early apostle reached the eastern extremity of Asia, if not the islands themselves of Japan?* Then the pomp and impressive ceremonials of the Roman church, and the frequency of its services, delighted the impressionable Japanese, who, in all probability, would have paid far less attention to a simpler form of worship. The first missionaries, moreover, were men of exemplary lives —modest, virtuous, disinterested, and most tender and charitable to the poor and afflicted. They sought out cases of distress; they attended the sick; and some knowledge they possessed of the superior science of medicine, as practised by the most advanced nations of Europe, was frequently of great benefit to the natives, and another means of facilitating their conversion. Xavier quitted Japan for China in 1551, and died on the second of December of the following year, at Shan-Shan, on the Canton river, not far from Macao;† but he left able and

---

* Meylan's Japan. "Quarterly Review," vol. lii. We believe that there is other evidence to show that the doctrines of Christianity were conveyed to India in the first century after the death of our Saviour.

† It is worthy of notice that poor Fernam Mendez Pinto, who by no means merits the very hard names bestowed upon him by a Spanish writer of romances and an English writer of plays, performed se-

enthusiastic missionaries behind him, and others soon repaired to the country.

It is said that the immediate successor of Xavier (he died in 1570) founded fifty churches, and baptized, with his own hands, more than 30,000 converts. These early missionaries are unanimous in their praise of the good, docile, kindly disposition of the natives ; and speak of them as eminently a grateful people. In one of his letters, the sainted Xavier says, "I know not when to have done when I speak of the Japanese. They are truly the delight of my heart."

The current of conversion, however, was not always smooth and unimpeded ; for, at this period of greatest success, we hear occasionally of a persecution, and, though less frequently, of an apostasy.

It was so much the more easy to the Portuguese to bring their trade into a flourishing condition, and at the same time to advance and support the conversion of the Japanese to the faith of our Saviour, as the neighboring city of Macao, in China, which they were then already possessed of, could furnish them at command with a sufficient stock of European and Indian commodities, and a competent number of priests. Their co-religionists the Spaniards, established at the city of Manilla, in the Phil-

---

veral voyages with the fearless missionary Xavier. He records, with great reverence, many of the learned father's deeds and disputations with the Bonzes, or native priests. It was not his fortune to be present at Xavier's death.

Not for the sake of my own humble performance, but for the sake of rescuing the fame of a brave, adventurous, and much-traduced sailor, I would recommend the reader to a short account of his life and adventures contained in my little book called the "Romance of Travel," vol. ii. p. 104 to p. 192.

ippine Islands, not very remote from Japan, were likewise at hand to assist them in case of need ; and the city of Goa itself, as the Rome of India, and the metropolis of all the Portuguese dominions in the East, though at a greater distance, yet could easily, and without prejudice to its own inhabitants, send over fresh recruits of ecclesiastics. Hence it is not matter of wonder that the Portuguese should, in a short time, attain to a high pitch of fortune in this insular empire.*

These local advantages and facilities of the Portuguese for any enterprise on the country were in themselves enough to awaken the jealousy of that Asiatic government; but many years passed ere any such feeling disturbed the intercourse. Perhaps, however, the comparative weakness of the central government, and insubordination and almost independence of many of the provinces, promoted the interests of the strangers as much as any other circumstance or cause then in operation. It is evident, from some of the early missionaries, that several of the princes or viceroys paid no attention to the edicts of the emperor.†

About the year 1566, the Portuguese first pointed out to the prince of Omura the great advantages of the harbor of Nagasaki over the ports they had been accustomed to frequent. Their suggestions led to the formation of a settlement, which, ere long, became an important city, and which retains a somewhat unhappy celebrity down to our own day.‡

---

* Kämpfer, "History of Japan."

† Fernam Mendez Pinto says that the emperor was recently dead, and that the Japanese were for some time engaged in a civil war.

‡ C. W. King, "Notes of the Voyage of the *Morrison* from Canton to Japan." New York, 1839.

The traders brought their cloths, silks, European stuffs, wines, drugs, medicines, and a great variety of other goods, and in return became possessed of "the golden marrow of the country." The missionaries had to struggle for some time with the difficulties of the language.

"At first, the fathers, being unacquainted with the policy, customs, manners, and language of the Japanese, were obliged to get their sermons and lessons to the people translated into Japanese by not over-skilful interpreters, and the Japanese words written in Latin characters, which being done, they read out of these papers what they did not understand themselves, and in a manner, as may be easily imagined, which could not but expose them to the laughter of the less serious part of their audience. But in process of time, when they came to familiarize themselves with the natives, learning their language, studying their religion, their customs, and inclinations, they then met with a success infinitely beyond their expectations. The number of converts, particularly upon the island of Kiusjú (Kewsew), where they first settled, was almost inconceivable, and this the rather, as the princes of Bungo, Arima, and Omura, did not only openly espouse the interest of the Christian religion, but were converted themselves and baptized."*

The Jesuits, after giving them a careful education, admitted a good number of young natives into their Society.

The Japanese Christians even went so far as to send an embassy, consisting of seven persons, well furnished with

---

* Kämpfer. See also Arnold Montanus and the other early Dutch writers; also Thunberg's travels.

letters and presents, to the city of Rome, there to do homage to Pope Gregory XIII., and to assure his holiness of their entire submission to his church. Being very long on their voyages and journeys, they did not reach the Eternal City until the year 1585, when they were present at the inthronization of Gregory's successor, Pope Sixtus V. Returning homewards, they did not reach Japan again until 1590, thus having been absent eight years from their country.* In the course of the two years which followed on their return (1591–2), no fewer than 12,000 Japanese are said to have been converted and baptized. It is even stated that the emperor then reigning, with many of his courtiers and of the chiefs of his army, professed a strong inclination to the Jesuits, and the doctrines which they had taught with such signal success. Yet the heathen priests, who found that they were losing both their revenues and their influence with the people, had influence enough at court to procure a proclamation, forbidding, under pain of death, the practice or profession of the Christian religion; and there were occasional and fierce outbreaks of fanaticism and persecution. It should appear, however, that these were directed solely against the native converts, and that the Portuguese remained exempt from any serious molestation. Many of them married native ladies of the best families—of course baptized. The merchants in their trade, and the priests in the propagation of their gospel, prospered equally well. The three ports that were most used were Bungo, Firando, and Nagasaki. The gain upon the goods imported was at least cent. per cent., and their profits on the goods they ex-

* An account of this remarkable embassy to Rome is given by Thuanus in his history.

ported were very high. It is confidently asserted that upwards of 300 tons of gold, silver, and copper were exported every year; for at that period the Portuguese had full liberty to import and export whatsoever they pleased, without limitation as to quantity. They traded in fine large ships, the arrival of which was always held as a holiday by the natives. "It is believed," says the valuable old German writer, whom we frequently follow, "that had the Portuguese enjoyed the trade to Japan but twenty years longer, upon the same footing as they did for some time, such riches would have been transported out of this Ophir to Macao, and there would have been such a plenty and flow of gold and silver in that town, as sacred writ mentions there was at Jerusalem in the time of Solomon."*

The Portuguese were at this period, with the exception of the Italians, as civilized a nation as any in Christendom; elegant in their attire and manners, fond of the arts and of music and poetry. Traces of their civilization are yet distinguishable among the upper classes of Japanese, curiously blended with the Chinese and Indian elements of civilization. Old Kämpfer, who loves to trace resemblances and affinities of races, says that there was a certain natural resemblance between the minds, dispositions, and inclinations of the Japanese and Portuguese, "both being born nearly under the same clime." The misfortune of the Portuguese was, that they allowed themselves to be overstocked with monks and missionaries, and fell themselves into a morbid state of ultra devotion.

If the English nation undertook as yet nothing, in this direction, on its own account, it was to the skill, science, and courage of an Englishman that the Dutch owed their

* Kämpfer.

first access to Japan, and the first advantages they acquired in the country. This remarkable man has left us a most curious and interesting account of himself and his adventures. He was born about the middle of the reign of Elizabeth. "Your worships shall understand that I am a *Kentish man*, born in a town called Gillingham, two English miles from Rochester, and one mile from Chatham, where the queen's ships do lie; and that, from the age of twelve years, I was brought up in Limehouse, near London, being 'prentice twelve years to one master, Nicholas Diggins, and have served in the place of master and pilot in her majesty's ships, and about eleven or twelve years served the worshipful company of the Barbary merchants, until the Indian traffic from Holland began, in which Indian traffic I was desirous to make a little experience of the small knowledge which God had given me.

"So, in the year of our Lord God 1598, I hired myself for chief pilot of a fleet of five sail of Hollanders, which was made ready by the chief of their Indian company, Peter Vanderhaeg, and Hans Vanderguct; the general of this fleet was called Jacques Mayhay, in which ship, being admiral, I was pilot."*

The fleet, or squadron, set sail from the Texel on the 24th of June, 1598, in the last years of Queen Elizabeth.

In those days long voyages were seldom attempted with impunity. Before the Dutch crossed the line, sickness broke out in their ships, and they were forced to touch at the coast of Guinea, where many of their men died. The admiral, or, as he was called in those days, the general, died before they reached the Guinea coast. After other

* Purchas, "His Pilgrimes."

calamities, they reached the Straits of Magelhaens at the beginning of April, 1599, "at which time the winter came, so that there was much snow: and our men, through cold on the one side and hunger on the other, grew weak." Though the straits had seldom been passed by ships from Europe, and were very imperfectly known, bold William Adams, our true English pilot, preferred going through them to doubling Cape Horn.

"We had the wind at N. E. some five or six days, in which time we might have passed through the straits; but, for refreshing of our men, we waited, watering and taking in of wood, and setting up of a pinnace of fifteen or sixteen tons in bigness. At length, we would have passed through, but could not by reason of the southerly winds, with wet and also very cold, with abundance of snow and ice. Wherefore, we were forced to winter and stay in the straits from the 6th of April until the 24th of September, in which time the most part of our provisions were spent, in so much that for lack of victuals many of our men died through hunger." At last they got through the perilous passage into the Pacific. But storms dispersed the fleet. After waiting on the coast of Chili eight-and-twenty days, in the hope of being joined by the others, the *Erasmus*, which was piloted by Adams, made sail for the island of Mocha. While they stayed on the Chilian coast, they found the natives "good of nature; but, by reason of the Spaniards, they would not deal with us at the first; but then they brought us sheep and potatoes, for which we gave them bells and knives, whereof they were very glad; but, in the end, the people went up from their houses into the country, and came no more unto us." Wherever these early navigators penetrated, they were met by the malice and sharp jealousy of the Spaniards and Portuguese, who had obtained a good footing in those regions before them.

"The 1st of November we came to the isle of Moka, lying in the latitude of 38°. Having much wind, we durst not anchor, but directed our course for the island of Santa Maria, where, having no knowledge of the people, our men went on land, and the people of the land fought with our men, and hurt eight or nine; but, in the end, they made a false composition of friendship, which our men did believe. The next day our captain and three-and-twenty of our chief men went on land, meaning for merchandise to get victuals, having wonderful hunger. Two or three of the people came straight to our boat in friendly manner, with a kind of wine and roots, making tokens to come and land, and signs that there were sheep and oxen. Our captain with our men, having great desire to get refreshments for the ship, went on land. The people of the country lay in ambush, a thousand and more, and straightway fell upon our men, and slew them all; among which was my poor brother Thomas Adams. By this loss we had scarce so many men whole as could weigh our anchor."

A day or two after this calamity they fell in with one of their missing ships, which had another story of woe to tell, having had the captain and twenty-seven men killed at the island of Moka.

"Now we took council what we should do to get victuals. To go on land by force we had no men; for the most part were sick. There came a Spaniard by composition to see our ship; and so the next day he came again, and we let him depart quietly. The third day came two Spaniards aboard us, without pawn (pledge), to see if they could betray us. When they had seen our ship, they would have gone on land again; but we would not let them, showing that they came without leave, and we would not let them go on land again without our leave; whereat they were greatly offended. We showed them that we had extreme need of victuals; and that if they would give us so many sheep, and so many beeves, they should go and land. So against their wills they made composition with us, which, within the time appointed, they did accomplish. Having so much refreshing as we could get, we made all things well again, our men being for the most part recovered of their sickness (by reason of the beef and mutton)."

The pilot of the other ship was also an Englishman, one Timothy Shotten by name, "who had been with Mr. Thomas Cavendish in his voyage round the world." Shotten and Adams were old friends, and about equally enterprising. They heard that the Spaniards had overpowered one of their fleet; but they could learn nothing of the fate of the other two ships that were missing. In all probability they had foundered at sea. A new captain being appointed in Adams's ship, a council was held as to what they should do to make their voyage most profitable. They had a great quantity of woollen cloths; and had evidently left Europe with no very decided plan as to the market they were to seek. "At last it was resolved to go for Japan; for, by report of one Dirreck Gerritson, which had been there with the Portugals, woollen cloth was in great estimation in that island; and we gathered, by reason that the Malaccas, and the most part of the East Indies, were hot countries where woollen cloths would not be much accepted. Therefore it was we all agreed to go for Japan."

It was on the 29th of November, 1599, that they shaped

their course, favored by the trade-wind, "which continued good for divers months." William Adams believed that they fell among cannibals. "In our way across the South Sea we fell in with certain islands, in 16° of north latitude, the inhabitants whereof are men-eaters. Coming near these islands, and having a great pinnace with us, eight of our men being in the pinnace, ran from us with the pinnace; and, as we suppose, were eaten of the wild men, of which people we took one."

In latitude 27° or 28° they encountered variable winds and very stormy weather. On the 24th of February, 1600, the ships lost sight of each other, and never met again. Poor Adams could only conjecture as to the fate of the other ship and his good friend the English pilot, Master Timothy Shotten. Of the five ships which had quitted Holland, there remained but one. Adams, however, did not give way to despair.

"Nevertheless, we still did our best, directing our course for Japan. The four-and-twentieth of March, we saw an island, called Una Colonna; at which time many of our men were sick again, and divers dead. Great was the misery we were in, having no more than nine or ten men able to go or creep upon their knees; our captain, and all the rest, looking every hour to die. But on the 11th of April, 1600, we saw the high land of Japan, near unto Bungo; at which time there were no more than five men of us able to go. The 12th of April we came hard to Bungo, where many country barks came aboard us, the people whereof we willingly let come, having no force to resist them. And at this place we came to an anchor."

It should appear that the Japanese were not then so remarkable for their honesty as they have since been found.

"The people offered us no hurt, but stole all things that they could steal; for which some paid dearly afterward.

"The next day, the king of that island sent soldiers aboard, to see that none of the merchants' goods were stolen. Two or three days after, our ship was brought into a good harbor, there to abide till the principal king of the whole country had news of us, and until it was known what his will was to do with us. In the mean time we got favor of the king of that place, to get our captain and sick men on land; and we had a house appointed us, in which all our men were laid, and had refreshing given them. After we had been there from five or six days, a Portugal Jesuit, with other Portugals, and some Japanese that were Christians, came from a place called Nangasaki; which was ill for us, the Portugals being our mortal enemies, who reported that we were pirates, and were not in the way of merchandising."

Whatever may have been the case in Master Adams's ship, most of the vessels, not Spaniards or Portuguese, that ventured into the Pacific and to these eastern parts of the world, at this period, certainly resorted to piratical or buccaneering expedients. Nor could it well be otherwise. In their restrictive commercial policy, the Spaniards and Portuguese, who, by virtue of a papal bull, claimed all the new, and good half of the old world, would not allow any share of the trade to Dutch, English, French, or any other nation of Christendom. If they found any weak unarmed vessel trading on the coast of South America, or elsewhere, they seized her as contraband, and treated all on board as thieves and smugglers. As it was not to be expected that their extravagant claim would be allowed, or that the bull of a pope (who did not, and who could not, at the time, understand the geography of the earth, or the extent of his donation) should be respected by nations of the reformed churches, who had long since renounced his authority, the adventurers to the South Seas took care to arm their ships, and to go generally in squadrons. In this way they traded where they could with the natives, boldly fought the Spaniards or the Portuguese, who would not allow a fair trade, seized and plundered their ships, and, not unfrequently, making descents on their coast, did the same by their towns and cities. These romantic adventures belong to the history of the buccaneers.* It is enough for our present purpose to say that these practices (provoked by Spanish and Portuguese presumption, jealousy, harshness, and, not unfrequently, atrocious cruelty) prevailed all through the reign of Elizabeth, James I., and Charles I., and that they did not entirely cease until the peace of Ryswick, in the time of William III., when a little freedom of commerce was allowed by Portuguese and Spaniards, and when other nations were becoming more powerful than they on the Pacific and in the East. During all the long period we have mentioned, it was the common saying of English sailors, that there was no peace beyond the Line, or that European treaties did not extend to the Spanish Main or the South Sea. But to return to honest Master Adams.

"The evil report of the Jesuits and Portuguese caused the governor and common people to think ill of us, in such manner that we looked always when we should be

---

* The best and most authentic history of these daring adventurers is that by Admiral Burney.

A condensed account will be found in MacFarlane's "Banditti and Robbers by all Nations."

set upon crosses, which is the execution in this land for piracy and some other crimes. Thus daily more and more the Portugals incensed the justices and people against us. And two of our men, as traitors, gave themselves in service to the king, being all in all with the Portugals, having by them their lives warranted. The one was called Gilbert de Canning, whose mother dwelleth at Middleburg, who gave himself out to be the merchant of the goods in the ship; the other was called John Abelson Van Owater. These traitors sought all manner of ways to get the goods into their hands, and made known unto them all things that had passed in our voyage."

As the Portuguese, who had got so firm an establishment in Japan, and who were desperately tenacious of the monopoly of that trade, were also animated to a fanatical height by the *odium theologicum*—as they detested the Dutch and English as much in their quality of heretics, as in that of interlopers, it is more than probable that they would have seen Adams, the captain, and some of the crew crucified, with much inward satisfaction. To their numerous Christian converts among the Japanese, they represented the strangers as unbelieving heathens, wretches, and blasphemers.

But, fortunately, the case being submitted to the imperial court, then at Osacca, the emperor was pleased to order that Master Adams, with one of the mariners, should be brought before him.

"So, taking one man with me, I went to him, taking my leave of our captain, and all the others that were sick, and commending myself into *His* hands, that had preserved me from so many perils on the sea. I was carried in one of the great king's galleys to the court at Osacca, about eighty leagues from the place where the ship was.

The 12th of May, 1600, I came to the great king's city, who caused me to be brought into the palace, being a wonderful costly house, gilded with gold in abundance. Coming before the king, he viewed me well, and seemed to be kind and wonderful favorable. He made many signs unto me, some of which I understood, and some I did not. In the end there came one that could speak Portuguese. By him the king demanded of what land I was, and what moved us to come to his land, being so far off. I showed unto him the name of our country, and that our land had long sought out the East Indies, and desired friendship with all kings and potentates in way of merchandise, having in our land divers commodities, which these lands had not; and also to buy such merchandises in this land as our country had not."

Had William Adams, the pilot and mariner, been indoctrinated in the axioms of political economy, he could not have explained himself better; had he been inflated with the pedantry and conceit of the staticians and economists of our own day, he would not have done it half so well. He continues:—

"Then the great king asked whether our country had wars? I answered him, yea, with the Spaniards and Portugals, being in peace with all other nations. Further, he asked me in what I did believe? I said, in God that made heaven and earth. He asked me divers other questions of things of religion, and many other things, as what way we came to his country. Having a chart of the whole world with me, I showed him through the Straits of Magelhaens; at which he wondered, and thought me to lie. Thus, from one thing to another, I abode with him till midnight. And having asked me what merchandise we had in our ship, I showed him samples of all.

In the end, he being ready to depart, I desired that we might have trade of merchandise, as the Portugals had. To which he made me an answer, but what it was I did not understand. So he commanded me to be carried to prison. But two days after he sent for me again, and inquired of the qualities and conditions of our countries, of wars and peace, of beasts and cattle of all sorts, of heaven and the stars. It seemed that he was well content with all mine answers. Nevertheless, I was commanded to prison again; but my lodging was bettered in another place."

We consider these scenes, in the naïve, sailor-like manner in which they are described, as perfectly delightful, and know not which the more to admire, the laudable curiosity of the semi-barbarous oriental despot, or the evident promptness and straightforwardness of the English mariner and pilot. Our sea diplomacy has been nearly always our best.

"So," continues Adams, "I remained nine-and-thirty days in prison, hearing no news neither of our ship nor captain, whether he were recovered of his sickness, nor of the rest of the company. . . . Now in this long time of imprisonment, the Jesuits and the Portugals gave many evidences to the emperor against us, alleging that we were thieves and robbers of all nations, and if we were suffered to live it should be against the profit of his majesty and the land; for then no nation could come there without robbing; but if justice were executed on us, it would terrify the rest of our nation from coming there any more. And to this intent they sued to his majesty daily to cut us off, making all the friends they could at court to this purpose."

Verily the Portuguese were merciless enough to the

new comers; and verily, also, when their hour came, the Dutch were equally merciless in their revenge. In their conduct towards each other, these people gave a practical denial to the blessed doctrines they professed, and discredited Christianity in the eyes of an interesting people, who seem to have been, in a most remarkable manner, open to Christian conversion.

"At length the emperor gave the Jesuits and Portugals this answer: That as yet we had done no hurt or damage to him nor to any of his land, and that therefore it was against reason and justice to put us to death; and if our countries and theirs had wars one with the other, that was no cause that he should put us to death. The emperor answering them in this manner, they were quite out of heart, that their cruel pretence failed; for the which, God be praised for ever and ever!

"Now, in this time that I was in prison, the ship was commanded to be brought so near to the city where the emperor was as she might, the which was done. So the one-and-fortieth day of my imprisonment, the emperor called me before him again, demanding of me many questions more, which are too long to write. In conclusion, he asked me whether I were desirous to go to the ship to see my countrymen? I answered, that I would very gladly do it; so he bade me go. Then I departed, and was freed from imprisonment. And this was the first news that I had that the ship and company were come to the city.

"Wherefore, with a rejoicing heart, I took a boat and went to our ship, where I found the captain and the rest recovered of their sickness. But at our first meeting aboard we saluted one another with mourning and shedding of tears; for they were informed that I was executed, and long since dead. Thus, God be praised, all we that were left alive came together again."

Everything was now taken out of the ship, the nautical instruments of our pilot being much prized. But the emperor ordered that these things should be restored to him, and that 50,000 reals, in ready money, should be given to the captain and his people, to buy food and other necessaries. After a short time the vessel was ordered round to the eastern coast of the island of Quanto, near to the city of Jeddo, where the emperor now was. To their supplications to be allowed to take their departure with their ship, his majesty turned a deaf ear. Matters were made worse by the Dutch sailors, who broke out into mutiny, and wanted all the money and all other things that were given by the Japanese. If the poor pilot and captain had put to sea with such a crew, they would in all probability have been lost or put to death. When they had been two years in Japan, they received a positive denial as to the ship, and were told that they must make up their minds to live happily and peacefully in the country all the rest of their days. The Dutch dispersed themselves on the island, every man going where he thought best. By the emperor's order each was allowed about two pounds of rice a day, and about twelve gold ducats a year,—no niggardly allowance in a country where the commodities of life were so cheap. They seem to have been a coarse, uneducated, dull set of fellows, incapable of doing anything good for themselves or for others. Not so our clever English pilot, who made himself friends with his ingenuity and ability, and gradually rose in the estimation of the emperor himself, and ultimately attained to almost the highest honors that could be conferred on a man who was not a native and a member of the hereditary aristocracy of the country.

"So, in process of four or five years, the emperor called me, as he had done divers times before, and would have me to make him a small ship. I answered that I was no carpenter, and had little knowledge thereof. 'Well,' saith he, 'do it so well as you can; if it be not good, it is no matter.' Wherefore, at his command I built him a ship, of the burthen of eighty tons, or thereabouts; which ship being made in all proportions as our manner is, he coming aboard to see it, liked it well; by which means I came in more favor with him, so that I came often into his presence, and, from time to time, he gave me many presents."

In this ship-building, little more could have been wanted from Adams than the *lines*, and his directing eye, the natives being excellent carpenters, good smiths, and intelligent and expert in nearly every mechanical art.

Shortly after building this vessel, William Adams greatly improved his condition by becoming tutor to his good-natured, liberal-minded master.

"Now being in such grace and favor with the emperor, by reason I taught him some points of *geometry* and the *mathematics*, with other things, I pleased him so, that what I said could not be contradicted. At which my former enemies, the Jesuits and Portugals, did greatly wonder, and entreated me to befriend them to the emperor in their business; and so by my means, both Spaniards and Portugals have received friendship from the emperor, I recompensing their evil unto me with good."

At the end of five years Adams, who had a wife and children in England, and who was evidently a man of warm affections, once more entreated to be allowed to take his departure, and try to get back to his own country and home. The emperor could, on no account, spare so clever and useful a man. But Adams's Dutch captain, not having made himself so useful, was permitted to go. Poor fellow! he would have done better to stay where he was. Being carried in a Japanese junk to a place which is called Patane, he stayed there a year waiting for the appearance of some Dutch ship; seeing that none came, he went to another place, which Adams calls Ior, where he found a fleet of nine sail; "of which fleet the Hollander Matleef was general; and in this fleet he was made master again." These, as we have intimated, were stirring times, when swords, muskets, and great guns, were constantly called into play; and when the bravest men had the best chance. The Dutch fleet sailed to Malacca, and fought with a whole armada of Portuguese. The Dutch, we believe, gained the victory; but our poor skipper lost his life in the battle. Adams, who did not receive the intelligence until long after the catastrophe, was very much affected; for he had hoped that his captain might, by some means or other, get back to Europe, and tell of his whereabouts. The two interesting letters from which we are quoting, and which contain nearly all that we have of his adventures from his own pen, were addressed, one to his wife, and one to his "unknown friends and countrymen," who might chance to receive it somewhere, and transmit it to England. The first is incomplete, and without date.* The second bears the date of the 22nd of

* The honest, laborious old compiler, Samuel Purchas, says, in evident anger, "The rest of this letter, by the malice of the bearers, was suppressed."

October, 1611. It will be remembered that poor Adams sailed from Europe in June, 1598.

In his yearning after his home, and his grieving for the death of his Dutch captain, he says,—" So now I think no certain news will be known in England, whether I be living or dead. Therefore my desire is, that my wife and two children may somehow learn that I am here in Japan. My wife is in a manner a widow, and my children fatherless; which thing only is my greatest grief of heart and conscience."

The passage which immediately follows is exquisitely simple and homely; and made all the more delicious by the admixture of self-importance. We love to see the mariner and pilot thus boasting of his east London acquaintance on the shores of a remote, mysterious island in Japan:—

"I am a man," quoth Adams, "not unknown in Ratcliff and Limehouse. I am well known to my good master, Nicholas Diggins, and Mr. Thomas Best, and Mr. Nicholas Isaac, and Mr. William Isaac; also to Mr. William Jones, and Mr. Becket. Therefore, should this letter ever come to any of their hands, or the copy of this letter, I know that good company's mercy is such, that my friends and kindred shall have news that I do as yet live in this vale of my sinful pilgrimage; the which thing, again and again, I do desire for Jesu's sake." The pathos at the close of this passage is made the more pathetic by the words which precede.

In the first ship he built for the emperor, he made a coasting voyage or two with Japanese sailors. He then, at the emperor's command, built a second vessel, of the burthen of 120 tons. In this second ship he made a voyage from Miaco to the Bay of Jeddo, which he estimates at a distance about equal to that from London to the Land's End. Shipwrecks are rather frequent on those rocky coasts, lashed by a stormy sea. In the year 1609, a large Spanish ship, called the St. Francisco, was cast away upon the coast in the night, during which 160 men were drowned. But 340, or rather more, were saved; and among these was no less a personage than the governor of Manilla, whom the unfortunate ship was conveying to New Spain. This shipwrecked party was treated with great kindness, and the larger of the two vessels which William Adams had built was appointed to convey the governor to Acapulco. Here was another chance of getting back to England, but our home-sick pilot was not allowed to avail himself of it. The ship set sail in 1610; and in the next year the governor returned another ship in her stead, with very rich presents in goods and money, together with an envoy to the emperor, to give thanks for his great friendship, and request a continuance of it. When Adams wrote (in 1611), the Spaniards had his Japanese-built ship at the Philippine Islands. By this time he was living like a lord, and might have been happy indeed, if he could have had his wife and children with him, or even have communicated with them.

"Now, for my service which I have done, and daily do, being employed in the emperor's service, he hath given me a living like unto a lordship in England, with eighty or ninety husbandmen, who are as my servants and slaves. The precedent was never done before. Thus God hath provided for me, after my great misery; to his name be the praise for ever. *Amen.* Now whether I shall come out of this land I know not. Until this present year there hath been no means; but now, through the trade of the Hollanders, there may be means. In the year of our Lord 1609 two Holland ships came to Japan. Their intention was to take the Portugal carrack (great ship) which comes yearly from Macao, and being some five or six days too late for that prize, they came to Firando, and went to the court of the emperor, where they were in great friendship received, conditioning with the emperor to send yearly a ship or two: and so they departed with the emperor's free pass. [The prevalent negotiator on this delicate occasion was William Adams himself; and to our good English pilot the Dutch are really indebted for their first permission and license to trade with Japan.] Now this year, 1611, there is a small Holland ship arrived, with cloth, lead, elephants' teeth, damask, black taffeta, raw silk, pepper, and other commodities; and they have showed cause why they have missed the former year, 1610, according to promise to come yearly. This ship was well received, and with great kindness entertained."

From these Dutchmen, whom he befriended at court and elsewhere, Adams learned for the first time that the English were now driving a fair trade in the East Indies, and attempting to set up humble factories on the Malabar coast.* By means of some of these Englishmen in the East—some of whom, he presumed, must needs know him—he hoped to be able to send intelligence to his dear family, and to receive their news. His deep-seated anxiety in this respect goes to the heart, and moves one almost to tears. Wife, or child, he had not seen for the dreary space of thirteen years, almost as long a time as

* Our first attempt at a settlement in the East Indies was made in the year 1608, in the reign of James I.

that other fine specimen of a brave, pious English mariner, Robert Knox, passed in captivity on the island of Ceylon, among the Cingalese. The Cingalese were incomparably a more barbarous and cruel people than the Japanese; but Knox was a young man, and had neither wife nor child to grieve and pine after.

"Thus," says Adams, in conclusion, "I am constrained to write, hoping that, by one means or another, in process of time I shall hear of my wife and dear children: and so with patience I wait the good will and pleasure of God Almighty, desiring all those to whom this my letter may come, to use the means to acquaint my good friends with it, that so my wife and children may hear of me; by which means there may be hope that I may see my wife and children before my death: the which the Lord grant, to his glory and my comfort. *Amen.*"

Alas! he never had this comfort. Detained by the emperor, he lived many years on the island after writing the letter, and he died there, at Firando, in the year 1619 or 1620.* By this time the Dutch had well established their trade with Japan, and secured considerable interest and influence in the country. We know not whether they showed their gratitude by marking the grave of this remarkable man with a monument and inscription, or whether they caused inquiries to be made in England after his family, in order to confer some benefit on them. It is most likely that they did neither.

---

* Writing in 1621, old Purchas says that the news of his death was received by the last India ship which had just reached London. Allowing for the long, tedious voyages of that time, and for the very roundabout way by which the news was, in all probability, transmitted, we cannot safely place the death at a later period than 1619.

Such were the truly romantic incidents which attended the opening of Japan to the Dutch. In all this time of bold maritime adventure, in no part of the interesting, exciting folios of Samuel Purchas, is there any matter more interesting than that which is contained in these two letters of William Adams.* Our mariner and pilot does indeed deserve a high place in the list of the heroes of naval discovery and enterprise, and equally so among the diplomatists of commerce and civilization.† If, with anything like a security of his letters reaching England, he had written out all that he knew of the country, and given an ample account of his experience in it during so many years of residence, we, no doubt, should have had as delightful a book as that of Robert Knox, and about a people in every way more interesting than the inner-dwellers of Ceylon. The little he says is favorable on the whole. After mentioning the abundance of precious metals, he adds:—

"This land of Japan is truly a great land, and lieth to the northward, in the latitude of eight-and-forty degrees, and the southernmost part of it in five-and-thirty degrees, and the length of it, east by north, and west and by south (for so it lieth), is 220 English leagues. The breadth, south and north, thirteen degrees, twenty leagues to the degree. . . . . The people of this land of Japan are good of nature, courteous above measure, and valiant in war. Their justice is severely executed, without any partiality,

---

* See Purchas, "His Pilgrimes," vol. i. from p. 125 to p. 132. This invaluable work was published in 1625, a very few years after the death of Adams. The adventures will be found reprinted in a more accessible book: Harris's "Collection of Voyages," vol. i. p. 856. Also in Rundall's Memorials of Japan.

† "Quarterly Review," vol. lii.

upon the transgressors of the law; they are governed in great civility; I think no land better governed in the world by civil policy. The people are very superstitious in their religion, but are of divers opinions. There are many Jesuits and Franciscan friars in this land, and they have converted many to be Christians, and have many churches in the land."

The first Dutch factory, on a very humble scale, was established at Firando, where Adams breathed his last. Having in vain attempted to prevent its establishment, the Portuguese intrigued and labored hard to bring about its destruction. The hatred between the two European nations was as irreconcilable as it was violent—no gust of passion, but a deep-welling perpetual hatred. If the Portuguese called the Dutch vile Lutherans, schismatics, accursed heretics; the Dutch were always ready to retort by calling the Portuguese worshippers of wood and rotten bones, lying papists, foul idolaters. The religious animosities certainly led to many melancholy occurrences, and rendered it impossible that the two nations should live peaceably together in the same country; but the Romanist writers are incorrect in asserting that it was owing to the malice of the Dutch that the missionaries of their church and their native converts were first subjected to Japanese persecution. That persecution had commenced before William Adams reached the country, and before the name of the Dutch was known to the natives; and it appears to have originated, in good part, from the enmities and dissensions which broke out among the different monastic orders in the East. If the work of Japanese conversion had been left wholly in the hands of those who began it and made so rapid and wonderful a progress in it, we think it at least probable that there would have been no persecution at all, and that the great bulk of the population would have been brought within the pale of the Church of Rome. But the politic, wary, and accomplished Jesuits were soon far outnumbered by a host of Franciscan, Dominican, Augustine, and other friars, of more zeal than discretion, who flocked in from Goa, Malacca, Macao and other Portuguese settlements, and who, instead of conciliating the government and people, set their laws and usages at defiance. The Franciscans quarrelled with the Dominicans, and all the orders together quarrelled with the disciples of Loyola. There was then frequently exhibited the unseemly spectacle of one body of papists intriguing with heathens against another, and, that which was scarcely more decorous, a Japanese convert laboring to reconcile these foreign Christian rivals.

The greatest vice of the Japanese is incontinence. It is hinted that the struggles of the missionaries to subdue this vice contributed very materially to the overthrow of their church. The princes and great men would not put away their numerous concubines,—for them, the harem must go with the church. According to one account, it was the passion of love that led to the religious catastrophe. A prince (some say the emperor himself) became enamored of a Christian lady, and was transported into fury at finding that the fair one would not conform to the old, easy customs of the country.

Orders were issued by the imperial court that no more friars or missionaries of any kind should be admitted into the country; and the Portuguese captains and traders were strictly commanded not to bring any more in their ships; nevertheless, they continued to smuggle in fresh recruits of ecclesiastics. Certain Franciscan friars, who came from the Spanish settlements in the Philippines, formed processions, preached in the public streets of Miaco, and built a new church there, contrary to the imperial edict, and contrary to the advice and earnest entreaties of the Jesuit fathers. They had nothing to plead in justification of their rashness, but an ardent, impatient longing after the crown of martyrdom. In vain the Jesuits urged that such conduct would prove in the end not only fatal to their own persons, but highly prejudicial to the advancement of Christianity and the good of the Church. It was this indiscreet zeal that brought on the first serious persecution, in the year 1597, or three years before Adams and the Dutch reached the country. Japanese tradition concurs with the early Dutch writers in representing the crisis as having been precipitated by the pride, rapacity, and sensuality of the religious orders. It is said that even the native converts were astonished, and grew impatient, when they saw that their spiritual fathers aimed not only at the salvation of their souls, but had an eye also to their money and lands, and that their pride was so great, that they refused the prescribed marks of respect to men of the highest hereditary rank. In the same view, it is said that their growing riches and unexpected success in the propagation of the gospel wonderfully inflated them; that those who were at the head of the clergy thought it beneath their dignity to walk on foot any longer, in imitation of the apostles; that nothing would serve them but they must be carried about in stately chairs, mimicking the pomp of the Pope and his cardinals at Rome; that they not only put themselves upon a footing of equality with the greatest men of the empire, but, swelled with ecclesiastical pride, fancied that even a superior rank was nothing but their due. As an example, the following story is told, as a thing that happened in 1596, and led immediately to the great persecution. It chanced one day that a Portuguese bishop met upon the high road one of the greatest officers of state, who was on his way to court. The haughty prelate would not allow his chair or sedan to be stopped, in order to alight and pay his respects to the great man, according to the usages of the country, but, without showing him the common marks of civility, or taking the least notice of him, he turned his head aside in contempt, and ordered his bearers to carry him on. It is added, that so imprudent a step, at a time when the Portuguese had already lost the best part of that esteem and favor in which they had formerly been held, could not but be attended with fatal consequences, highly prejudicial to the interest of the whole nation; that the grandee, exasperated at the affront, conceived a mortal hatred to the Portuguese, and forthwith drew to the emperor an odious picture of their vanity, pride, and insolency.*

Such an incident may really have happened, and there may have been individual cases of rapacity and sensuality. We doubt, however, whether these vices were at all common or prevalent among the missionaries.

"These vices are usually the attendants of long and undisputed possession rather than of the circumstances in which these missionaries of a religion struggling into life were placed. It is likely that the hostility of their Dutch rivals may have magnified individual instances of such errors, and that the zeal of triumphant persecution may have perpetuated the imputation."†

---

* Kämpfer. He here follows Arnold Montanus and other early Dutch writers and compilers.

† "Quarterly Review," lii.

In 1597, twenty-six professing Christians were executed on the cross, there being in the number one or two Jesuits and several Franciscan friars. But most of them appear to have been native converts. The friars flew out too violently against idol-worship. Their neophytes, with all the zeal of a recent conversion, not only told their countrymen that so long as they continued their heathen worship they had nothing to expect but eternal damnation; but they even proceeded to insult the bonzes or priests, to overthrow their idols, and to pull down their temples. This provoked further persecution. The emperor, and his hitherto tolerant government, could see in these demonstrations nothing but an intention to revolutionize the whole state.

In the year 1612, when Adams was living tranquilly at Firando, and when the Dutch were as yet only beginning to establish their influence, a dreadful persecution commenced.* It raged with still greater fury in 1614, when many of the Japanese converts, who would on no account recant, suffered cruel deaths. The monks and friars were scattered; many left the country for good; but, apparently, as many more either concealed themselves or returned stealthily.

The crosses they had erected were cast down and trampled under foot; their schools were closed; their churches razed to the ground; their faith was declared infamous, subversive of all ancient institutions, and of all authority and government.

For a long time the persecution did not reach the

* "Précis de la Vie du Père Charles Spinola, de la Compagnie de Jésus." Par le R. Père d'Orléans, de la même Compagnie.

According to the Père d'Orléans, who wrote in the year 1680, the persecution of the Romanists in Japan had not yet terminated.

Portuguese merchants and traders. The Japanese could not dispense with the foreign commodities they brought them, and the Dutch trade was not sufficiently developed to promise a regular supply. But as they continued to smuggle in missionaries, the Portuguese were no longer allowed the free use of the ports, but were strictly limited to, and confined in, the little islet of Desima, in the harbor of Nagasaki. In the year 1622 a frightful massacre of native Christians and some of their foreign teachers was perpetrated on a rock in the immediate neighborhood of that place. The Jesuit father Spinola, a Dominican friar, and a Franciscan, were in the number of those who suffered, having been convicted of returning to the country after the emperor had decreed their perpetual expulsion. Horrible tortures were employed, of which harrowing and revolting representations are given in the illustrations of the books of several of the old Dutch writers.* The heroic constancy of the poor Japanese to the faith which they had embraced is an indubitable historical fact, attested as well by the Lutheran or Calvinist Dutch as by the Portuguese and other Romanists.

At this time the power and consideration of the Portuguese in the East was rapidly declining in all directions: the splendid Indian empire, which the great Albuquerque

---

* See especially the old quarto (A.D. 1670) of Arnold Montanus. These engravings are as horrible as anything in the old editions of Foxe's "Book of Martyrs."

It was in this year, 1622, that the Dutch disgraced themselves in the Molucca islands, by that dark deed which is known in our history under the name of "The Massacre of Amboyna." They put eighteen Englishmen to the rack, and afterwards cut off the heads of nine of them. One Portuguese and nine Japanese were put to death at the same time, as accomplices with the English.

had created for them, was falling to pieces; the Dutch were dispossessing them of Ceylon and other rich settlements, and gradually obtaining nearly all the profitable trade which they had monopolized for nearly a hundred years. To blacken the Dutch in Japan, and drive them from that trade, they now represented them to the emperor and government as rebels to their former sovereigns, the kings of Spain—always a weighty argument in a despotic country—they renewed the accusations of robbery and piracy, which they had made on Adams's first arrival, and they resorted to every calumny that commercial and national jealousy and sectarian and personal hatred could suggest.* We have cleared the Dutch from unfounded aspersions; but we now reach a point where their conduct is proved to have been of a nature to excite feelings very unfavorable them. Few will agree with Kämpfer, who says, that "surely the Dutch were not much to be blamed for whatever attempts they made to keep up their own credit, to clear themselves of the calumnies of the Portuguese, and withal, to take what revenge they could upon their enemies." Even Kämpfer himself, like an honest man, afterwards condemns what he here excuses or extenuates.

A Portuguese ship, on its way from the East to Lisbon, was captured by the Dutch near the Cape of Good Hope. Among other matters found on board the prize were certain treasonable letters to the king of Portugal, written by a native Japanese, styled by the Europeans

* Every old writer, being a member of the Roman Church, seems to have considered himself in duty bound to keep up the charge of *piracy*. The Père Bouhours, in his life of St. Francis Xavier, and Père d'Orléans, in his life of the missionary and martyr Spinola, never mention either English or Dutch except as *pirates*.

Captain Moro. This man had long been a principal agent of the Portuguese in the country, a close friend of the Jesuits, and a great zealot for the Roman Church. Whether the Jesuits themselves, or others of the missionaries, were privy to this correspondence, is not clearly proved; but there is reason at least to suspect that the force of circumstances had induced, or compelled, the Jesuits (the real agents of that conversion) to associate themselves with the disaffected native Christians, and with a native political party, in some civil feud which then distracted Japan. Their converts were so numerous, and could be increased with so much facility, that they may have entertained the not very unreasonable hope of being able, with some assistance from Europe, to overturn the old empire, and establish a new Christian dynasty. In other eyes besides those of the disciples of Loyola, such an end would have gone far to justify the means. The Dutch, rejoicing in so excellent an opportunity of finishing the ruin of the Portuguese, lost no time in laying the intercepted letters before their patron, the prince of Firando, who communicated them to the governor of Nagasaki, as supreme director and judge in foreign affairs. Poor Captain Moro, the Japanese Christain, was forthwith arrested. He stoutly denied the charge and the letters; but his own hand and seal were against him. His letters laid open the whole plot, which the Japanese Christians, in conjunction with some Portuguese, had laid against the emperor's throne. They also showed that all they wanted was a supply of soldiers and ships, which had been promised them from Portugal;* and, unhappily, they

* According to some accounts, they expected, from Europe and from the Portuguese settlements in Asia, a vast supply of arms and ammunition, many ships of war, with flat-bottomed boats for landing

revealed the names of the Japanese chiefs who had entered into the conspiracy, the success of which was to be crowned by the benediction of the Pope at Rome. It is also asserted that these discoveries were afterwards confirmed by another letter, written by Moro to the Portuguese government at Macao, which was intercepted and brought to Nagasaki by a Japanese vessel. Poor Moro was burned alive at a stake; and in the course of the year (1637) an imperial proclamation was issued, decreeing that "the whole race of the Portuguese, with their mothers, nurses, and whatever belongs to them, shall be banished for ever."

The same proclamation set forth that no Japanese ship or boat, or any native of Japan, should henceforth presume to quit the country under pain of forfeiture and death; that any Japanese returning from a foreign country should be put to death; that no nobleman or soldier should be suffered to purchase anything of a foreigner; that any person presuming to bring a letter from abroad, or to return to Japan after he had been banished, should die, with all his family, and that whosoever presumed to intercede for such offenders should be put to death, &c.; that all persons who propagated the doctrines of the Christians, or bore that scandalous name, should be seized and immured in the common jail, &c. A reward was offered for the discovery of every padre or priest, and a smaller reward for the discovery of every native Christian.*

---

on the coast, and 20,000 soldiers. Nearly all the details may be incorrect; but it seems to us impossible to deny the existence of an extensive conspiracy.

* Kämpfer. A. Montanus. Charlevoix, Hist. Japan. P. L. Frois, "Nuovi Avvisi del Giapone."

Some of the Portuguese were scared away at once; but others lingered in their narrow factory or prison at Desima, hoping that the wrath would blow over, and that they might yet be allowed at least a little traffic. But the emperor was resolved to get rid of them entirely; and on the assurance of the Dutch that they would regularly supply the country with the goods and commodities required, he again declared the Portuguese enemies of the empire, and forbade them for ever to import even the goods of their own country.*

Thus the Portuguese lost their profitable trade with Japan; and they were totally expelled the country before the close of the year 1639. They accused the Dutch as the chief cause of their expulsion; and it is not easy to see how the charge can be either denied or doubted.

But worse followed. The Portuguese were rivals in commerce, and in every way implacable enemies; they would fain have done to the Dutch that which the Dutch succeeded in doing to them; but the poor Christian natives stood in no such position of rivalry, hatred, and unappeasable hostility.

Though deprived of their padres, or European teachers, and though menaced, not only with imprisonment, but also with torture and death, the converts persevered in their faith. Oppression drove them into open rebellion; and they took refuge, and made an heroical stand against the troops of the emperor in the province of Simabara. The imperial government called upon the Dutch to assist them in their war against these Christians; and the Dutch

---

* The imperial palate must have acquired a taste for port and sherry (no bad drinks in a cold Japanese winter), for the wines of Portugal and Spain were excepted in the prohibition.

promptly gave the aid required of them. The fact is admitted by all their own countrymen who have written about Japan, from their first writers in the middle of the seventeenth century, down to the year 1833. M. Fischer, the very last on the list, says that the Dutch were *compelled* to join in the persecution against the stubborn remnant of that Christian host. Others would soften the matter by saying that the Dutch *only* supplied the heathen Japanese with gunpowder and guns, taught them a little artillery practice, and sent ammunition, arms, and troops in their ships to the scene of action. But Kämpfer, who was only a German in the Dutch service, most distinctly and positively assures us that the Christian traders acted as auxiliaries and belligerents. The stronghold of the native Christians was an old fortified place, which the emperor's troops could not take.

"The Dutch, upon this, as friends and allies of the emperor, were requested to assist the Japanese in the siege ..... M. Kockebecker, who was then director of the Dutch trade and nation, having received the emperor's orders to this purpose, repaired thither without delay, on board a Dutch ship, lying at anchor in the harbor of Firando (all the other ships, perhaps upon some intimation given, that some such request was like to be made to them from court, set sail but the day before), and within a fortnight's time he battered the old town with 426 cannon-balls, both from on board his ship and from a battery which was raised on shore, and planted with some of his own guns. This compliance of the Dutch, and their conduct during the siege, was entirely to the satisfaction of the Japanese, and although the besieged seemed in no manner of forwardness to surrender, yet, as by this cannonading they had been very much reduced in number, and their strength greatly broken, M. Kockebecker had leave at last to depart, after they had obliged him to land six more of his guns for the use of the emperor."*

A recent writer, a right-hearted and right-minded American, says,—"The walls of Simabara were unquestionably battered by the Dutch cannon, and its brave defenders were slaughtered. Some apology might be made for this co-operation at the siege of Simabara, had its defenders been the countrymen of Alva, or Requesens, or John of Austria, or Alexander Farnese. But truth requires that the measures of Kockebecker should be regarded as the alternative, which he deliberately preferred to the interruption of the Dutch trade."†

It appears that the siege was converted into a long and close blockade, and that when the indomitable converts of Xavier were reduced and in good part exterminated by famine, a storm and an atrocious massacre ensued, none being spared, because none would recant and beg quarter; but men, women, and children being all butchered in heaps. In this war of religion, according to the most moderate estimate, there fell on both sides 40,000 men. According to the papists, the number of native Christians alone was far greater than this, and all the atrocities and horrors of the Diocletian persecution were repeated, exaggerated, and prolonged. The magnitude of the holocaust does indeed afford some measure of the depth and tenacity with which Christianity, in its Roman form, had struck its roots into the soil.

Over the vast common grave of the martyrs was set up this impious inscription:—"So long as the sun shall

---

* Kämpfer, vol. i. p. 324.

† C. W. King, "Notes of the Voyage of the *Morrison*, etc."

warm the earth, let no Christian be so bold as to come to Japan; and let all know, that the King of Spain himself or the Christians' God, or the great God of all, if he violate this command, shall pay for it with his head."

The Dutch were very far from deriving all the benefits they expected from their intrigues and mean compliances; they never attained to the consideration and liberty in the islands which had been enjoyed by the Portuguese; and they may be said to be, even at this moment, a despised set of traffickers. "By this submissive readiness to assist the Emperor in the execution of his designs, with regard to the final destruction of Christianity in his dominions, it is true, indeed, that we stood our ground so far as to maintain ourselves in the country, and to be permitted to carry on our trade, although the court had then some thoughts of a total exclusion of all foreigners whatsoever. But many generous and noble persons, at court and in the country, judged unfavorably of our conduct. It seemed to them inconsistent with reason that the Dutch should ever be expected to be faithful to a foreign monarch, and one, too, whom they look upon as a heathen, whilst they showed so much forwardness to assist him in the destruction of a people with whom they agreed in the most essential parts of their faith (as the Japanese had been well informed by the Portuguese monks), and to sacrifice to their own worldly interest those who followed Christ in the very same way, and hoped to enter the kingdom of heaven through the same gate. These are expressions which I have often heard from the natives, when the conversation happened to turn upon this mournful subject. In short, by our humble complaisance and connivance, we were so far from bringing this proud and jealous nation to any greater confidence, or more intimate friendship, that, on the contrary, their jealousy and mistrust seemed to increase from that time. They both hated and despised us for what we had done. In the year 1641, soon after the total expulsion of the Portuguese, and the suppression of Christianity among the natives, we were ordered to quit our comfortable factory at Firando, and to confine ourselves, under a very rigid inspection, to the small islet of Desima, which is more like a prison than a factory. So great was the covetousness of the Dutch, and so strong the alluring power of the Japanese gold, that rather than quit the prospect of a trade (indeed most advantageous) they willingly underwent an almost perpetual imprisonment, for such in fact is our residence at Desima, and chose to suffer many hardships in a foreign and heathen country, to be remiss in performing divine service on Sundays and solemn festivals, to leave off praying and singing of psalms, entirely to avoid the sign of the cross, the calling upon the name of Christ in presence of the natives, and all the outer signs of Christianity; and lastly, patiently and submissively to bear the abusive and injurious behavior of these proud infidels towards us, than which nothing can be offered more shocking to a generous and noble mind."*

To this wretched Desima the Dutch have been confined ever since. The place stands upon, and wholly covers a little artificial islet, about 600 feet in length, by 240 in breadth. The islet, shaped like a fan, is joined to the island and town of Nagasaki by a small stone bridge, at the end of which there is a strong Japanese guardhouse, with soldiers constantly upon duty, to see that none enter or come out without license. On the

* Kämpfer.

north side of the islet are two strong gates, called the water-gates; but these are never allowed to be opened except for the lading or unlading of the Dutch ships; at which seasons certain vigilant commissioners, appointed by the Japanese government, are always present with an armed guard. In the harbor, a few paces from the factory, are thirteen very high posts, at regular distances from each other, with small wooden tablets affixed to them, upon which is written the governmental order, that no boats or persons are to come within the said posts, or to approach the Dutch quarters, under very severe penalties. The whole islet is fenced in with a strong paling of high boards, with narrow roofs, on the top of which is planted a double row of iron spikes, in *chevaux de frise* fashion. The Dutch houses within this ugly inclosure are low and mean, and built of fir-wood and bamboos, the strangers not being permitted to build anything with stone. The place is at all hours open to the intrusion of the restless prying police of the town of Nagasaki, and is, or used to be occasionally, turned into a place of execution for smugglers,—smuggling being a capital crime in this empire. But besides the police, the Dutch are constantly watched by special guards, agents, spies and corporations, and they are obliged to pay these people for the annoyance they cause them. A more rigid *surveillance* was never devised by human ingenuity and suspicion. The men who are set to watch the Dutch are the more active in the duty, from being distrustful of one another. The Dutch are condemned to a life of celibacy, no female being allowed to arrive on board the annual vessel. Even their male Japanese servants must not be found in the factory between sunset and sunrise. All the servants, moreover, are frequently changed, lest they should become too much accustomed to Dutch manners and habits, and attached to their masters.

When a ship arrives, the first thing done is to remove her guns and ammunition. The Japanese then thoroughly visit every part of the vessel, and take lists of the goods and all other things on board. The people are then allowed to go on shore, to *refresh themselves* in the pleasant prison of Desima, where they generally remain, couped up like poultry afloat, for the space of two or three months. Guards are placed over them as soon as they land. Should any poor mariner, eager for a peep into the town of Nagasaki (a town with 60,000 inhabitants), attempt to pass the guard-house at the end of the little stone bridge, he gets into trouble, or is at least driven back. The poor Japanese people, sociable in their dispositions, and with no antipathy to foreigners, visibly regret all these harsh regulations, but dare not transgress the letter of the law, or give offence to their government.

All who serve the Dutch, or have any close dealings with them, are bound to take a solemn oath of renunciation and hatred of the Christian religion, once, twice, or even three times a year; and, at least at one of these ceremonies, they are made to trample under-foot crosses and crucifixes, with the image of the Redeemer upon them. The ill-meant, mocking, impious jests of Voltaire, as to the Dutch going through the same ceremony, may not have been, at every period, quite destitute of truth. As Lutherans or Presbyterians they may have entertained no more reverence for crosses and crucifixes and images of saints, than was felt by our English Puritans, who, in the days of their prepotency, found a rude delight in destroying such articles, and treating them with every imaginable disrespect.* The Portuguese, when driven to despair through their hated rivals, nearly involved the Dutch in their own ruin by announcing to the imperial government that they were Christians like themselves. It behoved the Dutch to convince the Japanese that there was the widest difference between them; that they belonged to a sect quite hostile to that of the Portuguese; that they hated Pope, Jesuits, Franciscans, Dominicans, and all manner of monks and priests. We can, therefore, easily credit that, if put by the Japanese government to that test, the Dutchmen would not much scruple to trample upon the cross in the manner described by Voltaire. A bigoted Presbyterian would even find a pleasure in so doing.† An old Nangasakian joke is, that a Dutchman, at the time of the great persecution, being surprised in some place by the Japanese police, and being asked whether he were a Christian, replied, "No! I am a Dutchman." We fear, indeed, that after any lengthened residence in the country, such religion as these Dutchmen carried with them was almost wholly evaporated. The life led in their prison at Nagasaki was little calculated to foster devotional feelings. Kämpfer says that in his time they lived like a set of heathens,—that the principles of Christianity were

---

* We ourselves once met in the island of Sicily a fanatical Presbyterian skipper, who wanted to pull down and burn all the crosses in the country, and who could never pass a wooden cross by the road-side without committing some assault upon it. He was a disagreeable and dangerous travelling companion; for his conduct greatly enraged the country-people, and might have led to very serious consequences.

† The Russian officer Golownin and the companions of his Japanese captivity found it expedient to deny, over and over again, that they followed the same religion, and exercised the same rites, as the Portuguese and Spaniards.

so little conspicuous in their lives and actions, that the Japanese were absurd in fearing that they would attempt the conversion of the heathens. But good and religious men have gone through this ordeal without any detriment to their faith or to their morals; so let not these remarks be taken as uncharitable, or as disrespectful to the Dutch.

Kämpfer is quite pathetic in his account of the imprisoned, uncomfortable way of life. "Thus we live all the year round little better than prisoners, confined within the compass of one small island, under the perpetual and narrow inspection of our keepers. It is true, indeed, we are now and then allowed a short escape, an indulgence which we can by no means suppose to be the effect of love and friendship, forasmuch as it is never granted to us unless it be to pay our respects to some great men, or for some other business advantageous for the government. . . . After the departure of our ships, the director of our trade, or resident of the Dutch East-India Company, sets out with a numerous retinue on his journey to the emperor's court, to make the usual yearly presents. . . . Upon this journey we are scarcely allowed more liberty than state prisoners might reasonably claim. We are not suffered to speak to any body, not even (without express permission) to the servants of the inns at which we lodge. As soon as we come to an inn, we are, without delay, carried up stairs, or into the back apartment, which has no other view than that into the small walled garden or court-yard. Our retinue, which is specially ordered and regulated by government, consists of interpreters, cooks, servants, porters, grooms, bailiffs, and soldiers in good number; and all these people, though ever so useless, must be fed and maintained at our expense. Before our departure for court, and again upon our return, we are bound to wait upon the governors of Nagasaki, to return them thanks for their favors, and to entreat the continuance of their protection. Now, not even this visit can be made without a numerous, expensive train of guards, soldiers, and bailiffs, the latter carrying *halters* in their pockets. We are often obliged to wait a good hour in the great guard-house before we are admitted to audience. Another visit, and with the like numerous attendants, is made to the governors upon a certain Japanese holiday, when it is usual to make them a present."

Of late years this severity has been materially relaxed. In 1822, when the Dutch mission went to Jeddo to pay their court to the emperor, and give him the presents, they were allowed considerable freedom of intercourse with the people. At the villages on the road fair damsels ran out to meet them, and to offer them spring water, tea, and other refreshments; and at Jeddo, the apartments allotted to them were crowded from morning till night by ladies and gentlemen, native doctors, and *savans*, and people of all classes, who asked them questions with wonderful volubility, and were always ready to answer the questions which the Dutch put to them. This intercourse, although under constant supervision on the part of the government, appears to have been sufficiently unrestrained. By the strict letter of Japanese law, the female sex were forbidden to enter the precincts; but the fair ladies went in such numbers, that it sometimes happened that there were six of them to a single male visitor. Their manners charmed the hearts of the Dutchmen—especially, it should seem the susceptible heart of the secretary, to whom we are indebted for the interesting account of this visit to Jeddo.*

The Dutch treated the Japanese beauties (and it is declared that some of them were very charming) with liqueurs and confectionary, and wrote Dutch words on their fans, as a substitute for albums. There was an agreeable interchange of presents. The secretaries of the government of Sadsuma brought an offering of twelve beautiful birds, fifteen rare plants, two lap-dogs, and a couple of rabbits, with some silks and other articles, conveyed in cages and Japan boxes, which in value and beauty far exceeded their contents. The whole of this recent account leaves on the mind the impression of a really delightful journey. It is to be noted, however, that the Dutch visit to Jeddo and court is no longer annual, but is now limited to once in four years.

In Kämpfer's time (1690–92), the few Dutch who remained at Desima after the departure of their ships, were permitted, once or twice in the year, to take a walk into the adjacent country, and to visit the temples about Nagasaki, the liberty being oftenest granted to their doctors and surgeons, under pretence that they were going in search of medicinal plants. But on these, as on two or three other rare occasions, on which they were allowed, for a few hours, to quit their narrow prisonhouse, they were narrowly watched, and obliged to incur heavy expenses. Every time they went to the temples their purses were severely squeezed, for they had to give a splendid dinner in one of the joss-houses, and to fee the priests of the temple besides.

---

* J. F. Van Overmeer Fischer, "Bijdrage tot de Kennis von het Japansche Rijk." Amsterdam, 1833.

Although the trade was reduced to two ships a year, it was so very profitable that the Dutch were anxious to retain it all for themselves; and, from first to last, they resigned themselves to many humiliations, in order to secure their monopoly.

At the beginning of the seventeenth century, when the English were beginning to make considerable commercial progress in India, our East India Company obtained what appeared to be a good footing in Japan. This was years before the great massacre of the Christians, and the total expulsion of the Portuguese. That truly remarkable man, William Adams, who led the Dutch to the country, and procured for them all their privileges, was also the real founder of the English settlement. The two letters which he sent to Batavia, were conveyed to London, and submitted to the "Worshipful Fellowship of the Merchants of London, trading into the East Indies."* They attracted immediate attention, and Captain John Saris, in command of the good ship *Clove*, was despatched on a mission to the emperor of Japan, being accredited with a letter, and charged with presents from our reigning sovereign, James I. Sir Thomas Smith, who was then acting as chairman of the infant company in London, appears to have taken a very active and spirited part in these measures.

The *Clove* came to anchor in the vicinity of Firando, on the 11th of June, 1613, not two years after the date of Adams's letters. The king of the island and his grandson went on board the ship and welcomed the captain, who "had prepared a banquet for them, and a good concert of music, which much delighted them." Captain

---

* This was the title then borne by the Honorable E. I. Company.

Saris immediately put himself in communication with Adams, whom the natives called *Auge*.

"The king was no sooner ashore, than all his nobility, attended with a multitude of soldiers, entered the ship, every man of worth bringing his present with him—some venison, some wild-fowl, some wild-boar, the largest and fattest that ever any of us had seen; some bringing fruits, fish, etc. They did much admire our ship, and made as if they could never see it sufficiently."*

His majesty soon returned to the ship, conducting with him his "four chief women." "These," says Captain Saris, "were attired in gowns of silk, clapped the one skirt over the other, and they were bare-legged, having only a pair of half-buskins, nicely bound with silk riband about the instep: their hair very black and very long, tied up in a knot upon the crown, in a comely manner; their heads nowhere shaven as the men's were. They were well-faced, well-handed and footed, clear-skinned and white, but wanting color, which they do amend by art. Of stature low, but rather fat; very courteous in behavior, not ignorant of the respect to be given unto persons according to their fashion. . . . . . The king's women seemed to be somewhat bashful, but he willed them to be frolicsome. They sang divers songs, and played upon certain instruments, whereof one did very much resemble our lute." The jovial skipper, who rejoiced in the double title of general and ambassador, treated them well in his cabin, and gave them some English manufactures to take on shore with them. The king was so pleased with the entertainment, that in a very few days he returned with divers other women "to make frolic." Saris goes on,—

* "Purchas his Pilgrimes."

"These women were actors of comedies, who pass from island to island to play, as our players do from town to town, having several changes of apparel, for the better grace of the matters acted, which for the most part were of war, love, revenge, and such like."

Early in July the king, or viceroy of another island came to visit "the excellent English ship." "So he was well entertained aboard, banqueted, and had divers pieces shot off at his departure, which he very kindly accepted, and told me that he should be right glad to see some of our nation come to his island, whither they should be heartily welcomed." Such was the freedom of intercourse only a few years before the political hurricane brought on by the Portuguese and the Dutch. In the month of August, 1613, Captain, or General Saris, set off for the imperial court of Jeddo, accompanied by our marvellous mariner and pilot Adams, and ten other Englishmen. They went from island to island in a royal galley, and performed nearly all the journey by water. The party stopped at several cities, which they describe as being densely peopled, and quite as extensive as the London of their day. "Everybody very civil and courteous; only at our landing, and so through the country, the boys, children, and worser sort of idle people, would gather about and follow after us, crying,—'*Coré, Coré, Cocoré waré*,' that is to say, '*You Coréans with false hearts*:' wondering, whooping, hallooing, and making such a noise about us, that we could scarcely hear one another speak, sometimes throwing stones at us (but that not in many towns); yet the clamor and crying after us was everywhere alike, none reproving them for it. The best advice I can give those who shall hereafter arrive is, that they pass on without regarding those idle rabblements; and in so doing they shall find their ears only troubled with the noise."

In most of the towns the general and his goodly company were most hospitably entertained; and they appear to have been freely admitted to the society of the Japanese ladies. In the latter stages of the journey, Saris was carried in a palankeen, on six men's shoulders, and had a spare horse, very handsomely caparisoned, whereon to ride when it so pleased him. The general, when in presence of the emperor, well maintained the honor of his country and his own personal dignity. There was no crawling like a crab, no humiliation, no ceremony unbecoming the representative of a powerful sovereign. Through the help and admirable diplomacy of Adams, a commercial treaty, or a series of privileges, more favorable than any ever enjoyed by Portuguese or by Dutch, was granted to the English, and apparently without any demur or delay on the part of the imperial court.

The first article in these original privileges of 1613 runs thus:—"We give free license to the king of England's subjects, Sir Thomas Smith, Governor, and Company of the East-India Merchants, for ever, safely to come *into any our ports* or empire of Japan, with their ships and merchandise, without hindrance to them or their goods; and to abide, buy, sell, and barter according to their own manner with all nations; and to tarry so long as they will, and depart at their pleasure."

The second article exempted English goods from all manner of customs or duties; the third granted to the English full freedom of building houses in any part of the empire, which houses, at their departure, they might freely sell; the fourth article placed the property of any English subject that might die in the empire under the sole control of the captain, merchant, or English resident, and exempted entirely all English subjects, whatever their offences, from the somewhat summary process of Japanese law; and the three remaining articles were all in the same liberal and most friendly spirit.*

These privileges were, however, somewhat modified in 1616, when the English, wherever they might arrive on the coast, were ordered to repair immediately to the port and of town Firando, there to sell their merchandise, and not to stay at, or trade, in any other port whatsoever. But it was ordered, at the same time, that, in case of contrary winds or bad weather, the English ships might abide in any other port, without paying anchorage duties; and the people were enjoined to treat such ships in a friendly manner, and to sell them whatsoever they might require. At the same time all the other valuable privileges of 1613 were confirmed. Captain Cock, who established himself at Firando, and remained in the country long after the departure of Saris, paid more than one visit to the imperial court at Jeddo.†

---

* See "Minutes of Evidence," appended to the "Report of the Select Committee of the House of Commons on Commercial Relations with China. 1847." Purchas, "His Pilgrimes," and the Notes to Mr. Rundall's valuable Memorials.

† MSS. in the East-India House (Japan Series), as quoted by Thomas Rundall, Esq., in "Memorials of the Empire of Japan, in the 16th and 17th centuries." Printed for the Hakluyt Society. London: 1850. Captain Cock was at Firando in 1620, when William Adams closed his adventours life. The captain took charge of the old pilot's will and property, and remitted the money to Adams's family in England. The original will is preserved in the East-India House, as is also the inventory of the estate of the deceased.

Too much praise can hardly be given to Mr. Rundall for his industrious researches into these matters.

Our factory at Firando, or rather, perhaps, those who managed their shipments in England, made an injudicious selection of merchandise, sending out commodities which were not in request in that country. In this manner, the trade was conducted, rather at a loss than profit, and this, with some other circumstances of discouragement, induced the East-India Company prematurely to abandon the experiment.

"Of the English," says a recent English writer, "it is simply to be observed that in their commercial project they failed, and that they retired with honor, and regretted, from the scene of their misadventure."* In the year 1623, after upwards of £40,000 had been uselessly expended, they entirely withdrew from that country, and trade. But though commercially unsuccessful, the English left an unimpeached character behind them, and worthy Captain Cock and his associates, honored by the esteem of the higher classes, were blessed and regretted by the humble in condition.† It was, perhaps, fortunate in more ways than one, that our countrymen were far from the empire long before the days of the terrible persecution, civil war, and slaughter. We should grieve to see our national fame blotted by conduct at all resembling that pursued by the Dutch at that dreadful crisis.

In 1673, when an English ship was sent to attempt a revival of intercourse, the first question asked by the Japanese authority was, whether it was long since the English king had married a daughter of the king of Portugal? Our Charles II. had married the Portuguese In-

---

* Thomas Rundall, Esq.; "Memorials of the Empire of Japan," &c.

† Id. id.

fanta Catherine of Braganza, twelve years before. The Dutch had made the Japanese acquainted with the fact; and this alliance with a hated nation led to a total refusal of the Japanese to permit any renewal of English intercourse, it being declared that "no trade could be permitted with the subjects of a king who had married the daughter of the greatest enemy of Japan, and the English ship must, therefore, sail with the first fair wind." The English captain was even denied permission to sell his cargo, which he had brought from so great a distance.* Yet, in other matters, our people were courteously received and hospitably entertained.

After this unsuccessful experiment there is no record of another English visit to Japan for considerably more than a century. Captain Cook, in his last voyage, merely coasted the western side of the empire.

But, in 1791, the "Argonaut," an English vessel employed in the fur trade with the northwest coast of America, made an attempt to trade and barter with the Japanese. She made for the western side of the islands, but met with no welcome. At the only port in which she anchored, she was immediately surrounded by lines of boats, and her people were cut off from all intercourse with the shore; and after getting a gratuitous supply of wood and water, she was obliged to sail away. The next English ship that touched the coasts was the "Providence," commanded by Captain Broughton, who was engaged on a naval survey, and who passed some time making obser-

* The name of this ship was the "Return." She had been despatched by the English East-India Company, with the sanction of Charles II. All on board of her appear to have been convinced that they were thwarted more by Dutch jealousy than by anything else.

vations, and refitting, on the coast of Yesso, north of Niphon, the main island. He was civilly treated by the inhabitants of Yesso, who were not very submissive to the central government. But Broughton had no commercial or political mission, and so made no attempt to establish any intercourse. In 1803, an English merchantman, the "Frederick," was sent from Calcutta with a rich cargo of goods; but her captain was refused admittance to the harbor, and enjoined to leave the neighborhood within the space of twenty-four hours.

The progress of our vast conquests and annexations on the Indian continent were of a nature to excite the jealous fears and increase the estrangement of people like the Japanese. They were uncommonly well informed of the particulars of that history, from the time of the great Lord Clive downwards. This complete information could be obtained only by means of the Dutch. To the people of that nation India was a sore subject. They had at one time aimed at supremacy in Hindostan, but Clive had shattered their talisman by the blow he struck at their settlement of Chinsura, above Calcutta, and under Warren Hastings their Indian continental power had dwindled to a mere shadow. They could not recover that power by criticising and condemning English ambition to the Japanese; but by this process it was certainly easy to excite the alarm of that people, to induce them vigilantly to bar their ports and harbors to the English, and so leave such trade as yet survived in Japan solely in the hands of the Dutch.

The French, though long powerful in India, and at one time all-powerful in Siam, made no effort in this direction. It appears, however, that when the celebrated Colbert took charge of the deranged finances of France, he projected an expedition to Japan, upon which he counted for a good supply of gold and silver, and for other advantages. But, from causes which are not explained, his project was never carried into execution.

Towards the close of the last century, Russia made more than one attempt to open an intercourse. Possessing one-half of the Kurile islands, while the Japanese possessed the other half, these two powers were, in a manner, next-door neighbors. About seventy-two years ago a Japanese vessel was wrecked on one of the Aleutian islands belonging to Russia; the crew were saved and conveyed to Irkutzk, where they were detained about ten years, well treated, and instructed in the Russian language, by order of the great Empress Catherine. On sending these Japanese back to their native country, Catherine directed the governor of Siberia to endeavor to establish such friendly relations as might tend to the mutual benefit of both countries. For this purpose, he was directed to despatch an envoy, in his own name, with credentials and suitable presents, taking especial care to employ no Englishman or Dutchman. The governor of Siberia fixed upon a lieutenant named Laxman, who, embarking in the "Catherina" transport, sailed from Okotzk in the autumn of 1792. Laxman soon made a harbor or bay on the northern coast of the Japanese island of Matsmai, where he passed the winter. In the following summer he went round to the southern coast of the same island, and entered the harbor of Chakodade, still having with him the natives whom the Russians had rescued from shipwreck. The officers of the Japanese government were exceedingly courteous; but all that Laxman could obtain from them was a declaration in writing to the following effect:—

"1. That although their laws inflict perpetual imprisonment on every stranger landing in any part of the Japanese empire, the harbor of Nagasaki excepted, yet, in consideration of the ignorance of these laws, pleaded by the Russians, and of their having saved the lives of several Japanese subjects, they are willing to waive the strict enforcement of them in the present instance, provided Lieutenant Laxman will promise, for himself and his countrymen, to return immediately to his own country, and never again to approach any part of the coast, but the harbor aforesaid.

"2. That the Japanese government thanks the Russians for the care taken of its subjects; but at the same time informs them, that they may either leave them or carry them back again, as they think fit, as the Japanese consider all men to belong to whatever country their destiny may carry them, and where their lives may have been protected."

During his stay, Laxman had been treated with the greatest civility; at his departure he was provided, without charge, with everything he wanted, and was finally dismissed with presents. The Empress Catherine, although she made no new attempt, kept her attention directed occasionally to Japan, and encouraged the cultivation of the language, which the shipwrecked Japanese had afforded some of her people the means of acquiring. Under her unfortunate, insane successor Paul, the matter slept; but her grandson, the Emperor Alexander, in the year 1803, sent the chamberlain Resanoff on a formal embassy, with imperial credentials and valuable presents to the emperor of Japan.

Resanoff proved himself ill qualified for so delicate and difficult a mission; after behaving perversely and ungraciously, he tamely submitted to be insulted by the Japanese government, who put him into a bamboo cage or narrow inclosure on the beach of Nagasaki, and in the end dismissed him very unceremoniously, with the notification that they had no wish for any Russian ships in any port of Japan. Although the ambassador of the Tzar bore all this very meekly while in his cage and in their power, he meditated vengeance; and on his return to Kamtschatka, applied to Chwostoff and Davidoff, each of whom commanded a small armed vessel in the service of the Americo-Russian company. These officers readily entered into the views of the chamberlain ambassador, and proceeded to retaliate the treatment which he had received at Nagasaki. But instead of going to that place to punish the offending party, they fell upon one of the Southern Kurile islands belonging to Japan, and wreaked their vengeance on the unoffending inhabitants, plundering their villages, killing some of the poor people, and carrying off others in their vessels. Resanoff died on his way back to St. Petersburg. Apparently no inquiry was instituted as to his mean and flagitious conduct; but his death could not obliterate the mournful recollections of the poor islanders.

In May, 1811, Captain Golownin was despatched in the imperial sloop of war the "Diana," to make a survey of the Kurile group. It has been suspected, though not proved, that there were ulterior objects, and that Golownin was instructed to make a new effort at establishing friendly relations with the Japanese government. But it was impossible that he could complete his survey without coming in contact with the Japanese authorities. By the 17th of June, Golownin had made his observations on the islands, from the thirteenth in the chain down to the eighteenth, when he found himself near the northern extremity of Ectoorpoo which he supposed to be inhabited only by

Kuriles. On landing, however, he was met by a Japanese chief, attended by some soldiers, who asked him if the Russians meant to treat them as the other island had been treated seven years ago. Golownin thought it best to take an immediate departure. He then went to the island of Kunaschier, which is the twentieth link in the chain, and separated from the thoroughly Japanese island of Matsmai, by a narrow strait. Entering the harbor of Kunaschier, two guns were fired at the "Diana" from a fort, hung round, in the fashion of the country, with blue and red striped cloth; and troops were seen in the town and on the seashore. Golownin endeavored by signals and ingenious symbols to intimate that he only wanted provisions and water. After various misunderstandings and adventures on the part of the Russians, and very great cunning on that of the Japanese, Golownin was tempted to land, with a weak party consisting only of a midshipman, a pilot, four Russian seamen, and a Kurile interpreter. He was received with great courtesy, and entertained at dinner, and treated with tea and sackee, a native drink distilled from rice; but when he and his party would have returned to their ships, they were all made prisoners, and bound with thick cords, and swung up by the arms and legs to a beam, their pockets having been first searched and emptied. The Japanese then sat down on their heels and coolly smoked their pipes for an hour. At the end of that period the party were loosened from the beam, the cords were removed from their legs, in order that they might be able to march, and they were led out of the castle and through a wood, each of them having a conductor holding the end of the main one of the ropes with which he still remained bound, and a grim-looking Japanese soldier by his side.

On ascending a hill, they heard a cannonade, and saw their ships standing away, under sail. "There goes our Diana!—Take a last look of her!" said the pilot. As they hurried him along, the rope round Golownin's neck became so tightened, that he was all but strangled. In the evening they arrived at a small village, and being carried into an empty apartment, were offered boiled rice and fish, the staple food of these people: they were then stretched on the floor, and the ropes by which they had been led, were made fast to strong iron hooks driven into the wall. Their conductors then sat down to smoke pipes and drink tea. Such is Japanese custom. At daylight the following morning Golownin was tied down to a plank or flat tray, like a sheep or dead pig, and carried away on the shoulders of two strong men, he knew not whither. He took a last farewell, as he fancied, of his companions in misfortune. In brief time, however, he found himself in a boat, into which all the rest of the Russians were brought, one by one, in the same manner, with an armed soldier between each of them. The boat shot across the narrow strait to the island of Matsmai, where they were placed in other boats. They proceeded along the shore, which appeared to be very populous, the whole of that day and the following night.

Though the Japanese would not relax the tight ropes with which they were bound, they were most attentive to their wants in all other respects, feeding them with rice and broiled fish, and constantly flapping away the gnats and flies which annoyed them. In a village a venerable old man brought them some sackee, and stood by while they were drinking it, with marks of pity in his face. But everywhere they experienced humane and kindly attentions from private persons, and Golownin, who, from his book, appears to have been rather a weak-headed, but a very right-hearted man, left Japan, after all his sufferings, with the most favorable impressions of the benevolence and generosity of the people. His testimony in this respect may be considered as conclusive and important.

The boats, which were thirty feet long and eight at the beam, were now dragged up a steep hill, on the other side of which they were launched into a sort of canal, which terminated in a large and beautiful lake. They crossed the lake, and then landed, boat and all. In this way, sometimes by land and sometimes by water, but always firmly bound, they were conducted on their way by about two hundred men. On the ninth day the cords round their wrists were so far loosened as to allow them to make some use of their hands. Hitherto they had been fed like helpless infants, the Japanese putting the rice and broiled fish into their mouths with little chopsticks. The prisoners now learned for the first time, that all the apparent inhumanity was intended as an act of kindness, to prevent them, in their despair, from committing suicide. This act not being considered either by the Chinese or Japanese as a crime, is very frequent in both countries; and as in both the officers of government are responsible for the health and safety of those delivered into their custody, their attentions are officious, incessant, and, in our eyes, extravagant. Woe to the escort if one of the Russians died! Their orders were to carry them alive and safe to Chakodade, and the orders of government must be executed to the letter, even in despite of natural sickness and disease. The humanity of these soldiers was, therefore, not altogether unselfish. Every night they carefully washed the feet of their prisoners with warm water; by day they would never suffer them to wet their feet in cold water, carrying them over every splash or streamlet they met. They would not allow them to eat strawberries and raspberries, lest their bowels should be deranged; when they smoked, they held their pipes for them, lest they should thrust the tube down their throats, and so kill or injure themselves.

At length they reached (a whole month after leaving the port in which they were captured) the well-peopled and prosperous-looking city of Chakodade, into which they were marched with great pomp, the sides of the road being crowded with spectators, men, women and children, who all behaved with the utmost decorum. "I particularly marked their countenances," says Golownin, "and never once observed a malicious look, or any sign of hatred towards us, and none showed the least disposition to insult us by mockery and derision."

They were conducted into a large wooden building, fenced round with bamboo palisades. It consisted of a long lobby or corridor, with a number of wooden cages arranged on each side, and into these the unfortunate Russians were thrust, each having his separate cage. These cages or cells were about six feet square and eight feet high, each having two small windows with iron gratings to admit light and air. A wooden bench and two or three mats formed the only furniture. Throughout the night guards came frequently along the passage to examine the cages, and, at intervals, the sentinels outside the prison plied their wooden rattles, to prove that they were vigilant. [We know not whether the Japanese borrowed the watchman's rattle from the Chinese, or the Chinese from the Japanese; but we took it, perhaps indirectly, from the Chinese. Our new police have suppressed its nocturnal music; but even in the days of the

"Charleys," few ever thought of the Oriental origin of the implement.] Every morning water for washing was carried to the prisoners, and a Japanese physician made his appearance to examine into the state of their health.

On the third day they were marched, with ropes round their waist, and under a strong guard, to the house of the governor of Chakodade. After being presented with tea and tobacco, they were asked a number of questions, all their answers being carefully written down. At length the governor desired to know if some change of religion had not taken place in Russia, "as Laxman (who had been here in 1793) wore a long pigtail, and had thick hair, covered all over with flour, whereas we had our hair cut quite short, and did not put any flour on our heads; and he could not believe us," says the captain, "when we told him that in our country religion had nothing to do with the cut of the hair."

But in Japan every custom is a religion. One question seems rather to have puzzled the Russians. They were asked why they had carried off wood and rice from a village where they had landed, without the consent of the owners; and whether, under the circumstances of leaving other articles in lieu, as they had done, any law existed in Russia to justify the deed? Golownin acknowledged that there was no such law; but added, that if a man took only what was necessary to support his existence, and left an equivalent, he would not be considered guilty. "With us," replied the Japanese, "it is very different; our laws ordain that a man must sooner die of hunger than touch, without the consent of the owner, a single grain of rice which does not belong to him."

At the expiration of fifty days, the Russians, again bound with ropes, were marched away from the coast to the capital of Matsmai, where they were caged as before. Here they underwent a multitude of examinations before the Bunyo or viceroy, who was far more inquisitive and minute than the governor of Chakodade, but mild and considerate, evidently feeling for their unhappy situation. They were well fed in their cages, and when the cold weather came on,—and it was *very* cold,—they were supplied with warm winter clothing. They were now visited twice a day by a physician, and if anything ailed them, he generally brought a second doctor with him.

The Russians were astonished to find how many trifling circumstances, unconnected either with themselves or with Resanoff, or Chwostoff, were brought to bear on the suspected views of the Russian government against Japan. The visit of Captain Broughton to one of the Kurile islands, and the visit of an English frigate to the Bay of Nagasaki, with some insinuations of the Dutch of that place, had confirmed the Japanese in their belief that the Russians and the English intended to divide China and Japan between them.

By the month of March, 1812, the prisoners were, however, permitted to walk about the town with a guard; and in April they were released from their prison, and removed to a private dwelling-house, surrounded by strong palisades. They resolved to escape from the town, get to the seashore, seize upon a boat, and stand across for the nearest part of the Asiatic continent. Having burrowed the ground beneath the palisades, one night, at the end of April, they crept out, one by one, and, favored by darkness, struck across the country towards the sea, directing their course to the northward, and ascending hills covered with snow. Hiding by day, they, for eight nights, wandered through thickets or scrambled among rocks and precipices, to the great risk of their necks or limbs. At length they reached a village on the shore and found two boats, but they were hauled up on the beach, and, weak and famishing as they were, they could not launch them. A little farther on they saw a boat afloat, and near it a tent. One of the famishing sailors thrust his hand into the tent, but instead of finding something eatable, he grasped the head of a Japanese who was sleeping within. The fellow roared out, and the Russians, fearing that the noise would alarm the villagers, hastened back to the hills. On the next morning, when they were completely exhausted and helpless, they found themselves surrounded by soldiers, who came upon them very quietly, bound their arms behind their backs, and led them to a house, where they refreshed them with sackee, boiled rice, radishes, and tea. The Russians had been regularly tracked day by day. Golownin fancied that the old fear about suicide had prevented the Japanese from seizing them sooner. They were marched back to Matsmai, and safely lodged in the castle. The viceroy showed no anger at this escapade: he merely told Golownin that his plan was ill contrived, and that if he had succeeded, and the Russians had got off, he and other Japanese must have answered for it with their lives.

They were soon sent from the castle to a new prison, and put into separate cages. But at last, when the second year of their captivity was well advanced, they were restored to liberty, and sent off for their own country.

The officers of Golownin's ship, the "Diana," on finding that the water was too shallow to allow of their getting near enough to use the small guns (with which the vessel was mounted) with any effect, had hauled off, and had remained three days near Kunaschier, the place where their captain was entrapped, in the vain hope of learning what had become of him. They then landed, at a lonely village, some linen and other articles for the captives, and returned with all speed to Okotzk, to lay before the government an account of what had occurred. Captain Rikord, of the Russian navy, immediately set off for Petersburgh. At Irkutzk he learned that the governor had already despatched a report to the capital. But the distances from Japan to Petersburgh were long; political events of the greatest magnitude were in progress, and before the report could reach him, the Emperor Alexander was fully engaged in preparations to meet the invasion of his dominions by Napoleon Bonaparte. Orders, however, were at length sent for the "Diana" to return to Japan. Captain Rikord took with him seven Japanese, six of whom had been shipwrecked on the coast of Kamschatka, in the hope of exchanging them for the seven Russians. They soon made the coast of Japan, but found that nobody would communicate with them from the shore. At Kunaschier, the Japanese opened their batteries upon them. Captain Rikord then resolved to seize any vessel he might meet. A bark was soon captured, but as the crew jumped overboard, and escaped by swimming, nothing could be learned from them. But, next morning, they intercepted a Japanese ship of the largest size, as she was making for the harbor. On being brought to, several of the crew threw themselves into the sea; of these, some were picked up by the "Diana's" boats, some swam ashore, and nine were drowned. But the captain, a lady, and all the rest of the crew, were secured. Fortunately, the captain was a great shipowner and merchant, a person of much influence and ability. He and the lady, his inseparable companion in his voyages, bore their misfortunes with wonderful composure. With the exception of four men, all the Japanese sailors were liberated, and allowed to proceed in their own vessel. The captain assured Rikord that Golownin and his companions were alive, and in the city of Matsmai. The season being now too far advanced to allow him to remain in those stormy seas, with no port open to him, Rikord steered back to Kamschatka, where he landed with his interesting captives on the 12th of October. In the middle of the dreadfully cold winter of that country two of the poor Japanese died. But all were treated with the greatest hospitality and kindness, and many prejudices which they had previously entertained against the Russians were removed. The captain betook himself to the study of the Muscovite language, and was never heard to utter a word of complaint.

On the approach of fine weather, the "Diana" put again to sea. She arrived in Kunaschier Bay in June, but nobody would communicate with her, and not a living being could be seen along the whole line of coast. Upon Rikord's insisting that the Japanese captain should act in a manner which he thought the most likely to open communications, the captain, in a tone, the earnestness of which could not be mistaken, threatened to kill him and then kill himself. But when the Russian officer left this resolute and clever man to act in his own way, all went well on shore; and Golownin and his comrades were soon liberated. Being landed, on his promise to do his best, he exhibited a declaration—which had been procured, by his advice, from the Russian governor of Irkutzk,—that the violent proceedings at the Kurile island had been wholly unauthorized; and of his own knowledge and experience he bore testimony to the good feelings of the Russians towards Japan. No doubt he was aided by his affluence and his connections; but it would appear that, but for his extraordinary address and abilities, even he would have failed.

On the 16th of August, Golownin and those with him were set at liberty. They soon reached the "Diana," which had been allowed to come round to the port of Chakodade. It must have been long ere they forgot their caging.*

Some of the last attempts of the English to open a friendly intercourse, were attended with melancholy consequences, and ended in thorough failure. In October, 1808, a European vessel under Dutch colors appeared off Nagasaki. The usual Dutch trader was expected at the time; and therefore the president of the Dutch factory,

---

* "Narrative of my Captivity in Japan, during the years 1812 and 1813; with Observations on the Country and People." By Captain Golownin, R.N.; to which is added "An Account of the Voyages to the Coasts of Japan, and of the Negotiations with the Japanese for the release of the Author and his Companions." By Captain Rikord. London: 1818.

These very amusing volumes have been recently republished by Messrs. Colburn and Co. We recommend to general attention the worthy Russian captain's minute narrative of his own adventures and sufferings. They throw much light on the manners of this remarkable people, and bear the stamp of sincerity and thorough truthfulness. When he describes what he saw himself he is entitled to implicit reliance. The portions of the work called "Recollections of Japan, comprising a particular account of the religion, language, government," &c., is chiefly compiled from Kämpfer, Thunberg, and other voyagers; but it occasionally presents original remarks, which appear to us to be of considerable value. Very few will take up the book without reading it through.

M. Doeff (who has since written much about Japan), without any suspicion, sent off two of his subordinates. Instead of returning, the two Dutchmen were detained on board the ship. This circumstance excited both suspicion and alarm. Preparations were instantly made by the Japanese for a warlike collision; but their governor found, to his consternation and horror, that a strong garrison placed at a commanding point on the harbor, were nearly all absent without leave; that the commander of the garrison himself was nowhere to be found; and that only sixty or seventy men could be collected on the spot. The governor shuddered at the intelligence, for he foresaw his inevitable lot—death by the knife. About the hour of noon a letter was brought from one of the absent Dutchmen, with these words only, "A ship has arrived from Bengal. The captain's name is Pellew; he asks for water and provisions."

The Dutch president dared not comply, without the concurrence of the Japanese governor. At midnight, the first secretary of that high officer visited him, and informed him that he had orders to rescue the two Hollanders. M. Doeff asked him how he proposed to do this? The secretary replied, "Your countrymen have been seized by treachery; I shall therefore go alone, obtain admission on board by every demonstration of friendship, seek an interview with the captain, and on his refusal to deliver his prisoners, stab him first, and then myself." The Dutch president dissuaded him from an enterprise hopeless in itself, and dangerous to his two captured countrymen. The Japanese governor, adopting the same view, the secretary's desperate scheme was abandoned.

The plan next adopted was to detain the ship till all the junks, boats, and forces of the neighboring princes or viceroys should be collected for attack; and the night passed away in military preparation, which, as M. Doeff says, bore marks of the effect of a want of warlike practice of two centuries' duration. In the afternoon of the following day, Gozeman, one of the *detenus*, was landed, and brought with him the following note:—"I have ordered my own boat to set Gozeman on shore, to procure me water and provisions; if he does not return with such before evening, I will sail in to-morrow early, and burn the Japanese and Chinese vessels in the harbor."

The Japanese functionary was unwilling to allow of Gozeman's return to the vessel; but was persuaded by M. Doeff, who considered that measure the only means of recovering the other man. Gozeman did return on board with the provisions, and shortly afterwards, both he and his captured companion reappeared on shore. It now became the object of the governor to execute, if possible, that clause of his commission, which enjoins every one to detain, till the pleasure of the head government of the province be known, any foreign vessel which comes too near, or commits any act of violence or illegality on the coast. The Dutch president was again consulted. M. Doeff considered the Japanese not strong or warlike enough to detain by force a well-armed British frigate (for such the stranger was), and told them so plainly; but he advised them to detain the vessel by some other means, long enough to permit a number of native vessels, laden with stones, to be sunk in the narrowest part of a passage through which the stranger must go on her quitting the port to put to sea. The Dutchman calculated that this scheme might be executed in the course of the next day and night, without being discovered by the English. The Japanese harbor-master declared that the scheme was feasible, and received the governor's orders to make the necessary preparations. A favorable east wind was blowing; but it was expected that the frigate would wait for a further supply of fresh water, which had been promised, with the view of detaining her

On the following morning, about daylight, the Prince of Omura arrived, at the head of his troops, and proposed to the governor to endeavor, with 300 boats, each manned with three rowers, and filled with straw and reeds, to burn the frigate. The rowers were to escape by swimming. The Prince offered to lead the enterprise in person. But during this consultation, the frigate weighed anchor, hoisted her white canvass, and sailed out of the harbor with a fresh breeze.

In other countries the adventure, once over, would have excited little more than laughter, at the *ruses de guerre;* but in Japan, it was no laughing matter for those on shore. The rules and laws of government had been broken, and for this, those who had offended must die the death. Within half an hour of the frigate's departure, the governor redeemed himself from impending disgrace, and his family from forfeiture and an inheritance of infamy, by the terrible expedient which Japanese custom dictates on such occasions. The officers of the neglected post followed the example, and ripped open their bowels. These men were under the orders, not of the governor of Nagasaki, but of the governor of the province (Fizen), who was residing at the time in the distant capital (Jeddo); yet that absent functionary was punished by an imprisonment of one hundred days, for the delinquency of his subordinates.

The British frigate was the "Phaeton," and her commander Captain Pellew (subsequently the second Lord Exmouth), who had been ordered by Admiral Drury, the head of our fleets in the Eastern Seas, to cruise off the Japanese Islands, for the purpose of intercepting the Dutch traders to Nagasaki. We were at war with Holland, which for some years had been a mere dependency of France. Her troops were fighting in the armies of Bonaparte, her ships were conveying his troops and stores, and her war-ships and privateers were doing us all the mischief they could. After cruising in vain for a month in these stormy seas, Captain Pellew, thinking that the Dutch traders had reached the harbor of Nagasaki, had determined to look for them there; and being there, and finding no Dutchmen, he had merely endeavored to have some little communication with the shore, and to ask for provisions and fresh water. He assuredly never would have gone thither had he been aware of the mischief his visit would entail on the Japanese authorities.*

In the summer of 1813, two vessels bearing the Dutch flag, and showing a private Dutch signal, approached the coast. A letter was sent on shore, announcing the arrival of M. W. Waardenaar, formerly president of the factory, and M. Cassa, appointed to replace M. Doeff, with three

* M. Doeff's account of these occurrences is marked with considerable prejudice, animosity, and unfairness to the English. But something must be pardoned in the poor Dutchman, who found himself, for a number of years, completely cut off from all communication with Europe and with his countrymen in the east, by the conquering ubiquitous fleets of Great Britain. He and his companions, at Nagasaki, wore out their last coats, their last pantaloons, and their last shoes, and were obliged to go half naked, or to dress themselves like natives. They drank out out all their schiedam, and (woe for jovial Dutchmen!) they could get no more gin.

A moderate and excellent article on this subject will be found in the "Quarterly Review," vol. lvi. p. 415.

assistants. No suspicion crossed the mind of M. Doeff, who sent an officer and clerk of the factory on board. The officer soon returned, saying that he had recognized M. Waardenaar and the Dutch captain, Voorman, but that things looked very strange on board the ship, and that Waardenaar had told him he could deliver the papers with which he was charged to none but M. Doeff in person. It was observed that nearly all the people on board spoke English, but thence it was only concluded that the vessels were Americans hired by the Dutch, who, during the war, had very frequently sought security for person and property under the flag of the United States. To ascertain the truth, M. Doeff boldly went on board. There M. Waardenaar, with evident embarrassment, handed him a letter. Doeff declined to open the letter till he should return to his residence, whither he was presently accompanied by Waardenaar and his clerk. Being opened at the factory, the letter presented matter that astounded and bewildered the poor Dutch president, who for nearly four years had been cut off from the world by the successful operations of our fleets, and kept in total ignorance not only of the occurrences in Holland and the rest of Europe, but also of what was passing in the Indian Seas. The letter, which announced that M. Waardenaar was appointed Commissary in Japan, with supreme power over the factory, was signed, "Raffles, Lieutenant-Governor of Java, and its dependencies." "Who is Raffles?" said the puzzled president, who had never heard the name, and who believed Java to be still in the hands of the Dutch, as the rich and magnificent island had been for ages. In reply, M. Doeff was informed that Java had been captured by the English; that Holland had lost her nationality, and had been incorporated with the French empire; and that Waardenaar, together with an Englishman, Dr. Ainslie, had been appointed by the British government as Commissioners in Japan. Doeff instantly refused any compliance with the order set forth in the letter, maintaining that they came from the government of a colony in possession of the enemy, and that Japan was not to be considered as a dependency of Java, or affected by any capitulation into which the Dutch in Java might have entered with the English.*

This ingenious and bold attempt to get a footing in the Dutch factory, and to smooth the way for future intercourse with the exclusive Japanese, proceeded from the spirit of enterprise which distinguished Sir Stamford Raffles, one of the many very remarkable men sent out to the East by the Hon. East India Company. His views extended all over this vast Archipelago; his darling object was to establish an insular empire, as magnificent, and even more extensive, than our continental empire in India. Sir Stamford was a great man, yet we cannot but agree with those (persons friendly to him) who think that his zeal in this instance overstepped his discretion, and that he arranged his scheme without a sufficient knowledge of the country and of the character of the government and people of Japan. Success could be gained only by entire acquiescence and collusion on the part of M. Doeff; and the lives of the crews and of all on board the two ships (which were only weak trading vessels), were

---

* Herinneringen uit Japan,—"Recollections of Japan." By Hendrick Doeff, formerly President of the Dutch factory at Desima. 4to. Haarlem, 1835.

This curious Dutch work has not been translated into English, but numerous passages from it have been given in the "Quarterly Review," vol. lvi. 1836.

placed in the hands of that Dutch functionary, who, by a word, could have given them over as Englishmen and enemies to the vengeance of a nation revengeful beyond measure, and still furious with the recollections of the visit paid to them by the Phaeton frigate.

It appears to us that Doeff, whose hatred to the English was intense, and had been increased by years of segregation, suffering, and absolute privation, would really have taken this course, but for the happy circumstance that M. Waardenaar was not only his countryman, but his very old friend and patron. Fortunately, too, Waardenaar was known and respected in Japan, having formerly been president of the factory; the ships bore the Dutch flag, and no suspicion that the English had a Dutch agent in their service had as yet reached the Japanese authorities. This rendered it comparatively easy to keep the secret if M. Doeff would only connive; and this, upon certain conditions of commercial profit to his country, he consented to do. The cargoes of the two ships were delivered to him in the usual manner, and copper was obtained in return, and these transactions being completed, the "Charlotte" and "Mary" sailed away with all speed. Those on board were certainly not out of danger until they were well out at sea, for they were too weak to defend themselves against an attack which would certainly have taken place if the Japanese government had made any discovery. At the court of Jeddo was established, at this very moment, in great power and favor, the son of that governor of Nagasaki who had committed suicide in consequence of the visit of the English in 1808. At Nagasaki itself, the garrison consisted of the troops of the Prince of Fizen, who had suffered 100 days' arrest for his imputed negligence in the same affair; and doubtless the friends and relations of the other victims of the transaction were living there and panting for vengeance on any Englishmen that might fall into their hands.

But what would have happened if M. Doeff had obeyed the orders of Sir Stamford Raffles, and had left his appointed successor and the English surgeon Ainslie to explain to the Japanese the British authority under which they were appointed? Nothing less, in all probability, than the destruction of the factory, the execution of its officers, and the final cessation of all intercourse with Europe. And these are consequences to be at least apprehended, from the armament of the United States, whether it succeed or fail. Success by diplomacy, we consider an impossibility. If their force be sufficient, they may possibly hold for a longer or shorter period, one of the smaller islands of the group; but, so sure as the Americans effect this by force of arms, the Dutch will be expelled, and the ports of Japan will be closed and barred more strongly than ever against the shipping of foreign nations.

In the following year (1814) Sir Stamford Raffles renewed his attempt by sending the Dutch agent Cassa, in the "Charlotte," to Nagasaki; but although the enterprise was conducted with rare skill and circumspection, it failed most completely.*

In June, 1818, Captain Gordon, of the British navy, entered the Bay of Jeddo, in a little brig of sixty-five tons. He was visited immediately by two Japanese officers, whom he supposed to be of high rank. He told them he had come merely to obtain permission to return

* In relating these English attempts, we have followed M. Doeff's own account, in his "Recollections of Japan," and the remarks thereon, by the able writer in the "Quarterly Review," vol. lvi.

to them with a cargo of goods for sale. They said he must unship his rudder and allow it, with all his arms and ammunition, to be taken on shore. The vessel was then surrounded by a circle of about twenty small boats, and beyond them, by another circle, of about sixty larger guard and gun-boats, besides two or three junks, which mounted a number of guns. Two interpreters then came on board, one speaking Dutch, the other knowing something of Russian, and both a little English. They inquired if the vessel belonged to the East-India Company, if the English were now friends with the Dutch. They knew the names and uses of our various nautical instruments, and said that the best of these, and other articles of manufacture, were made in London. At a subsequent visit, they firmly, but politely, told Captain Gordon that he could not be permitted to trade to Japan, as by their unalterable laws, all foreign intercourse was interdicted, except at Nagasaki, and even there allowed only with the Dutch and Chinese, and that the governor of the province desired they would take their departure the moment the wind should be fair. They declined some trifling presents which the captain offered, saying, that they were prohibited from accepting them. The rudder, with everything else that had been taken on shore, was carefully returned, and about thirty boats were sent to tow the vessel out of the bay. Ten years had now passed since the visit of the "Phaeton" frigate, and, very fortunately, Gordon had put into a very different port, on a different island. He speaks in high terms of the polite and affable conduct of the Japanese towards him and his people, and towards one another. He also speaks of the great mineral riches of Japan, and thinks that, if their government would only consent, a profitable trade might be carried on with them in our woollen cloth and manufactures. The worthy officer is praised by those who have seen the details of his expedition, for admirable prudence and conduct. Perhaps, under an inferior guidance, the expedition of the little brig would have ended in some other tragical catastrophe.*

The recent and rapid growth of the whale-fishery in the Pacific, has caused a much more frequent resort to the coasts of this empire. Many of the whalers of the United States have killed their fish in the waters of Japan. The most recent of all our English writers on the subject says,—"It appears that the American whalers have already come into collision with the Japanese government. The rising trade between California and Hong Kong, from which latter place the Chinese proceed in crowds to the new Dorado (California), joined to the general increase of navigation and business in the Pacific, must end in either opening European intercourse with Japan, or in greatly increasing the pains of the government to prevent it. It is a circumstance in favor of the English and Americans that, in common with the Dutch, they do not profess the *Romish* religion, against which the jealousy and hostility of the Japanese has been principally directed."†

---

* MS. Journal of Captain Gordon, as cited in "Quarterly Review," vol. xx. p. 119.

We met, a quarter of a century ago, a person who had been at Japan in the little brig, and who thought that the people would hospitably receive the English and gladly trade with them, if they did not stand in such dread of their arbitrary government. We believe so, too; but how is that dread to be removed?

† Sir John Francis Davis, Bart., F.R.S., late her Majesty's Plenipotentiary in China; Governor and Commander-in-Chief of the colony

The results of the British war in China were fully reported to the Japanese government, and if they have increased its fears of foreign intercourse, they must, at the same time, have inspired it with some degree of caution as to the treatment of foreigners, and the degree of respect to be shown to visitors. It is assumed that this has been proved by the conduct of the authorities at Nagasaki to Captain Sir Edward Belcher, on his visiting that harbor in the "Samarang," during the year 1845. As the ship drew near the port, numerous guard-boats pushed off, and one of them handed a letter on board. The letter, written in Dutch, as well as French, contained instructions "to anchor off the entrance of the harbor in a convenient position, until visited by the proper authorities." This was done, the pilots and minor guard-boats showing great anxiety that the "Samarang" should not enter the port. The officers at length came off, and their conduct was extremely civil. They stated that notice had long since reached them, through the Dutch, of the probability of this visit; that in 1843 they had letters from Packunshan, relating all the movements of the "Samarang" among those islands. That they had recent letters from Loo Choo describing the visit there, and that they knew their intentions to be good and well-disposed. Sir Edward Belcher, in following up his main object, wished to make astronomical observations on a neighboring island. Great opposition was started by the officers, but permission was, at last, obtained to land at night to determine some point by the stars, and complete certain

---

of Hong-Kong,—"China, during the War and since the Peace; to which are added observations on Japan and the Indo-Chinese nations."

magnetic observations. They, however, earnestly implored that this might not be repeated until they received instructions from their superiors. They took down a list of every article required by the "Samarang," promising that the whole should be immediately procured; and they were given clearly to understand that the English would pay for these things, and would not accept them as a humiliating gift. They were anxious to prevent the immediate departure of the ship, and requested the captain to delay it two days. On being told that the "Samarang" would stay four days if they would consent to farther observations on the island, they were much disconcerted, and said that such a measure would certainly lead to their punishment. During the delay of taking in water, the chief interpreter stated (cautiously, and while others were absent), that the Japanese would be very glad to see English ships at Nagasaki.

Our officers were much impressed by the manners of the people. "The gentlemen of Japan were most polite and courteous, conducting themselves with refined and polished urbanity; and exhibiting in their actions a dignified and respectful demeanor, that put to shame the ill-breeding of the seamen who ventured to laugh at them."*

They had an evident dislike to speak about the Dutch, but stated that their vessel was in port. All the time the "Samarang" remained, the hills and outlines of the villages were marked by batteries, dressed in striped canvas, in the fashion observed by Golownin. The English sailors laughed, and said that the Japanese had put their batteries in petticoats. Nothing, in a warlike sense, is

* Voyage of H. M. S. "Samarang." 1845.

more contemptible than these batteries! The guns (of brass) were laid on level platforms, without parapet or protection of any kind, unless we accept as such the petticoats, or striped cloth. It was remarked to the official people on board the "Samarang," that they had previously fired on an American vessel and driven her off the coast, when she came, in humanity and friendship, to restore some shipwrecked Japanese. This happened in 1837. In the course of the year 1831, a Japanese junk was blown off the coast into the Pacific Ocean, and, after drifting for a long time, was cast ashore in America, near the mouth of the Columbia river. [This incident alone may help to show how the West may have been peopled from the East—how the population of the New World may have sprung from that of the Old.] The poor castaways were kindly treated, and after four years of varied adventures, they were conducted to Macao, where they were taken care of by the English and Americans. It was reasonably supposed, by those who did not know the imperial decree of 1637, or who could not conceive that that decree would still influence the conduct of the Japanese authorities,* that, to carry the poor people back to their own country, would be a good and sufficient reason for appearing at Japan. An American merchantman, called the "Morrison," was excellently equipped for the purpose; but, unfortunately, her guns and armament were taken out of her, as a recommendation to the confidence of the Japanese. This very circumstance became the cause of her unceremonious expulsion and bad treatment. The defenceless ship, with a medical missionary

* The second clause of that decree is simply to this effect:—"All Japanese, who return from abroad, shall be put to death."

on board, to administer to the sick, reached the Bay of Jeddo. The first care of the officers who visited her from shore was to inspect her keenly, and ascertain her strength, by rowing round and peering in at the sides. When it was discovered that she was wholly unarmed, the greatest contempt and insolence were betrayed by these official visitors, and early the next morning the "Morrison" was saluted by a discharge of shotted guns from the shore, at very short distance. Badly as the guns were directed, their point-blank range, and the unarmed condition of the ship, made it necessary to weigh anchor with all speed. The Americans then ran westward to the neighborhood of Kagosima, the principal town of the island of Kiutsu, or Kewsew, where they anchored in a deep and spacious bay.

Mr. C. W. King, a highly respectable merchant of New York, conducted the negotiations with tact, good humor, and ability. On his arrival in the port, he prepared a paper to be laid before the emperor. "The American vessels," said he, "sail faster than those of other nations. If permitted to have intercourse with Japan, they will communicate always the latest intelligence. . . . . . Our countrymen have not yet visited your honorable country, but only know that, in old times, the merchants of all nations were admitted to your harbors. Afterwards, having transgressed the law, they were restricted or expelled. Now we, coming for the first time, and not having done wrong, request permission to carry on a friendly intercourse on the ancient footing."

The natives seemed very friendly, and it was thought at first that the negotiations for landing the shipwrecked Japanese was in a fair train; but after a period of uncertainty, striped canvas cloths were seen stretched along the shore. Their Japanese passengers, in great dismay, told the Americans that these were warlike preparations; lines of this cloth repeated, one in the rear of the other, being used to deaden the effect of shot, and to conceal the gunners. The anchor was again weighed, when a battery on shore opened savagely on the defenceless ship. Nothing was left for it, but to return to Macao with the shipwrecked people.* On these circumstances being recalled to the mind of the Japanese authorities at Nagasaki, by Captain Sir Edward Belcher, they merely said, "We never allow any Japanese to return under such circumstances. We sent a junk-full back to the Emperor of China, and *he* is our ally." Upon the day of the "Samarang's" intended departure, the chief officers, accompanied by a numerous suite of attendants, came on board, bringing the articles the captain had required. The purser was directed to pay for them, but the officer said, "If we dared to disobey the mandate of the Emperor, our heads would answer for it. We must not even discuss such a matter." After sundry manœuvres, all betokening the jealousy of the government, and the dread of punishment in its officials, the "Samarang" quietly took her departure. Of the people, Sir Edward Belcher speaks very favorably, praising their good manners, gentleness, and urbanity. As far as *they* are concerned, there can be little doubt that a free and open intercourse would be a matter of no great difficulty; but then this embarrassing

---

* C. W. King, "Notes of the Voyage of the 'Morrison' from Canton to Japan." New York, 1839.

We have the testimony of Mr. Lawrence, the United States Minister, now in this country, to the excellent character and thorough truthfulness of Mr. King. Both his works upon Japan are exceedingly interesting.

question presents itself,—Are we, for the sake of the desired end, to teach these people to revolutionize a government which, at the least, has given an unwonted degree of peace, order, and tranquillity to an extensive empire, with a population of many millions, for the space of two hundred and more years?

In the same year, 1845, three Japanese were carried to Ningpo, in China, by the American frigate "St. Louis." These three men had been blown or drifted right across the Atlantic, in a little junk, from the coast of Japan, all the way to Mexico, where they had remained two years.* The Chinese authorities were ready and willing to return these men to their native country, by the annual

* "After this," says Sir John F. Davis, "there can be little difficulty in accounting for the original peopling of America from Asia."—"*China during the War and since the Peace*," &c.

It should really appear that some Chinese junk was drifted to the coast of Mexico, and that America was known to that singular people many centuries before its discovery by Christopher Columbus. In the year 499, a Bonze wrote an account of a country in the far west, which he called Fou-Sang, and the description of which closely agrees with what we know of Mexico in its flourishing and most civilized time. The only thing that startles belief is this: the Bonze speaks of horses, and it has always been assumed that there were no horses on any part of the American continent, until they were carried thither by the Spaniards. The Bonze mentions a sort of deer which the natives of the country employed as beasts of burden. This was clearly the Alpaca. The Bonze, though a great traveller, was evidently no great naturalist and may have described some other animal as a horse. On this curious subject the reader may be referred to "Recherches sur les Navigations des Chinois du Côté de l'Amérique, &c." Par M. de Guignes "Mémoires de l'Académie des Inscriptions," &c., vol. xxviii. p. 503 Paris: 1761; and to "L'Amérique sous le Nom de Pays de Fou Sang," &c. Par M. de Paravey. Paris: 1844; and to "Nouvelle Preuves que le Pays du Fou-Sang, mentionné dans les livres Chinois est l'Amérique," by the same author.

junks which go from Cheepoo to Nagasaki; but one of the Japanese objected, on the ground of personal fear of the consequences to himself. No doubt the poor fellow knew the law of 1637. It is astonishing that such a law—a law punishing misfortune as crime, and repelling men who ought to be endeared by their perils and adventures, and who would be welcomed back and cherished by every other country in the world—should continue to be pitilessly enforced; but such, it appears, is the fact.*

In 1846, seeing the absolute necessity of protecting their own subjects frequenting those seas, the United States made an attempt to open negotiations with the obstinate court of Japan. The "Columbus," of ninety guns, Commodore Biddle, attended by the United States frigate "Vincennes," arrived at the entrance of the Bay of Jeddo on the 20th of July. The ships were immediately surrounded by about four hundred guard-boats, each containing from five to twenty men, who were generally without arms. Going on board the "Vincennes," the smaller of the ships, a man placed a stick with some symbol on it at the head, and another stick of the same sort at the stern. As the Americans thought that this looked rather like taking possession, they ordered the stick to be removed; and this was instantly done, without any objection on the

---

* An interesting account of these poor Japanese mariners is given by the American medical officer Dr. Pickering, in his "Races of Man, and their Geographical Distribution." According to Dr. Judd, an American Missionary, who had previously had some communication with educated Japanese, these poor fellows were fishermen of the lowest class. Their boat resembled the flat-bottomed skiffs of New England. Dr. Pickering shows how naturally and almost inevitably a bark, carried away from Japan in a storm, would drift to the coast of Mexico, or California.

part of the Japanese. Sir J. F. Davis thinks, that in this respect, the Japanese resemble their Chinese neighbors: "They go as far as they dare, until a check occurs. Thus they tried at first to prevent communication between the 'Columbus' and 'Vincennes,' and a triple line of boats made no attempt to move; but, on the seamen being ordered to cut the connecting ropes, no opposition was made." The interpreter was a Japanese, who, like many of his countrymen at Nagasaki, understood Dutch perfectly. The superior officers were very civil, well-conducted, sociably, and even jovially inclined. The Americans thought them generally a much better-looking people than the Chinese. Although the two ships remained ten days at anchor, not a soul went on shore. A reference being in the mean while made to the Emperor, the written reply arrived in about seven days. It was sufficiently curt:— "No trade can be allowed with any foreign nation, except Holland." On their departure, the "Columbus" and "Vincennes" were towed out by the whole fleet of boats.

Here is the substance of the letter of the President of the United States to his Imperial Majesty of Japan,—a letter in which we can see nothing to condemn or criticise:—

"I send you, by this letter, an envoy of my own appointment, an officer of high rank in his country, who is no missionary of religion. He goes by my command to bear to you my greeting and good wishes, and to promote friendship and commerce between the two countries.

"You know that the United States of America now extend from sea to sea; that the great countries of Oregon and California are parts of the United States; and that from these countries, which are rich in gold and silver and precious stones, our steamers can reach the shores of your happy land in less than twenty days.

"Many of our ships will now pass in every year, and some, perhaps, in every week, between California and China; these ships must pass along the coasts of your empire; storms and winds may cause them to be wrecked on your shores, and we ask and expect from your friendship and your greatness, kindness for our men and protection for our property. We wish that our people may be permitted to trade with your people; but we shall not authorize them to break any law of your empire.

"Our object is friendly commercial intercourse, and nothing more. You may have productions which we should be glad to buy, and we have productions which might suit your people.

"Your empire contains a great abundance of coal; this is an article which our steamers, in going from California to China, must use. They would be glad that a harbor in your empire should be appointed to which coal might be brought, and where they might always be able to purchase it.

"In many other respects commerce between your empire and our country would be useful to both. Let us consider well what new interests may arise from these recent events, which have brought our two countries so near together, and what purposes of friendly amity and intercourse this ought to inspire in the hearts of those who govern both countries."

Also in the same year, 1845, Nagasaki was visited by Admiral Cécille, in the French ship "Cléopâtre." The French met with no better success than the Americans and English have done. Under such circumstances, Sir J. F. Davis thinks it impossible to do otherwise than subscribe to the opinion of a correspondent at Paris:—"I do not believe that the moment is yet come for entertaining much hope of the commerce of this part of the world. There will be many bowels opened, and many official suicides, before European flags will be able to float freely at Jeddo or at Nagasaki."

"Yet," adds Sir J. F. Davis, "the inevitable collisions which will arise with the increased frequentation of the Japanese seas, can scarcely fail to raise questions which must be solved either by negotiation, or, failing that, by the *ultima ratio ;* and the Japanese have already shown some disposition to avert the latter. A case occurred in 1849, of several American seamen wrecked or put ashore from a whaling ship. The *China Mail* records " the return of the U. S. ship 'Preble' from Japan, whither she had been despatched by Commodore Geisinger, to take away some men belonging to the American whaler 'Lagoda.'" As the " Preble" approached the Japanese harbor, she was warned away by what was meant to be a tremendous display of batteries in petticoats. A paper fixed to the end of a long split bamboo, and containing certain directions in the English language, was tendered to the captain, who would not take it, and who continued his course in spite of some strong attempts which were made to stop the progress of the ship. An interpreter soon appeared, with orders that the vessel should stop and anchor at a particular spot ; but the captain, unfolding a chart, showed where he intended to anchor. Some very inferior officers being sent on board to inquire into his business, the captain, very properly, refused to confer with them. When more befitting functionaries came off and learned the object of the visit, delays were urged on account of the unavoidable necessity of referring the matter to the emperor ; but the American captain limited a time, beyond which he could not defer applying to his commander for further and more decisive instructions. The Japanese understood the menace, and in a very short time all the wrecked American seamen were sent safely on board. The Japanese then offered to supply the wants of the ship, but as they would not, or could not, receive payment, the offer was, with proper dignity, declined.

We have no authentic information before us, but we believe that, since the expedition of the " Preble " in 1849, some other American whalers have been wrecked on the coast, and confined in cages like the Russian Golownin.* We apprehend that the refusal to deliver up such subjects of the United States, or even a perseverance in the systematic imprisonment and harsh treatment of such subjects, constitutes a *casus belli*, and justifies a recourse to arms. As we proceed, we will endeavor to show the other strong incentives which impel the Americans towards these islands, and which are connected with the commerce and civilization of the whole globe. We heartily wish that our trans-Atlantic brethren may proceed in their mission with circumspection, gentleness, moderation, and humanity; but we really cannot call in question either the justice, or the expediency, of their interfering in the affairs of Japan.

Whether a nation which, like Japan, refuses all intercourse with the rest of the world, may claim all those privileges of neutrality for its harbors which other civilized nations have created and sanctioned for their mutual convenience, is a point of international law very open to discussion and doubt. Whether any nation—barbarous, semi-barbarous, or civilized—has the right to cut herself off from all other nations, to shut her ports and harbors of refuge against the foreign mariner, buffeted by those stormy seas and struggling on those dangerous coasts, is very much to be questioned. Can a government which repudiates the law of nations, and which has never en-

* It is said that some English as well as American whalers have been put to death for merely landing on the coast. On the other side it is asserted that some parties of these whalers have attacked and plundered Japanese villages, killing men and carrying off young women. We have no authentic information, as yet; but we can easily credit both stories.

tered into that compact (for compact it is, or it is nothing), claim the benefit of that law when it suits its own particular and immediate purpose? We think not. Even if the rights of nations justified a government playing the part of the dog in the manger, it would be found that men are not quite so patient as oxen. The instincts of nature, the natural law, stronger than all others, will impel mankind to invade and break up such excluding systems as those which obtain in Japan, China, and Annam.*

Japan lies on the high road of nations, and cannot, by any possibility, be left long in the condition of a barrier and impediment on that road. She possesses in the bosom of her own soil that mineral which gives wings to trade and intercommunication, and which is gradually linking together all the remotest parts of the earth. Assuredly no link in that chain will be allowed to remain incomplete out of deference to the whim and tyranny of one or two ultra-absolute Oriental governments.

It is, indeed, a pity that the civilized world should not be better represented at the court of Jeddo than it is by the Dutch, who have submitted to the very extremities of degradation.

Kämpfer, an eye-witness, has told us how the chief of the Dutch factory was received at court in his time (1691), and we believe that the ceremonial of the reception has not been materially improved since then.

"Having waited upwards of an hour in a large lofty, rather dark room, the emperor having in the meanwhile

---

* This is the proper designation of the Indo-Chinese nation, which we rather absurdly continue to call Cochin-China. Sir J. F. Davis remarks:—"It might be as well if the latter unmeaning designation (the authority for which is very obscure) were abandoned, and the true name, Annam, adopted."

seated himself in the hall of audience, Sino Cami and the two commissioners came and conducted our resident into the emperor's presence, leaving us behind. As soon as he came thither, they cried out aloud, 'Now, *Hollanda Capitan!*'* which was the signal for him to draw near and make his obeisances. Accordingly, he crawled on his hands and knees to a place showed him, between the presents ranged in due order on one side, and the place where the emperor sate, on the other; and there, kneeling, he bowed his forehead quite down to the ground, and so crawled backwards, like a crab, without uttering one single word. So mean and short a thing is the audience we have of this mighty monarch."

This, surely, is not the way to deal with a haughty, half-civilized government; it is not by crawling backwards, like a crab, that the onward march of civilized man is to be represented. Among all governments in this condition, the more a European or Christian debases himself, the more humiliation is put upon him, and the more difficulty raised in the way of the interest he is sent to represent and promote. This, quite down to our own day, was the case at Constantinople, where the ambassadors, to that decrepit and dying empire, from the greatest and most powerful nations in Christendom, verily ate dirt. We have taught the Turks a better lesson, and the same good teaching must be given to the Japanese, if we would bring them to any reasonable arrangement. There is, indeed, scarcely any limit to the evil consequences of implicit submission to their will and caprice. With the Americans, the necessity of negotiation has now become un-

---

* It appears that the Japanese commonly turn the *ll* into *rr*, and pronounce "Horranda Capitan."

avoidable, and very much will depend on the manner in which they may manage these negotiations. They have taken the field on a scale, or with a display of power, which will obviate any chance of insult. But this alone will not secure success, or lead to a treaty, which ought to be conceived in a large and liberal spirit, so as to be beneficial alike to Americans, English, Dutch, French, Portuguese, and Spanish interests. Sir J. F. Davis, whose consummate ability and very long experience in China and the neighboring countries, give great weight and value to any opinion he may deliver on these matters, concludes some valuable remarks in these words:—

"Much depends on the commencement in Japan, and, therefore, it seems highly impolitic to permit lines of guard-boats round our ships. From the treatment of British and other vessels of war during the last few years, the Japanese have shown an evident desire to stave off extremities, and are now, probably, more amenable to reason. Still, the difficulties are not trifling, and it would be far better not to attempt anything than to fail, as others have done, were it only for the influence in China.

"But should circumstances alter, and the Saigoun or Kubo head of the executive government at Jeddo find it necessary to relax the old restrictions, the strange constitution of the country would have to be considered. Anything like a treaty might be invalid, unless it bore the seal of the Dairi at Miako, as well as the Kubo;* and this, besides, must guarantee the adhesion of all the minor

* In this singular government there are two emperors, reigning conjointly: the Daïri, or spiritual emperor, who resides at Miako; and the temporal or lay emperor, who usually lives in the great city of Jeddo. See Chapter on Government and Laws.

princes, without which it might be mere waste paper. The land is divided into innumerable principalities, each with its seignorial rights. In the sixteenth century, each of the smaller potentates bordering on the sea appears to have vied with his neighbors in attracting the greatest amount of foreign intercourse.

"A treaty once concluded with Japan would, certainly, not be observed with worse faith than in China; for the Japanese are, at least, as straightforward as their neighbors, if not more so.

"Some of the interpreters attached to our consulates in China have undertaken the study of the Japanese language; and there will be teachers enough if Japan foolishly persists in excluding all her subjects who have been driven from the country by accident or necessity. Nothing could more completely defeat its own purpose than this sullen policy, for it supplies means and appliances against itself. With pure Chinese and Japanese, and the addition of Dutch or even English translations, it would be most important to avoid the assistance of their official interpreters,—a class objectionable on every account, and, if admitted into negotiations, capable of defeating every object. Many of the expatriated Japanese have learned English, and could be employed in a foreign dress.

"Considering Japan as one of the most advanced nations of Asia, with a territory and lines of coast equal to those of the British islands, it would, no doubt, be important to open such a mart for our capital and enterprise. Supposing anything should occur to induce Japan to alter its present policy of entire exclusion, a treaty, modelled on that of Nanking, with such modifications as past experience or local differences might suggest, would answer every legitimate object. With the perfect knowledge that the Japanese possess of all external matters, it is not likely that they would go beyond what has been done by China. To do even this, the first step constitutes the great difficulty."*

In every case, we earnestly hope that the American expedition may be conducted with firmness, but also with prudence and gentleness. Should our very enterprising and energetic brethren begin with a too free use of Bowie-knives and Colt's revolvers, the history of their mission will all be written in characters of blood; slaughters and atrocities will be committed, and an interesting people will be plunged back into complete barbarity. Though unable to contend in the field even with a small disciplined force well provided with artillery, and good artillerymen, the Japanese, if we are correctly informed as to their character, will brave death, and die in heaps. We would not make any positive assertion, but we apprehend the Americans will find that little or nothing can be done by negotiation. Should force be resorted to, the best means of proceeding would probably be to take possession of one of the smaller islands, or of some peninsula or promontory that might be easily fortified on the land side. A line of intrenchments sufficiently strong to keep off any native force, might soon be made, and easily strengthened afterwards. On this strong basis negotiations might probably be carried on with a better chance of success.

The very last English visit to Japan, of which we have any account, was made as late as May, 1849, when the "Mariner" sloop of war, Commander Matheson, anchored off the town of Oragawa, twenty-five miles from Jeddo. On the approach of the ship, some officers came off and

* "China during the War and since the Peace," &c.

presented a paper in French and Dutch, desiring that she should neither anchor nor cruise about the bay, but remain out at sea. On this being declined, as the wind fell light, they offered their boats to tow the ship to her anchorage. The maritime town of Oragawa appears to be the key of Jeddo, the capital city, the whole trade of which touches there at the custom-house, and, with a moderate force, might be completely stopped by any naval power. Commander Matheson found the native officers extremely courteous and obliging: they were very anxious to gain every sort of information from their visitors, but they would give none in return, being afraid to speak of their own country or government.*

As we have an official report of this our last visit of all, and as it is as brief as it is curious, we will here give it in full:—

"*Extract of a letter from Commander Matheson, of H. M. S.* "*Mariner,*" *to Captain E. M. Trowbridge, of H. M. S.* "*Amazon;*" *dated* 14*th July*, 1849, *at Shanghae. Communicated by the Admiralty.*

"SIR,—I have the honor to inform you, for the information of the Commander-in-Chief, that, in obedience to orders from his Excellency, dated 14th May last, I proceeded in H. M. S. "Mariner," under my command, on the 17th of that month, to the coast of Japan, and anchored on the 29th May, off the town of Oragawa, situated twenty-five miles from the capital of the empire, three miles further than any other vessel has been allowed to proceed, sounding all the way across and along the shore of Japan.

"Having a Japanese on board, who acted as interpreter, he informed the authorities of the object of my visit. I sent my card written in Chinese, ashore, to the Governor, requesting him to name the time he would receive me. His reply was, that, out of courtesy to me, and curiosity to himself to see the ship, he would have liked very much to pay me a visit, and also entertain me ashore; but it

* "Journal of Royal Geographical Society," vol. xx. p. 136.

was contrary to the laws of their country for any foreigner to land, and that he would lose his life if he permitted me to go ashore, or to proceed any further up the bay.

"When about eight miles from Cape Misaki, which forms the southwest end of the bay, ten boats came alongside, manned with twenty men and five mandarins in each, all armed with muskets and swords. The mandarins wore a sword and dagger.

"I allowed the latter on board, when they presented me a paper written in French and Dutch, desiring me not to anchor or cruise about the bay, but remain at sea. Finding, however, that I was determined to proceed, and the wind falling light when within two miles of the anchorage, at half-past eight o'clock they offered their boats to tow us up, which I accepted.

"When the mandarins left the ship, several boats were stationed all round us during the night. Forts were lighted up, and about 400 boats, all manned and armed, collected along the shore, each carrying a lantern. By means of my interpreter, who was very much frightened, I made them keep at a respectful distance; had the guns loaded, and kept a watch on deck, armed, during the night, in case of any treachery on their part. Othoson, our interpreter, said he would not land on any account; that they would murder all of us, and as for himself, they would torment him all his life.

"Oragawa appears to be the key of the capital of the empire; contains 20,000 inhabitants, and could hold 1,200 junks. All the junks going and returning from Jeddo arrive here to pass the custom-house; and, with a moderate armed force, the trade might be completely stopped; for Jeddo depends upon its supplies by sea. From the advantage a steamer has over a sailing vessel, there would be no difficulty in her surveying or sounding the passage up to Jeddo, which you can approach, as I am informed, within five miles. There is a very good road between the two towns.

"The mandarins appear of an inferior class. They treated us civilly; were anxious to gain every information, but to give none in return. They took sketches of different parts of the ship; sent us some water, vegetables, and eggs; after which they were continually inquiring when I intended to depart.

"I directed Mr. Halloran, the master, to make a survey of the anchorage, which I beg to forward along with his remarks, and some of my own. The day was fortunately clear and fine; generally speaking, it is very foggy and misty.

"On the 31st May I weighed, and proceeded to Semodi Bay, where I remained four and a half days, to enable the master to take a more accurate survey of the bay, a copy of which I transmit herewith.

"There are three fishing villages at this anchorage, where I landed for a short time; but the mandarins followed, begging and entreating me to go on board. They supplied us with plenty of fish, and sent fifty boats to tow us out, so anxious were they to get us away. The weather detained me, however, two days at this anchorage, and the governor of the province came on board on the third; he lives thirteen miles off, at a town called Miomaki. He was evidently a man of rank, from the respect shown to him by his followers.

"The Dutch interpreter, from Oragawa, and two other mandarins, made their appearance (after the second day) to watch our proceedings. They appear to be spies one upon the other, and would exchange scarcely anything, and that only by stealth.

"On the 7th of June I again weighed and returned to this anchorage on the 2nd of July."*

The attention of the whole civilized world is now fixed on the American expedition. This cannot be made a merely national object; its character must be essentially cosmopolitan. We rejoice to see that the subject has

* "Journal of the Royal Geographical Society," vol. xx. p. 136. London, 1851.

We observe that our English and American writers are in the habit of calling the grandees of Japan by the Chinese name of mandarins, which is very unsuitable to them, and by no means descriptive of their hereditary rank. Mr. C. W. King (committing the common error) gives an amusing anecdote:—"We had inquired of the Japanese how their officers were to be distinguished—whether they wore any badges besides the ever-famous 'two sabres.' The answer was, *If you see a man come on board that trembles very much, he is a mandarin*."—"Notes of the Voyage of the 'Morrison,'" &c. New York. 1839.

claimed the attention of our own mercantile classes, and that efforts are making to diffuse authentic information concerning it. We must not be outstripped in the East even by the Americans.

It was the opinion of the illustrious Humboldt, that an opportunity for opening a liberal and honorable communication between Europe and Japan, would not occur until the two great oceans (the Atlantic and the Pacific) should be united by a canal cut across the Isthmus of Panama, when the productions of the west and northwest coasts of America, China, and Japan, would be brought more than 6,000 miles nearer Europe and the United States, and when alone any great change could be effected in the political and commercial policy of eastern Asia. "For this neck of land," said Humboldt, "has been for ages the bulwark of the independence of China and Japan."

A very recent English writer says, "Since, however, this opinion was expressed, the bulwark has been breached, and various circumstances have transpired to alter the features of the case, and to bring about a rapid change in the tide of commerce, and the progress of trade. The British have established themselves on the frontiers of China, and in the heart of the Eastern Archipelago, and have compelled respect to their flag and freedom to their trade. Energy and enterprise have constructed a railroad across the Isthmus of Panama, and the gold discoveries of California, and the colonization of Vancouver's Island, have settled a vast and industrious population on the western sea-board of the American continent, and led to the establishment of new lines of steam navigation, and an immense tide of commerce and emigration. The opening of the Nicaragua, Tehuantepee, and other practicable routes of intercommunication between different points on the Atlantic and Pacific, has been undertaken by various companies. Steam communication has been extended from India to China, and recently to our Australasian settlements, by the way of Singapore and Java. There has also been a great increase in the European and American shipping employed in the India and China trade in general commerce, and the whale-fishery on the Pacific. The Americans, particularly, have largely extended their whaling fleet, and prosecuted the fishery very successfully to the seas and coasts of Japan and her northern dependencies, to the gulfs of Tartary and Okotsk, the Sea of Kamtschatka, Behring's Straits, and the Arctic Ocean.

"The port of San Francisco, California, is destined to become the great mart and entrepôt for American commerce on the Pacific, with China, Japan, and all the maritime countries of Asia, Polynesia, Oceanica, and Australasia, which embrace an aggregrate population of upwards of six hundred millions. Our own excellent port and harbor of Sidney, from proximity and central situation, having now the advantages of regular steam communication, possesses even superior advantages for carrying on a most extensive and lucrative trade with the coasts and islands of Asia and the Eastern Archipelago.

"Japan is directly opposite the American possessions on the Pacific coast, and the two great islands of Niphon and Jesso from the Strait of Sangar, through which hundreds of its whale fleet are compelled annually to pass. To land, however, on any of the shores of this empire for supplies of wood, water, or the necessaries of life, or to be forced upon them by stress of weather, subjects the unfortunate whaler to robbery and death.

"Japan not only refuses to hold commercial intercourse

with the rest of the world—a very questionable right; but she goes further; and, occupying, as she does, an enormous extent of seacoast, not only refuses to open her ports to foreign vessels in distress, but actually opens her batteries upon them when they approach within gun-shot of her shores. And when driven upon them by stress of weather, she seizes upon, imprisons, exhibits in cages, and actually murders the crews of such ill-fated vessels.

"The world, however, is one of progress; and in the march of human events it is highly probable that the Japanese will be persuaded of the error of their present policy, and induced to pursue a more liberal course.

"The insular geographical position of Japan, her excellent ports and harbors, dense and industrious population, her boundless productive resources and vast capabilities for commerce, the superior intelligence and refinement of her princes and nobles, together with the skill, energy, and enterprise of the Japanese people, justly entitle her to rank above every other Asiatic nation. By a judicious relaxation of her restrictive policy, all these unrivalled, natural, and political advantages, could be made available for couducting a very extensive and profitable trade with various countries both on the Atlantic and Pacific, without compromising either her sovereignty, national religion, or peculiar institutions.

"This isolated and mysterious empire, which has been since 1637 hermetically sealed to all foreign intercourse and trade, except with the Chinese and Dutch, will now be compelled by force of circumstances to succumb to the progressive commercial spirit of the age, and the Japanese islands will eventually become in the East what the British islands are in the West."*

* "Lawson's Merchant's Magazine, Statist, and Commercial Re-

American papers state that there exists further south a route vastly superior to the Panama, Nicaragua, and the Tchuatessed, inasmuch as the new route offers peculiar facilities for the cheap construction of a canal. They allude to that of the rivers Atrato and San Juan, in the republic of New Grenada. The Atrato extends from the Gulph of Darien, in latitude 8° in a southerly direction, to latitude 5°, where it approaches very near the head-water of the river San Juan, which empties into the Pacific Ocean in latitude 4°, a short distance from Buena Ventura. Humboldt, when in New Grenada some fifty years ago, stated that not only was a canal practicable across the dividing ground between the head-waters of the two rivers, but that one of small dimensions had actually been constructed by the natives, who, by its means, had carried on for many years an extensive traffic between the towns on the Pacific coast and those on the Atlantic.

A New York company has obtained from the govern-

---

view," edited by B. H. Strousberg, author of "Practical Finance," "Nummus," &c., vol. i. No. 1. London: May, 1852; published by Robert Hastings, 13, Carey-street.

We hail with very much pleasure the appearance of this very useful, well-conducted work. The first number, which is all that we have as yet seen of it, does great credit to the editor and his contributors. Some such work was really a desideratum in our literature. Our brethren across the water have long had a periodical work of the same nature, entitled, "The Merchant's Magazine and Commercial Review," published at New York. We have before us the first volume, which appeared in 1839, and which contains some valuable information about Japan. Of the editor and writers of the English work we know nothing personally, but we very cordially wish them success.

ment of New Grenada a grant for the construction of a canal along this route; and an able civil engineer, Mr. J. J. Williams, has been selected to make the necessary surveys. In this connection, we may also give the following extract from a Report by the Committee on Naval Affairs to the last Congress, in relation to a line of steam-ships to connect San Francisco with Macao, or some other port in China:—

"The acquisition of California presents facilities for trade and intercourse with China which ought not to be neglected. It is believed that steamers can regularly make the voyage from the Bay of San Francisco to China in twenty days; and by the circuitous route over the isthmus, now necessarily used, communication is maintained between the western coast of our Atlantic cities in little more than thirty days. Thus the establishment of a line of steamers on the Pacific would place New York within less than sixty days of Macao. The trade with China in sailing vessels, which go round the Cape, now labors under a great disadvantage in the length of time required for the voyage. It may be assumed that an average of ten months is required to make the return; and the voyage from Europe to China and back may be considered as occupying an average of full twelve months. With the facilities now existing, and with the addition of the Pacific line proposed by the memorialists, the communication between Liverpool and China would be reduced to sixty days, and the return of an adventure from London to China might be received by the way of the United States in less than five months, less than half the time now required."

This report to Congress has been followed by various other papers, which have not yet reached this country. The magnitude of the subject is in every way imposing. If viewed on this scale, commerce assumes the character of romance or of lofty poetry.

A recent American writer says:—

"The commerce of India has always enriched the nation enjoying it. The exports of China have so much value in proportion to their bulk, that they can well afford to bear the cost of steam transportation.

"With all the advantages which will be possessed by a line of six steamers of enormous capacity for freight, wearing the flag of the United States, commanded by officers of the navy, making their trips with regularity, and much more speedily than on any other routes, it is certain that the rich stream of eastern commerce would flow into the United States; that new markets would be opened among the dense population of the East for our varied productions; and that a great increase of public revenue would result from increased importations; and if the goods imported be not entered, but warehoused, vast advantage would follow to our commercial and shipping interests. Shippers of goods to be warehoused and sent to a more favorable market, would necessarily draw on their consignees, and the additional great commercial advantage of exchange would thus be secured to our merchants.

"The competitors for the China trade are the British and American merchants. The commerce of the United States with China has been steadily increasing, and it can scarcely be doubted that the contemplated facility of communication by steam will give to our enterprising countrymen advantages which cannot be countervailed by those of any European nation.

"One of the greatest and most important effects of the concentration of this commerce at some point in the Bay of San Francisco (where must necessarily be located the depôt on the Pacific), and the extension of our intercourse with the Asiatic nations, would be to hasten the adoption of some practicable plan for connecting the two oceans by a railroad across the continent; thus binding together two widely-separated members of our confederacy, not only by the moral influence of the same constitution and laws, but by another link in that vast system of improvement by which the common welfare is to be so greatly promoted, and by which alone the remote state of California and the coterminous possession of the United States can be brought into those easy and intimate relations, and that constant intercourse which ought to subsist between all parts of the same government."

Mr. J. J. *Williams*, in a recently published work, gives the following as the different distances to California:—

	NAUTICAL MILES
From England to San Francisco, round Cape Horn .	13,624
From England to San Francisco, *viâ* Panama . . .	7,502
From England to San Francisco, *viâ* Nicaragua . .	7,401
From England to San Francisco, *viâ* Tehuantepec .	6,671
From New York to San Francisco, round Cape Horn	14,194
From New York to San Francisco, *viâ* Panama . .	4,992
From New York to San Francisco, *viâ* Tehuantepec .	3,804
From New Orleans to San Francisco, round Cape Horn	14,314
From New Orleans to San Francisco, *viâ* Panama .	4,505
From New Orleans to San Francisco, *viâ* Nicaragua	3,767
From New Orleans to San Francisco, *viâ* Tehuantepec	2,704

Mr. Allen M'Donnell, also an eminent English engineer, in discussing the project of a railroad from Lake Superior to the Pacific, says, in reference to the isthmus route:—

"Through her geographical position, the United States can more readily avail herself of the benefits to be derived from this course than any other nation. Her fleets would steam in one unbroken line through the Gulph of Mexico: her naval power would overawe our settlements upon the north-west coasts; and her influence extend itself throughout all our Indian possessions. The Marquesas Islands, in case the project be carried into effect, lying directly in the route of the navigation to India, would, at a step, advance into one of the most important maritime ports in the world, whilst the Society Islands, also in the possession of France, would enhance immensely in their value; more than all, returning back, the vessels of all Europe would ere long procure their tropical productions from the newly-awakened islands in the Pacific Ocean: in just the degree that their value would increase, the West India possessions would depreciate. . . . The power and advantage of St. Helena, Mauritius, Cape Town, and the Falkland Islands, commanding the passage round Cape

Horn, would be transferred to New Orleans and other cities of the United States bordering upon the Gulph of Mexico."*

Enough has been here quoted to show the lofty aspirations of the citizens of the United States, and the necessity of vigilance, activity, and energy on the part of the merchants and navigators of Great Britain.*

* For these interesting American extracts we are indebted to "Lawson's Merchant's Magazine," vol. i. No. 1, May, 1852.

* See Appendix A.

THE FUDSI-JAMMA.

BOOK II.

GEOGRAPHICAL SKETCH OF JAPAN.

THIS country was altogether unknown to the Greeks and Romans of the ancient world; and to the modern world it was first mentioned, under the Chinese name of Zipangu, by that truly illustrious traveller Marco Polo, who was in China, and engaged in the service of the great conqueror Kublaï-Khan at the close of the thirteenth century.

It is to be noted that Marco Polo did not visit the country in person. He collected his information in China, at the court of the great Khan. This is his brief description:—

"Zipangu is an island in the Eastern Ocean, situate at the distance of about fifteen hundred miles from the mainland or coast of *Manji*. It is of considerable size; its inhabitants have fair complexions, are well-made, and are civilized in their manners. Their religion is the worship of idols. They are independent of every foreign power, and governed only by their kings. They have gold in the greatest abundance, its sources being inexhaustible; but as the king does not allow of its being exported, few merchants visit the country, nor is it frequented by much shipping from other ports. To this circumstance we are to attribute the extraordinary richness of the sovereign's palace, according to what we are told by those who have had access to the place. The entire roof is covered with a plating of gold, in the same manner as we cover houses, or more properly churches, with lead. The ceilings of the halls are of the same precious metal; many of the apartments have small tables of pure gold considerably thick, and the windows also have golden ornaments. So vast, indeed, are the riches of the palace, that it is impossible to convey an idea of them. In this island there are pearls also in large quantities, of a red (pink) color, round in shape, and of great size; equal in value to, or even exceeding, that of the white pearls. It is customary with one part of the inhabitants to bury their dead, and with another part to burn them. The former have a practice of putting one of these pearls into the mouth of the corpse. There are also found there a number of precious stones.

"Of so great celebrity was the wealth of this island, that a desire was excited in the breast of the Grand Khan

Kublaï, now reigning, to make the conquest of it, and to annex it to his dominions."*

A glance at the map will show the advantageous geographical position of this empire. From the great Corean Peninsula, to the jutting promontories of Tarakay, there is a succession of islands in contiguity—being one vast volcanic chain—and this line is continued by the Kurile Islands, which join, or almost touch, the great peninsula of Kamtschatka. On the map, these islands look like so many stepping-stones, to pass from Corea to Kamtschatka.†

Japan consists of an unknown number of these islands, of very different dimensions. Some of the Kurile group belong or pay tribute to her, while others are occupied by Russia, and governed by the Russian authorities in Kamtschatka.‡

These islands may be considered as constituting the western boundary of the Pacific between 31° and 45° N.

---

* "Travels of Marco Polo,' as edited by the late William Marsden, Esq. An invaluable work to all who are engaged in studying the remote countries of the East.

† See particularly "Outline Map of North Eastern Asia and the Asiatic Islands of the Northern Pacific Ocean," drawn from the latest accessible authorities, by Aaron H. Palmer, to illustrate his memoir, geographical, political, and commercial, on Siberia, Manchuria, &c., addressed to his Excellency James K. Polk, President of the United States, under date of the 10th of January, 1848, and printed by order of the Senate of the United States.

‡ This government has long paid a very laudable attention to the Japanese language, &c. Even so far back as the time of the adventurous Count de Benyowsky (A. D. 1771) there were several Russians, in Kamtschatka and Siberia, who had learned the language from shipwrecked Japanese. See "Benyowsky's Memoirs and Travels," vol. i. 4to. London. 1790.

lat.; but the Japanese settlements on the island Tshoka, or Tarakay, better known by the name of Takhalia, seem to extend as far north as 47° or 48° N. lat. Between these islands and the continent of Asia, is a closed sea, called the sea of Japan, which at its southern extremity is united to the Tong-Hai, or Eastern Sea of the Chinese, by the Strait of Corea, and at its northern with the sea of Okhotsk, or Tarakai, by the still unexplored strait which divides the island of Tarakai from Manchuria. The Sea of Japan is united to the Pacific by several straits, which divide the Japanese islands from one another. The most remarkable is the Strait of Sangar, between the large islands of Niphon and Jesso. Japan is situate between 129° and 150° E. long. from Greenwich. It is divided into Proper Japan and the dependent islands.

Proper Japan consists of three large islands,—Kioosioo or Kewsew, Sitkokf, and Niphon or Nifon, which are surrounded by a great number of smaller islands. Kioosioo, the most western, may be about 200 miles long, with an average breadth of 80 miles, which would give it a surface of 16,000 miles, nearly equal to that of the island of Sardinia. On its western coast are two deep bays; that of Simabara in the middle, which is by far the largest, and that of Omoora, north of it; at its southern extremity is the Bay of Kangosima. Kioosioo is separated from Sitkokf by the Bungo Channel, and from Niphon by the Suwo Sound and the Strait of Simonoseki. Sitkokf may be 150 miles long, with an average breadth of 70 miles; it probably contains more than 10,000 square miles, and is much larger than the island of Corsica. The long strait which divides it from Niphon on the north, is in some places hardly more than a mile wide, but about the middle a large bay enters deeply into the island of Sitkokf. The eastern extremity of this is separated from Niphon by the Bay of Osacca, which contains the island of Awadsi. Niphon, the largest and the principle of the Japanese islands, has the form of a curve, or, as Kämpfer says, of a jawbone. Its length, measured along the middle of the island, exceeds 900 miles, and its average width may be estimated at more than 100 miles; its surface may, therefore, cover an area of about 100,000 square miles, or considerably more than that of Great Britain. Its largest bays are along the southern coast; as Osacca Bay, Mia Bay, and Yedo, or Jeddo Bay.

The dependent countries are the large island of Yesso, with some of the Kurile Islands, and the southern districts of Tarakay. Yesso has a very irregular form; its length, from west-south-west to east-north-east, is more than 250 miles, and its average width, perhaps, does not fall short of 100 miles. This gives a surface of 25,000 square miles, or somewhat less than that of Ireland. Only the two southernmost of the larger Kurile Islands, Kunashir and Uturup, are now regularly occupied by the Japanese; the others, as we have said, belong to the Russian empire. The island of Tarakay, whose southern portion is called Tshoka, is divided from Yesso by the Strait of La Perouse. It is certain that the Japanese have formed some settlements here, but it is not known how far they extend northward. According to this rough estimate, and excluding the settlements on the island of Tarakay, the Japanese empire contains about 160,000 square miles.

All these islands are very imperfectly known; not even the coasts are laid down with any degree of correctness. This arises partly from natural causes. Nearly all the coasts are very difficult of access, being surrounded by numerous rocks and islands, and by a very shallow sea.

6

This shallowness is most remarkable in the numerous inlets and bays with which the southern coast is indented. The harbor of Jeddo or Yedo, for instance, is so shallow, that even small boats cannot approach the beach: the larger Japanese vessels keep far out to sea, and a European ship would be obliged to anchor at five leagues' distance. The harbor of Osacca is not much better. This circumstance may, in some measure, account for the smallness of Japanese vessels.

The sea, besides containing numerous rocks, has some very dangerous whirlpools, two of which especially have been noticed by navigators: one near the island of Amakoosa, at the entrance of the Bay of Simabara, and the other near the southern extremity of Niphon, between the bays of Osacca and of Mia.* To this must be added, that no part of the ocean is subject to heavier gales than the sea which surrounds Japan.

Some of our travellers (Thunberg, for instance) assert that the whole surface of these islands is only a succession of mountains, hills, and valleys; but Kämpfer expressly says that he passed-through several plains of considerable extent: as that which runs from the town of Osacca to Miaco, a distance of about seventy miles; and a similar plain west of Jeddo, and extending to that town. A large plain occurs also along the northern shores of the Bay of Mia, and numerous smaller plains are noticed by Kämpfer. But generally the hills run down close to the sea, or leave only a narrow strip of level ground between them and

* Striking descriptions of these phenomena will be found in Kämpfer's valuable old book. The Japanese give the most fabulous account of them. They appear to be constantly mentioned by their poets and other writers.

the seashore. Though Japan is doubtless a very hilly country, it can hardly be said to be monntainous, as by far the greatest number of the eminences are cultivated to the very top, and those few which are not cultivated are left in their natural state on account of the sterility of the soil. The Dutch have observed only one single peak of great elevation,—the Fudsi Jamma, not far from the Bay of Tomina, west of the Bay of Jeddo. They compare it in shape with the Peak of Teneriffe, and observe that the snow seldom melts on its top. Recent Dutch writers estimate the height of this remarkable peak at 11,000 to 12,000 French feet. According to the accounts of navigators, however, it would seem that the northern part of Niphon is traversed by a continuous chain of mountains with several peaks. Volcanoes, either in an active state or extinct, are numerous; to the latter class the Fudsi Jamma certainly belongs. Some active volcanoes occur on the islands scattered in the Strait of Corea; as the Sulphur Island, noticed by Captain Basil Hall.

From the peculiar form of these islands, it may be presumed that they have no large rivers; and the rapidity with which the streams run down shows that the country in the interior rises to a considerable height. Many of them are so rapid that no bridges can be built over them, and they are not passed without danger. Several others are less rapid, and though they cannot be navigated, timber and wood are floated down them. A considerable number, however, seem to be navigable for small river-boats to a distance of some miles from the sea. The most considerable and important of those which are known is the river Yedogawa, in Niphon, which rises in the Lake of Oity, a sheet of water sixty miles in length but of inconsiderable width. After leaving this lake, it traverses the fine plain which extends from its shores to the harbor of Osacca, and in all this course it is navigated by river-barges. Boating is a favorite pastime with the Japanese ladies and gentlemen. It appears from the accounts of several travellers, that they have rendered some of their rivers navigable for considerable distances by artificial means, and that they have some canals connecting their rivers and lakes.

We are, of course, very imperfectly acquainted with the climate of Japan, the meteorological observation made by Thunberg at Nagasaki only extending over one year. The southern part seems to resemble, in many points, the climate of England. In winter it does not freeze and snow every year, though in most years it does. The frost and snow, when there is any, lasts only a few days. In January, 1776, the thermometer descended at Nagasaki to 35° Fahr., but it was considered a very mild winter; in August, it rose to 98°, and that was considered as the average heat of the season. The heat would, consequently, be very great but for the refreshing breeze which blows during the day from the south, and during the night, from the east. The weather is extremely changeable, and rains are abundant all the year round; but they are more heavy and frequent during the *satkasi*, or rainy season, which occurs in June and July. Storms and hurricanes seem to occur very frequently, and the descriptions of them in Kämpfer and Langsdorf are truly terrific. Thunder-storms are also common, and earthquakes have successively destroyed a great part of the most populous towns. Only a few spots appear to be exempt from these terrible phenomena. It is observed by Kämpfer that waterspouts are nowhere of such frequent occurrence as in the seas inclosing Japan.

All travellers speak of the populousness of the country, and the extent of the villages, which frequently occupy two English miles and more in length. In some more fertile districts, they are so close to one another as to form nearly one continuous street; as, for instance, in the plain which extends from the harbor of Osacca to Miaco. The smaller towns commonly contain five hundred houses, and the larger two thousand and upwards; and though the houses have generally only two stories, they are occupied by a comparatively large number of persons.

I. The island of Kioosioc or Kewsew, is extremely well cultivated and generally fertile, with the exception of its eastern coast, bordering on the Bungo Channel, where it is mountainous, barren, and comparatively thinly inhabited. The best-known towns of importance are, Nagasaki, Sanga, and Kokoora.

Nagasaki, sometimes pronounced Nangasaki,* the only place open to foreigners, lies on a peninsula formed by the deep Bay of Omura, in 32° 45′ N. lat. and 129° 15′ E. long, Its harbor is spacious and deep, extending in length about four miles, with an average width of more than a mile. At its entrance is the small island of Papenberg, where the water is twenty-two fathoms deep, but it grows shallower as it proceeds inward, so that, opposite to the town, it has only a depth of four fathoms; so far it runs north-east, it then turns north, and has less depth. The town is built on its eastern shores, in a narrow valley which runs eastward. It is three quarters of a mile long, and almost as broad, and inclosed by steep,

* The proper name is certainly Nagasaki. We find it written and printed in a perplexing variety of ways. The old Spanish and Portuguese writers frequently turn it into Langasaki, or Lampsaki.

though not lofty, hills. There are some good buildings in the town; as the palaces of the two governors, and those of some princes and noblemen of the empire, but especially the temples, which were sixty-two in number, within and without the town, in the time of Kämpfer (1692.) The population may amount to 40,000 or 50,000 souls. It is one of the five imperial towns of the empire.

Sanga, situated on a fine and well-watered plain at the northern extremity of the large Bay of Simabara, the capital of the fertile province of Fisen, is a very large and populous town, with canals and rivers running through its wide and regular streets.*

Kokoora, built near the entrance of the Strait of Simonoseki, has a shallow harbor, but carries on a considerable trade. The town, which in the time of Kämpfer had much decreased, was found in a thriving state, in 1775, by Thunberg.

II. The island of Sitkokf, according to a Japanese geographer, cited by Kämpfer, contains many mountainous and barren districts, and is, on the whole, less fertile than the other large islands.

III. Nipon, or Nifon, or Niphon, which constitutes the main body and strength of the empire, is, as far as it has been seen by Europeans, well cultivated and fertile, with

* We are indebted for most of this well-condensed information to that excellent work the "Penny Cyclopædia," art. Japan. The geographical articles in that publication are particularly admirable. The whole work has now an established reputation in every part of the civilized world. We cordially wish its enterprising projector and publisher, Mr. Charles Knight, every encouragement and success in his new and greatly improved edition, which will bear the name of the "Imperial Cyclopædia," and will be dedicated to Her Gracious Majesty Queen Victoria, who greatly admired the original work.

the exception of a few barren tracts of moderate extent. The name *Nipon*, commonly applied by the Japanese to the whole of their empire, signifies source or fountain of light (*Fuente de luz*). The island contains the largest towns, and the manufactured articles produced in this island are considered the best. The important towns visited by Europeans, along its southern side are,—

Simonoseki, built at the foot of a mountain, on the shore of the narrow strait which bears its name, and which is only one mile and a half wide. It is not very large, but it carries on a very active coasting trade with all the districts to the east of it.

Muru, opposite the north-eastern coast of Sitkokf, consists only of about 600 houses; but its harbor is very safe, being well defended by a mountain; for which reason it is resorted to by the coasting vessels, of which frequently more than 100 are anchored there. It is noted for its tanneries, where horse-hides are tanned in the manner of the Russian leather.

Osacca, one of the five imperial towns, and the most commercial place in the empire, is situate in the northern angle of the Gulf of Osacca, on the banks of the river Yedogawa, which, near the town, divides into three branches, and, before it falls into the sea, into several more. The middle or principal branch of the river, though narrow, is deep and navigable. From its mouth, as far up as the town, and higher, there are seldom less than a thousand barges going up and down. Several navigable canals, which derive their water from the river, traverse the principal streets of the town, and serve as means for conveyance of goods. The banks of the river and of the canals are of freestone, coarsely hewn, and formed into ten or more steps, so as to resemble one continued staircase.

Numerous bridges, built of cedar-wood, are laid over the river and canals, some of them are of large dimensions, and beautifully ornamented. The streets are narrow, but regular, and cut each other at right angles; though not paved, they are very clean. A narrow pavement of flat stones runs along the houses for the convenience of foot-passengers. The houses are not above two stories high, and built of wood, lime, and clay. At the north-east extremity of the city is a large castle. The population is very great. According to the exaggerated account of the Japanese, an army of 80,000 men may be raised from among its inhabitants. Many of the residents are very wealthy men, especially the merchants, artists, and manufacturers. The Japanese themselves call Osacca the universal theatre of pleasure and diversion; and plays are daily exhibited in public and private houses. South of Osacca, on the shores of the same gulf, is Sakai, another imperial town.

Miaco, or Kio, the residence of the ecclesiastical emperor, or Daïri, is about twenty miles from Osacca, and contained, in the time of Kämpfer, according to a census, more than 500,000 inhabitants, besides the numerous court of the Daïri. From the latest Dutch accounts, it should appear that the population has greatly diminished, while that of Jeddo has greatly increased. All the authorities we have consulted agree in representing this holy city as the most immoral, profligate place in the Japanese empire. It is nearly four miles long and three wide. The Daïri resides on the northern side of the city, in a particular ward, consisting of twelve or thirteen streets, and separated from the city by walls and ditches. On the western part of the town is a strong castle, built of freestone, where the Kobo, or secular emperor, resides when he comes to visit the Daïri. The streets are narrow, but regular, and always greatly crowded. Miaco is the principal manufacturing town of the empire, where every kind of manufacture is carried to the greatest perfection. Nearly every house has a shop, and the quantity of goods which they contain is astonishing; at the same time, it is the centre of science and literature, and the principal place where books are printed. The town is united by a wide canal to the river Yedogawa, which flows not far from its walls.

Kwano and Mia are two very considerable and thriving towns on the Gulf of Mia, each containing 2,000 or 3,000 houses.

Yedo, or Jeddo, the capital of the empire, is situated at the northern extremity of the gulf of the same name, in an extensive plain. According to the Japanese, it is about ten miles long, seven wide, and nearly thirty miles in circuit. All travelers agree that it is the largest and most populous town in the empire, but no one of them has recently ventured to state the number of its inhabitants. M. Fischer, however, states that the populousness, activity, and bustle of the place reminded him of London; and there can be no doubt that the census would reach an enormously high figure. An old Portuguese writer roundly asserts that, in his time, the population amounted to 2,000,000. Some of the old Dutch writers fix it at 1,500,000. A large river runs through the town and sends off a considerable arm, which incloses the imperial palace, or that of the Kobo, or secular emperor. There are several good bridges over the river. The principal is called Niponbas, or the Bridge of Japan, and from it the milestones are counted, which are erected along the principal roads that traverse the empire. Jeddo is not so regularly built as Miaco, and the private houses do not differ from those of Osacca; but as the families of all the hereditary princes, lords, and noblemen are obliged to reside at the court the whole year round, the town contains a great number of fine palaces. Rows of trees are planted along the numerous canals which traverse the town, to prevent the fires from spreading. The Japanese have several curses in common with their cognate race the Turks. Fires are as frequent at Jeddo as at Constantinople; and, as the houses are chiefly of timber and bamboo, thousands of them often perish in one conflagration. Jeddo is not less famous for its manufactured goods than Miaco. The palace of the Kobo is built in the middle of the town. It consists of five palaces or castles, and some large gardens behind it, and is more than eight miles in circumference.

IV. The island of Yeso is very imperfectly known. On its western coast are lofty mountains. Its eastern and southern coast seem to be very thickly inhabited. Near the Strait of Sangar are two considerable towns, Kokodade* and Matsmai. The latter is the capital, and the residence of the governor.†

The Portuguese, Dutch, and other writers, are unanimous in representing the Japanese as an active, enterprising, commercial people. According to recent writers, some of their merchants are possessed of enormous capital, and are truly, "merchant princes."‡ Their liberality keeps pace with their riches.

All over the empire the inland trade is very considerable. The coasting trade is much favored by the great number of small harbors, and the interior commu-

---

* Often written Chocodada

† "Pen. Cyclopædia."

‡ MM. Doeff and Fischer.

nication by well-planned and well-maintained roads, which are always thronged with carriages and people. Most of the roads are wide, and ornamented with lines of trees. The foreign commerce is now limited to the Dutch and Chinese.

The Chinese, like the Dutch, are shut up in a small island, but are permitted to visit a temple in the town of Nagasaki. Their trade is much more extensive. About seventy junks arrive annually from the ports of Amoy, Ningpo, and Shanghae.

In the time of Kämpfer, there was still some trade carried on with Corea, and the Loo-Choo Islands: but this trade had ceased at the time of Thunberg (1775), and Siebold (1830) speaks of it as no longer existing. A few Coreans occasionally steal into the country in Chinese junks. Their race or nation is bitterly hated by the Japanese, who once held dominion over them.

Notwithstanding the rigid prohibitions of their laws, Japanese vessels occasionally carry on trade with foreigners covertly at Quelpaert's Island, the Majicosiana group, the Philippines, and the Loo-Choo and Bonin Islands. The latter are about 500 miles from the coast of Japan, possess safe harbors, and have been recently brought into a good state of cultivation by a small colony of English, Americans, and persons of other nations, who have made settlements and afford supplies to whalers, &c.*

After a careful comparison of authorities, we are inclined to think that the entire population of the Japanese empire can scarcely be taken at less than 25,000,000.†

---

* Lawson's "Merchant's Magazine."

† Mr. J. R. MacCulloch says that the population has been fixed by some writers at rather more than 50,000,000. See "Geographical,

To give a clearer idea of the towns, we subjoin the description of *one* of them by an old Dutch voyager:—

"Nanguesaque (Nagasaki) lies in 33° 15′ northerly latitude, in a very pleasant landship, and is both very great and populous; but like most of the towns of Japan, lies without walls. It is seated upon a very commodious bay, or road, fit to receive ships of the greatest burthen. It has a very magnificent prospect from seaward, having an infinite number of towers, temples, and spacious palaces. The houses are mostly built of wood, for the ground is weak, and frequently subject to earthquakes, so that they cannot use stone. But the poorer sort have little cottages made of twigs and plastered over with clay, as in Brabant, Germany, and other countries. They are covered with planks, which shoot far out over the walls like a pent-house, to shelter them from sun and rain. They have upon each house several tubs with water, which is kept in case of fire, to which such buildings are liable. And certainly, were it not for the great benefit of the water running through the town in ditches, as it does in most towns in Holland, it would be suddenly reduced to ashes, and for this reason have they built several houses of stone where to secure their goods upon such occasions. The houses in the city are uniform, and the streets regular, there being eighty-eight streets, each 400 feet long, which are all fenced off with palisades at the end, and lanterns set up. Here they have also their watch-houses, and none are suffered to pass by night; no, not to fetch either doctor or midwife, without a pass from

---

Statistical, and Historical Dictionary," vol. ii. We consider this number to be exaggerated, particularly as it excludes the inhabitants of the Japanese dependencies.

the governor. This watch is set always at ten o'clock, after which hour few people are seen upon the streets. This is a good means to prevent theft and mutiny, but is a great inconvenience if fire do happen to break out; for no street or ward can have the assistance of another in such a case; besides the great danger that the people themselves are in, being sometimes so narrowly pent up. An instance of this happened in the year 1646, when a dreadful fire happened in a house where several Dutch had their lodgings, which, on a sudden, had consumed a great part of the street and several houses on both sides, burnt down to the ground. The Dutch then seeing themselves in such peril, chose rather to hazard the effects of the governor's displeasure for that time, than to be roasted alive, and so broke up the fence and saved themselves."*

As there is considerable variety of opinion as to the climate of Japan, we will quote a passage from the Russian writer who resided a considerable time on one of the islands:—

"On a comparison of the geographical situation of the

---

* Struys. The title is not the least curious part of this rare and very curious old book. Here it is at full length:—

"The Voyages and Travels of John Struys, through Italy, Greece, Muscovy, Tartary, Media, Persia, East India, Japan, and other countries in Europe, Africa, and Asia; containing remarks and observations upon the manners, religion, politics, customs, and laws of the inhabitants, and a description of their several cities, towns, forts, and places of strength, together with an account of the author's many dangers by shipwreck, robbery, slavery, hunger, torture, and the like, and two narratives of the taking of Astracan, by the Cossacks, sent from Captain D. Butler, illustrated with copper plates, designed and taken from the life by the author himself.—Done out of Dutch, by John Morrison. London. 4to. 1684."

Japanese possessions, with that of the countries of the Western hemisphere, under the same degrees of latitude, it might be imagined that the climate, the changes of the seasons, and the atmosphere, were alike in both; but such a conclusion would be very erroneous.* The difference of these two parts of the world, in this respect, is so striking, that it deserves particular notice. I will take, as an example, Matsmai, where I lived two years. This town lies in the forty-second degree of latitude, that is, on a parallel with Leghorn in Italy, Bilboa in Spain, and Toulouse in France.

"In these places, the inhabitants hardly know what frost is; and never see any snow except on the tops of high mountains: in Matsmai, on the contrary, the ponds and lakes freeze, the snow lies in the valleys and plains, from November till April, and gales, besides, in as great abundance as with us in St. Petersburgh. Severe frosts are, indeed, uncommon; yet the cold is often fifteen degrees of Reaumur. In summer, the parts of Europe under the same latitude as Matsmai enjoy serene warm weather; in Matsmai, on the contrary, the rain pours down in torrents, at least twice a week, the horizon is involved in dark clouds, violent winds blow, and the fog is scarcely ever dispersed. In the former, oranges, lemons, figs, and other productions of the warm climates, thrive in the open air; in the latter apples, pears, peaches, and grapes, hardly attain their proper ripeness.

"I have not, it is true, been in Niphon, the principal

---

* Charlevoix states that the Japanese are much prejudiced in favor of their own climate, and acknowledges that it must be very healthy, since the people are long-lived, the women very prolific, and diseases very uncommon.

island of the Japanese possessions; but I have heard from the Japanese that, in Jeddo, the capital city of the empire, in the thirty-sixth degree of latitude, snow often falls, in the winter nights, to the depth of an inch or more. It is true it melts immediately the next day; but if we consider that Jeddo is under the same latitude as Malaga, in Spain, we shall be convinced that the climate of the Eastern hemisphere is much ruder than that of the Western. The Japanese assured me that, on the southern part of Sagaleen, in the forty-seventh degree of latitude, the ground is often thawed, during the summer, only to a depth of a foot and a half. If we compare with this the climate of a place in Europe, the latitude of which corresponds, for example, Lyons, in France, how different are the results! That the accounts given by the Japanese are true, I cannot doubt, for we ourselves met with great fields of ice, so late as the month of May, off the Kurile island, in latitude 47° 45′. At this season, no ice is to be seen with us in the Gulf of Finland, in 60° north latitude; though the water there, from being so confined, has not power to break the ice, which vanishes more in consequence of the rays of the sun. Off Japan, on the contrary, the waves of the ocean must break it up much sooner, if the sun acted with the same power.

"This great difference of the climate proceeds from local causes. The Japanese possessions lie in the Eastern Ocean, which may be truly called the *Empire of Fogs.* In the summer months, the fog often lasts three or four days without interruption, and there seldom passes a day in which it is not, for some hours, gloomy, rainy, or foggy. Perfectly clear days are as rare in summer there, as fogs in the Western Ocean. Though the fine weather is more constant in winter, yet a week seldom passes without two or three gloomy days. These fogs, and this gloomy weather, make the air cold and damp, and hinder the beams of the sun from producing so much effect as in other countries, which enjoy a clear sky. Besides this, the northern parts of the islands of Niphon, and Matsmai, and Sagaleen, are covered with extremely high mountains, the summits of which are mostly above the clouds, whence the winds that blow over these mountains bring an extraordinary degree of cold with them. It is also to be noted that the Japanese possessions are separated from the continent of Asia by a strait, the greatest breadth of which is 800 wersts, and that the country of the Mantchous, and Tartary, which from the east frontier of Asia, towards Japan, are nothing but immense deserts covered with mountains and innumerable lakes, from which the winds, that blow over them, bring, even in summer, an extraordinary degree of cold. These may be the three causes of the striking difference of climate in the countries situated on the eastern side of the old world, and those of the western hemisphere under the same degree of latitude."*

It appears, however, that, taking its whole extent, from south to north, and counting all its islands, Japan will afford the cultivator all the productions both of tropical and temperate climates; and that it is a most healthy country to live in. "The air of all these islands," says an

* Captain Golownin, "Recollections of Japan." We believe, as we have already declared, that this Russian officer is entitled to full credit whenever he speaks of the things which came under his own observation. It must, however, be borne in mind that he was a prisoner all the time he was in Japan. The atmosphere of a prison does not improve one's notions of the climate of any place.

old Spanish writer, "is very salubrious. The soil is very fertile, the fruits are most delicious."*

The abundance of running water affords everywhere the means of irrigation; and, in this art, the Japanese seem even to surpass the Chinese. The longevity of the people appears to be a well-established fact.†

---

* Don Pedro Hurtado de Mendoza, "Espejo Geographico." Madrid. 1690.

Count Benyowsky speaks of the excessive heat of the climate in the month of July.

† "Ambassades Mémorables," &c. By Jacob Van Meurs; Kämpfer's "History of Japan;" Charlevoix, "Histoire et Description Générale du Japon;" Thunberg's "Travels in Europe, Africa, and Asia;" Benyowsky, "Memoirs and Travels;" Adventures and Recollections of Captain Golownin; Siebold's "Japan;" Extracts from Fischer and Meylan; "Journal of Education," vol. vi. p. 370; and vol. x. p. 184. For some further geographical notices, see Appendix B.

THE CRATER OF THE FUDSI-JAMMA.

DIVINITIES

BOOK III.

RACE—PROBABLE COURSE OF MIGRATION—SUMMARY OF HISTORY.

If you ask a Japanese of what race they are, or whence they came, he will tell you with great pride, that they are lineally descended from the gods, and had their origin in the islands which they now inhabit. They consider themselves affronted by those who attempt to draw their descent from the Chinese. Because a good many Chinese usages prevail among them, the belief in this descent long obtained in Europe. The stock to which they really belong is the great Mongol race, which has peopled so vast a portion of the Eastern world, and which now fills the undefined country of Tartary, a great part of the Russian empire and central Asia, and is found, in other offshoots, in the Turkomans, Calmuks, Turks, Tongus, and the like. The same race conquered China, but at a period long subsequent to the peopling of Japan.

Ethnologists are now agreed as to this Mongol assimilation. Although the Japanese, in their writing and printing, frequently drop in a Chinese character, to express a Chinese thing or idea, the two characters, however identical in their origin, are now totally distinct. Nor is there any affinity between the two languages, although the Japanese frequently borrow Chinese terms, rather to parade their learning than from any deficiency of equivalent expressions in their own tongue.

There can scarcely be a greater difference than in the pronunciation of the two peoples: it should seem, as Kämpfer remarks, that the very instruments of voice are different in the Japanese to what they are in the Chinese. The pronunciation of the Japanese language, in general, is sharp, articulate, and distinct, there being seldom, according to our alphabet, more than two or three letters combined together in one syllable; the pronunciation of the Chinese, on the contrary, is nothing but a confused noise of many consonants, pronounced with a sort of sing-song accent, very disagreeable to the unaccustomed ear. The same strong difference appears with regard to particular letters. Thus the Chinese pronounce our letter *h* very distinctly, but the Japanese can give it no other sound but that of an *f*. Again, the Japanese pronounce the letters *r* and *d* very distinctly, while the Chinese always make an *l* of them, even such as are well skilled in the European languages. There are other instances equally striking. We allude to the language in this place merely as connected with the question of race, reserving for a future chapter some ampler observations on it, and on the characteristic literature of Japan.

Another argument against the descent of the the Japanese from the Chinese, is drawn from the difference between the ancient religions of the two nations. If the Japanese were a colony of the Chinese, they would have brought with them into these islands the faith and worship of their mother country. But the original religion of the Japanese, by them called *Sintoo*, is peculiar to their own country, and has not the slightest resemblance to the ancient belief of the Chinese. Buddhism exists in both countries, but is to both of exotic growth, and was not introduced into either until a comparatively recent period. Besides, the Japanese say that they received Buddhism not from China but from Corea.

There are also differences in physical conformation. Although strongly marked with the Mongol type, the Japanese bear a stronger resemblance to the European family, and their eyes are not so deeply sunk in their heads as those of the Chinese. Generally, it may be said that the Japanese are not so strong as Europeans; but they are well made and have stout limbs. Their eyes show their Mongol origin, not being round, but oblong and small. Their hair is black, thick, and shining, and their noses, although not flat, are rather thick and short. Their complexion is yellowish. They seem to resemble most the inhabitants of Corea and the Ainos, on the island of Tarakai. In a country so vast and so various in climate as China, there are great differences between the inhabitants of the several provinces; but, in general terms, it may be admitted that the Japanese are a stronger, hardier, and a braver race than the Chinese.

In some parts of the islands, even the common people, if dressed in our costume, might pass for Portuguese, or southern Italians, or Sicilians. Many of the Upper classes, or members of the old families, are tall exceedingly handsome in figure and countenance, and are far more like Europeans than Asiatics.

Then again the Japanese greatly differ from the Chinese in many of their customs and ways of life, as in eating, drinking, sleeping, dressing, shaving of the head, saluting, sitting, and many others. There is also a remarkable difference in the national characters of the two. The Chinese are peaceable, timid, much given to a sedate, ruminating way of life; cunning, suspicious, greedy, and much addicted to fraud and usury; the Japanese are quick and volatile, daring, fond of an active, exciting life, frank, liberal, and open-handed, having many of the virtues of the nomadic tribes. Of course we speak of the people and not of the government.

In their governmental and municipal institutions, in their law of primogeniture, in their hereditary nobility, and in many other institutions, they widely differ from the people of the Celestial Kingdom.

Although this singular people seem always to have been somewhat jealous of intermixture, or even of intercourse, with foreigners, they appear to have admitted from time to time small colonies from China, Corea, and perhaps from some other neighboring countries.* The Japanese themselves make frequent mention in their histories of learned Chinese, who brought over into Japan their books, and the knowledge of useful arts and sciences, though not until the latter ages, when their own original stock had vastly increased and multiplied, and Japan had already become a powerful empire. "And, indeed," says old Kämpfer, "since so few foreign words have been brought into the Japanese language, that it is hardly visible that there hath been any alteration at all made in it, and since the religion and old customs subsist

* Nothing was done by war, or invasion and conquest. The Chinese never made good an invasion of Japan. But the Japanese invaded, and for a time occupied, Corea, or, at least, the maritime parts of that peninsula, and made frequent inroads on China. As we speak of virgin fortresses, so we may call Japan a virgin empire, for it has never been conquered by any foreign foe. This, in spite of the oppressiveness of their internal government, no doubt contributes materially to the independent bearing of the people.

till now, it appears plainly that whatever foreign colonies did from time to time voluntarily or by chance come over into Japan, their number must have been very inconsiderable with regard to the bulk of the Japanese nation."

The same ingenious old writer, whose facts are still invaluable, and whose theories are deserving of all respect, draws a pleasant and very creditable itinerary. At the confusion of languages, or dispersion of peoples, he brings the Japanese family, by slow marches, from Mesopotamia, to the shores of the Caspian Sea, where they would find a large and fertile country extending itself far eastward, offering abundance of pasture to their cattle and their flocks, and the means of easily and leisurely pursuing their journey. He supposes that they then proceeded through the valleys of the Yenisi, Silinga, and parallel rivers until they came to the Lake of Argueen, where the cold northern climate would not invite a long stay. From that lake arises a large river of the same name, the valley of which would bring them to the still more considerable river, the Amoor, which runs E.S.E., and the long valley of which would bring them to the eastern coasts of Asia, into the then uninhabited peninsula of Corea, where the Amoor loses itself in the Eastern Ocean. Once at Corea, the passage over to Japan was neither long, nor (in the summer weather) dangerous, especially as there are many little islands at almost regular distances between the main and the large islands which constitute the Japanese empire. In fact they might have crossed over in common fishing-boats. In the many broad rivers and vast lakes they had crossed, or on whose banks they had sojourned during their long migration, they must have made themselves familiar with the use of boats, and a short residence in Corea, on the coast of a sea abounding with fish, must soon have made fishermen and expert boatmen of these pastoral tribes.

It is not supposed that this immense march was made in one, in fifty, or in a hundred years. The ancestors of the Japanese would probably remain in any favorable region until they felt their rear pressed upon, or their flank annoyed, by other nomadic tribes. Then they would collect their flocks and herds, and move forward in quest of other regions and "pastures new." They could make a home wherever they could find streams of pure water and pasture for their flocks and herds. Something of the same sort may still be seen in many parts of the East. Even so near as Asiatic Turkey, when certain pastoral tribes are oppressed in one pashalic, they move on, with all that they possess, to another; and should the same inconvenience follow them, they go on to a still greater distance; and were the countries in their front not occupied (however thinly), it would be difficult to put an imaginable limit to their migrations. What Kämpfer fancies is, that from the purity or freedom from admixture of the Japanese language, that people could not have made any very considerable stay in any one country, or with any one people then existing. Had they made such stay, they must have adopted some words of the language of that nation into their own. Having brought them across the seas to Niphon, the most considerable of their islands, he carries them from the western coast to the southern extremity of the land, where the soil is most fruitful, the air most mild and salubrious, and where every advantage was offered in the way of security, tranquillity, and pleasant abode. To this day the Japanese look upon this part of their country as the place where their ancestors first dwelt, and as such they honor it with frequent pilgrimages and other acts of devotion.

Whatever may have been their original course and the time of their arrival in the islands, it appears to be in a high degree probable that the Japanese, at a remote period, peopled at least a part of the great American continent.*

The Japanese have in their literature many histories, if that name can be conferred on wild chronicles and semi-fabulous annals. Though pretending to a descent from the gods, and of course to a remote antiquity, their writers are not so ambitious in the latter respect as are those of the Celestial Empire. Passing over the obscure times when the country was divided into clan or tribe governments, they fix the foundation of their monarchy, under Syn Mu, about the year before Christ 660. The government was strictly hereditary and theocratical: Syn Mu

---

* "The Polynesian groups are everywhere separated from South America by a vast expanse of ocean, where rough waves and perpetually adverse winds and currents oppose access from the west. In attempting, from any part of Polynesia, to reach America, a canoe would naturally and almost necessarily be conveyed to the northern extreme of California; and this is the precise limit where the second physical race of men makes its appearance. So well understood is the course of navigation, that San Francisco, I am informed, is commonly regarded in Mexico as 'being on the route to Manila.' Again, the northern extreme of California is as favorably situated for receiving a direct arrival from Japan. At the present day, owing to a change in national policy, Japanese vessels are only by accident found at large. But, within a few years, one has been fallen in with by a whale-ship in the north Pacific; another has been wrecked on the Sandwich Islands; and, a case more in point, a third has been drifted to the American coast, near the mouth of the Columbia river."—"The Races of Man, and their Geographical Distribution." By Charles Pickering, M.D., Member of the United States Exploring Expedition.

was at once the high priest, or representative of the divinities, and king or emperor of the people. He civilized the inhabitants of Japan, introduced chronology among them, dividing the time into years and months, and reformed the laws and government of the country. Having fully secured the throne to his posterity, and attained to the fabulous age of 156 years, he died, full of honor and sanctity. If there were troubles in the islands, they appear not to have been recorded; one theocrat quietly succeeding to another in their annals. But when the empire was about 200 years old, a civil war is first mentioned by their historians. For a long succession of years, nothing is chronicled but an occasional earthquake, volcanic eruption, meteoric phenomenon, comet, or fiery dragon, always excepting, however, great efforts made by emperors and sages to discover the philosopher's stone, or the elixir vitæ, or some compound which should make the life of man immortal. In the same ages, and long after, the same fancies haunted the imaginations of the emperors and philosophers of the Celestial Empire. From the east, the whim flew to Europe; and, as an old writer slily observes, the Europeans were not more unsuccessful than the Japanese in their pursuit of the means of transmuting metals and prolonging life.

In the nineteenth year of the reign of the Emperor Siunsin (before Christ 78) merchant ships and ships of war were first built in Japan; and under Siunsin's son and successor, "it rained stars from heaven in Japan." It is also noted that in this same reign of Synin, the Japanese first began to make fish-ponds in their islands, and to cultivate rice-fields, and to inclose the same with ditches. This emperor was on the throne at the time of our Saviour's birth, and also at the time of the Crucifixion.

These emperor-theocrats, called in the language of the country Mikados, claimed to rule by divine right and inheritance. They were high priests as well as kings; they were held as representatives of the gods upon earth, and like gods they were worshipped. No subject ever addressed them except on his knees. They were thoroughly despotic; and even after they had ceased to head their own armies, and intrusted the military command to sons and kinsmen, their power long remained undisputed and uncontrolled. "Even to this day," says Kämpfer, "the princes descended from the family, more particularly those who sit on the throne, are looked upon as persons most holy in themselves, and as Popes by birth. And, in order to preserve these advantageous notions in the minds of their subjects, they are obliged to take an uncommon care of their sacred persons, and to do such things, which, examined according to the customs of other nations, would be thought ridiculous and impertinent. It will not be improper to give a few instances. The ecclesiastical emperor thinks that it would be very prejudicial to his dignity and holiness to touch the ground with his feet: for this reason, when he intends to go anywhere, he must be carried thither on men's shoulders. Much less will they suffer, that he should expose his sacred person to the open air; and the sun is not thought worthy to shine on his head. There is such a holiness ascribed to all parts of the body, that he dares to cut off neither his hair, nor his beard, nor his nails. However, lest he should grow too dirty, they may clean him in the night when he is asleep; because, they say, that what is taken from his body at that time, hath been stolen from him, and that such a theft doth not prejudice his holiness or dignity. In ancient times, he was obliged to sit on the throne for some hours every morning, with the imperial crown on his head, but to sit altogether like a statue, without stirring either hands or feet, head or eyes, nor indeed any part of his body, because, by this means, it was thought that he could preserve peace and tranquillity in his empire; for if, unfortunately, he turned himself on one side or the other, or if he looked a good while towards any part of his dominions, it was apprehended that war, famine, fire, or some other great misfortune, was near at hand to desolate the country. But it having been afterwards discovered, that the imperial crown was the palladium, which, by its immobility, could preserve peace in the empire, it was thought expedient to deliver his imperial person, consecrated only to idleness and pleasure, from this burthensome duty, and therefore the crown, alone, is at present placed on the throne for several hours every morning. His victuals must be dressed every time in new pots, and served at table in new dishes: both are very clean and neat, but made only of common clay, that, without any considerable expense, they may be laid aside, or broken, after they have served once. They are generally broken, for fear they should come into the hands of laymen; for they believe religiously, that if any layman should presume to eat his food out of these sacred dishes, it would swell and inflame his mouth and throat. The like ill effect is dreaded from the Daïri's sacred habits; for they believe that if a layman should wear them, without the emperor's express leave or command, they would occasion pains in all parts of his body."*

The latest Dutch accounts leave it doubtful whether the

* Kämpfer. See also A. Montanus; Mr. Rundall's excellent "Memorials of the Empire of Japan;" Titsingh, "Illustrations," &c.

Daïri, or ecclesiastical emperor, is not still kept a perpetual prisoner in his palace in the city of Miaco, and still precluded from setting his foot to the earth, or allowing the sun to shine upon him.*

In the twenty-third year of the reign of Keikoo (about A.D. 93), there was great volcanic action, and a new island rose up from the bottom of the sea. Perhaps all the islands, both great and small, had no other origin. This particular island was called Sikubasima, and consecrated to Nebis, the Neptune of the Japanese. Three years afterwards a Mia or temple was built upon it in honor of Nebis, and a sufficient number of bonzes or priests were sent to attend it. This temple, in the course of ages, became very famous and rich, and the island itself is said to have been always free from those terrible earthquakes which have waved and tossed the rest of the empire, and which, at this day, are of unpleasant frequency.

Women can sit on the throne of the ecclesiastical emperor, and the Japanese have had many brilliant female reigns. The system, which is found to prevail in various parts of southern India, has obtained occasionally in Japan; a decided preference being shown to the female line. Usually on the death of a Mikado, the ministry and council put upon the vacant throne whomsoever they thought the nearest heir, without regard had to age or to sex. Hence it often happened that princes under age, or young unmarried princesses, ascended the throne. It is also said that there are instances of the widow of a deceased emperor succeeding her husband on the throne.

Singukogu was an empress of great renown, who began her reign with the third century of the Christian era

---

* Fischer.

She was the widow of the Emperor Sin Ai, and his blood relation in the fifth degree. She is described as an Amazon. She carried on war against the Coreans, and at the very beginning of her reign went over to that country with a numerous army, which she commanded in person. But, finding herself in an interesting situation, she hastened back to Japan, and was delivered of a son, who, in due course of time succeeded her, and was so renowned a monarch that at his death he was honored with the divine title of the "God of War." This empress, according to the ancient annals, consulted by Kämpfer, reigned gloriously for the space of seventy years, and dying, in the hundredth year of her age, was placed by her grateful people among the gods and goddesses of the country.

It may be here noted that the Japanese bestow a marvellous longevity on all their good and great sovereigns. An age equal to that of Methusalem is by no means a rarity in their earlier mortal reigns. Their celestial kings reigned their millions of years.

Frequently allusions are made to the contemporary history of China, and there appears to have been, through a long series of years, a free and active intercourse between the two nations. Under the Emperor Kin Mei—a very religious prince, who reigned about the middle of the sixth century—there was a great importation of priests and idols from China, and the Buddhist worship was spread with great success in Japan. Abundance of idols, idol-carvers, and priests, also came over from several other countries beyond the sea. At the end of the sixth, and beginning of the seventh century, there was another female reign. In the sixth year of this empress, some crows and peacocks were brought over from beyond sea as presents to her. "Both kinds of birds are still subsisting, and the crows particularly multiplied to such a degree that at present they do a great deal of mischief."* During her reign all Japan was shaken by earthquakes in a dreadful manner, and vast numbers of buildings were overthrown and swallowed up. The next year after these calamities, fire fell from heaven, and after that there fell such a quantity of rain, that many towns were laid under water. It is said that during the reign of this empress gold was brought over into Japan from the "barbarous country of Corea." After the death of her son, who reigned from A.D. 629 to 642, the succession fell to another female, the widow of the late monarch, and a very few years after this an unmarried princess ascended the throne.

About the year 672, the succession was disputed by two brothers, and a mournful civil war took place.† But the younger brother being entirely defeated in battle, put an end to the war by ripping open his bowels, *more Japonico.* At short intervals we find several other female reigns. About the end of the eighth century, a foreign people, "who were not Chinese, but natives of some more distant country," came over to invade Japan in an hostile manner. The Japanese did what they could to get rid of them, but as their losses in battle were constantly made up by fresh recruits who arrived from beyond sea, this work was very difficult, and the strangers were not entirely defeated and dispersed till eighteen years after their first arrival. Some have thought that these strangers proceeded from the Malayan Peninsula, others that they

---

* Kämpfer.

† It will be understood that we speak rather doubtingly of these dates in early Japanese history. In fact their whole chronology, as well modern as ancient, abounds in difficulties. Mr. Edwin Norris's valuable notes upon the Japanese era will be found in Appendix C.

came from the Peninsula of Kamtschatka, or from Siberia and the regions round the Baikal Lake. Between the ninth and twelfth centuries several new religions or idolatries are mentioned as being introduced by foreign priests, or by Japanese returning from foreign countries. About the year 987, the Emperor Quassan, a very young man, was suddenly seized with such a desire of retirement and a religious life, that he left his palace privately in the night-time, and retired into the lone monastery of Quansi, where he changed his name, and caused his head to be shaved like the rest of those monks or bonzes. He lived twenty-two years in this manner, and was only forty years old when he died. From various causes, abdications of the throne were very frequent. This need not excite surprise if we reflect upon the imprisoned, constrained, monotonous kind of life the Japanese emperor then led in the palace at Miaco. He was allowed for his solace one wife and twelve concubines, plenty of pipes for smoking, and such diversion as music, poetry, and study could afford him. He certainly was nothing more than the shadow of sovereignty. All the powers of the state were in the hands of the court and council, formed of a long hierarchy of spiritual officials. Sometimes the father resigned the crown successively to one or more of his children, in order that he and their mothers, while yet alive, might enjoy the pleasure of seeing them fill the throne. All this was done at court with as little trouble and noise as possible. A Mikado might die or resign, and another be put into his place, without anybody, beyond the precincts of the court, knowing anything of the matter until it was all over and settled.* It, how-

---

* Kämpfer. Charlevoix.

ever, occasionally happened that those members of the imperial family who considered themselves entitled to the succession, but were excluded, maintained their rights or pretensions by force of arms, endeavoring to turn out the emperor whom they thought unlawfully possessed of the throne. Hence arose civil wars very prejudicial to the empire. The princes of the empire espoused different interests, and these quarrels seldom ended but with the entire destruction of one of the contending parties, followed by a cruel extermination of whole families. It would appear, however, that these civil wars in Japan were of rarer occurrence, and were waged with far less ferocity than similar contests in the Celestial Empire. We nowhere read of such wholesale massacres, such suicides by thousands and tens of thousands at a time, as cast so deep a shade of horror over Chinese history.

Horace Walpole might have swelled his catalogue of royal authors from the annals of Japan. Several of the emperors, while sitting on the prison-throne, or after their abdication, wrote books. Nearly all of them encouraged letters, and such sciences as the country possessed. The reign of the emperor Itsi Sio (987—1012) was famed for a great epidemic and mortality all over Japan, and for many eminent and learned men who then flourished at court. His grandson and successor set the fashion of ecclesiastics being drawn in covered chariots by two oxen, "which was so well liked, that the whole ecclesiastical court soon followed the example." His reign was further illustrated by the appearance of two moons, another dreadful plague or epidemic, and a fall of snow which covered the ground to the height of five feet. Under the reign of Go Rei Sen (1046—1069) there was a rebellion in the province of Osju. The rebels kept their ground for five years, till a great general, the commander-in-chief of all the imperial troops, defeated them, and slew their two great leaders. This rebellion is described at great length in the Japanese book, called "Osju Gassen," or, the Wars in Osju. In the reign of To Ba (1108—1124), a strange noise was heard in the air, as if drums (fifes are not mentioned) had been beating, which continued for several days together; aud a rebellion was made by Kijomori, a prince of the blood, very famous in Japanese story. He assumed the title of Daïri, or Emperor, and made himself a court and government. But not being able to maintain his title and dignity, he was forced to fly to the celebrated monastery of Midira, on the mountain Jeesan, where the monks protected him against the imperial court. He changed his name, got his head shaved, and turned monk. He lived fourteen years in this condition, unmolested and safe, but when he died, it was of a malignant burning fever, which made the body look red, as if it had been all on fire, a just punishment according to the Japanese history, for his presumptuous revolt against his lawful sovereign.

Some of the Japanese traditions, though included in their histories, and placed under comparatively modern dates, are sufficiently startling, and have a smack of the fabulous history of the Greeks, and the twelve labors of Hercules. Thus, under the emperor Konjei (1142—56), there lived Jorimassa, a prince of the blood, and another Japanese Hercules. By the assistance of the God of War, Jorimassa killed with his arrows the infernal dragon *Nuge*, who had the head of a monkey, the tail of a serpent, and the body and claws of a tiger. This monstrous beast inhabited the emperor's own palace, and was exceedingly troublesome, both to his sacred person and to all his court, particularly in the night-time, making very improper noises and frightening them, and disturbing the poor courtiers out of their sleep. This is, of course, a myth, upon the interpretation of which we need hardly venture. The Japanese take the story in its natural, or rather, non-natural sense; and they have many such. The same dragon-slayer, Jorimassa, bore an heorical part in the civil wars carried on between the four most powerful families of the empire, and was slain in battle, after which his whole family was extirpated. But these sharp executions did not put an end to the dissensions of the country. In fact, Japan seemed on the point of resolving herself into her primeval condition,—or that of a congeries of small independent states, with about as many princes and governors as there were provinces in the islands. The early Portuguese and Spanish writers, speaking of the state of the country in the old times, enumerate as many as sixty or sixty-eight principalities, or, rather kingdoms (*Reynos*), which all managed separately their own affairs, and did little more than acknowledge the nominal suzerainty of the *one* emperor. About the middle of the twelfth century, during the reign of the above-named emperor, Kon Jei, these provincial potentates formed confederacies hostile to the central government. "It was about this time," says Kämpfer, "that the supreme and unlimited authority of the Daïri, or ecclesiastical hereditary emperor, began to decline. The princes of the empire, governed by ambition, jealousy, and envy, abandoned by degrees the duty and allegiance they owed to their sovereign, assumed an absolute power in the government of their dominions and principalities, entered into alliances for their own defence, and carried on war one against another." In this situation of affairs, the court thought it expedient to entrust the command of its entire army to the celebrated Joritomo, a young soldier of high birth (he was a scion of the ancient imperial stock), very valorous, successful and ambitious. He was the first that received the office and title of *Ziogun*, or generalissimo of the crown. Men intrusted with extraordinary power seldom care to part with it. "This," adds Kämpfer, "was the case with Joritomo, who gladly embracing so favourable an opportunity, increased his power to that degree, as not only to arrogate to himself an absolute authority in the decision of all the secular affairs of the empire, but to leave to his successors a plausible pretext to claim and exercise the same. Thus, in the twelfth century, the power of ecclesiastical hereditary emperors received at first a fatal shock by the disobedience and quarrels of the princes of the empire, and was at last entirely taken from them by the usurpation of their crown generals, though without prejudice to their supreme dignity, rank, holiness, and some other rights and prerogatives."

The office of Ziogun, or generalissimo, soon became strictly hereditary, and though that high functionary did not, for a very long time, assume the title, he was, in effect, a joint emperor with the Daïri, and had the supreme management of all affairs not ecclesiastical.* Abdications became still more frequent. The brother and successor of the emperor Kon Jei shaved his head and turned monk. The following is a remarkable instance of the accessibility

* In Turkey, we have given the name of a place or building (the Sublime Porte) to the government. In Japan, Europeans have given the name of the palace to the ecclesiastical emperor. The word *Daïri* means court or palace. The proper style and title of this emperor would be *Daïri-Sama*, or Great Lord of the Palace.

to high places and commands afforded to ladies in Japan. On the death of the first great Ziogun Joritomo, his widow renounced the world and became a Buddhist nun. But an infant being called, by hereditary right, to succeed to the post of generalissimo, the widow returned from her convent, and governed for the minor, retaining all that high military and political authority until the day of her own death. The Japanese annalists call her the Ama Ziogun, or Nun General. An empress, as we have seen, had gone to the wars, but this lady, the widow of the great Joritomo, appears to be the only instance of a female generalissimo.

The conquest of China by the Mongol Tartars (A.D. 1260—81) carried alarm to Japan, and induced that cautious government to break off all intercourse with the Chinese. In the year 1268, the great Mongol conqueror, Kublai Khan, sent a letter and envoys to Niphon to call upon the Japanese emperor for his alliance, offensive and defensive, and to apprise him of the far-spreading power and the irresistibility of the Mongols. "I apprehend," said Kublai, "that the true state of things is not, as yet, well known and understood in your land, and, therefore, I send envoys with a letter, to acquaint you with my views. I hope we may understand each other. Already philosophers desire to see all mankind form one family. But how may this one-family principle be carried into effect if friendly intercourse subsist not between parties? I am determined to call this principle into existence, even though I should be obliged to do so by force of arms. It is now the business of the *wang* (king) of Niphon to decide what course is most agreeable to him." The course most agreeable to the Japanese emperor and the Ziogun, was to have nothing to do with Kublai Khan or his Mongols.

They refused to admit the envoys to an audience at court, and dismissed them without any answer to their great monarch's epistle. Two other missions dispatched by Kublai, one in the year 1271, and the other in 1273, were treated precisely in the same manner. The haughty conqueror then resorted to arms. In 1274* a Mongol-Chinese fleet and army, with a contingent drawn from a part of Corea which had been conquered by Kublai, appeared off the coast of Japan. But the Japanese had taken warning, and were well prepared. The Ziogun came down to the coast with an immense army, and the ecclesiastical emperor, in the quiet recesses of his palace, put up prayers to the gods, and appointed general prayer days to be observed throughout the empire. Some of the old Japanese annalists assert that the enemy merely ravaged a small part of the island of Kewsew, and then retreated in dismay and confusion; but others affirm that the Mongols were defeated, with great loss, in a general action. Marco Polo, the great Venetian traveller, who was, afterwards, actively engaged in the service of Kublai Khan has left us a short but very curious account of the expedition.

"In order to effect his purpose, the khan fitted out a numerous fleet, and embarked a large body of troops, under the command of two of his principal officers, one of whom was named *Abbacatan*, and the other *Vonsancin*. The expedition sailed from the ports of *Zaitun* and *Kinsai*, and crossing the intermediate sea, reached the island in safety; but in consequence of a jealousy that arose between the two commanders, one of whom treated the plans of the other with contempt, and resisted the execution of his orders, they were unable to gain possession of

* Marco Polo dates this expedition a few years earlier.

any city or fortified place, with the exception of one only, which was carried by assault, the garrison having refused to surrender. Directions were given for putting the whole to the sword, and in obedience thereto, the heads of all were cut off, excepting only eight persons, who, by the efficacy of a diabolical charm, consisting of a jewel or amulet introduced into the right arm, between the skin and the flesh, were rendered secure from the effects of iron, either to kill or wound. Upon this discovery being made, they were beaten with a heavy wooden club, and presently died.

"It happened after some time that a north wind began to blow with great force, and the ships of the Tartars, which lay near the shore of the island, were driven foul of each other. It was determined thereupon, in a council of the officers on board, that they ought to disengage themselves from the land; and accordingly, as soon as the troops were re-embarked, they stood out to sea. The gale, however, increased to so violent a degree that a number of the vessels foundered. The people belonging to them, by floating upon pieces of the wreck, saved themselves upon an island lying about four miles from the coast of Zipangu. The other ships which, not being so near to the land, did not suffer from the storm, and on which the two chiefs were embarked, together with the principal officers, or those whose rank entitled them to command an hundred thousand or ten thousand men, directed their course homewards, and returned to the Grand Khan. Those of the Tartars who remained upon the island where they were wrecked, and who amounted to about thirty thousand men, finding themselves left without shipping, abandoned by their leaders, and having neither arms nor provisions, expected nothing less than to become captives or to perish; especially as the island afforded no habitations where they could take shelter and refresh themselves. As soon as the gale ceased, and the sea became smooth and calm, the people from the main island of Zipangu came over with a large force, in numerous boats, in order to make prisoners of the shipwrecked Tartars, and having landed, proceeded in search of them; but in a straggling, disorderly manner. The Tartars, on their part, acted with prudent circumspection, and being concealed from view by some high land in the centre of the island, whilst the enemy were hurrying in pursuit of them by one road, made a circuit of the coast by another, which brought them to the place where the fleet of boats was at anchor. Finding these all abandoned, but with their colors flying, they instantly seized them; and, pushing off from the island, stood for the principal city of Zipangu, into which, from the appearance of the colors, they were suffered to enter unmolested. Here they found few of the inhabitants besides women, whom they retained for their own use, and drove out all the others. When the king was apprised of what had taken place, he was much afflicted, and immediately gave directions for a strict blockade of the city, which was so effectual that no person was suffered to enter or to escape from it, during six months that the siege continued. At the expiration of this time, the Tartars, despairing of succor, surrendered upon the condition of their lives being spared. These events took place in the course of the year 1264. The Grand Khan having learned some years after that the unfortunate issue of the expedition was to be attributed to the dissension between the two commanders, caused the head of one of them to be cut off, the other he sent to the savage island of Zorza, where it is the custom to execute criminals in the following manner. They are wrapped round both arms in the hide of a buffalo fresh taken from the beast, which is sewn tight. As this dries, it compresses the body to such a degree, that the sufferer is incapable of moving, or in any manner helping himself, and thus miserably perishes."*

Kublai Khan, however, would not forego his "one-family" principle. In the very next year he sent fresh envoys to Japan. This time the Tartars were admitted to the presence of the Ziogun, or crown general; but the answer they got from him was not very satisfactory: "Henceforth no Mongol subject shall set foot upon this soil under pain of death." In spite of this warning, Kublai sent over some other ambassadors; and the Japanese, firm in their resolution, cut off the head of every man of them!

In the year 1280, when Kublai had completed the conquest of China, and reduced all the neighboring nations to pay him tribute, he resolved to take vengeance on Japan; and orders were forthwith given for the preparation of a mighty Mongol Chinese armament, with contingents from Corea and other regions.

This great expedition took its departure for Japan in the summer of 1281, under the command of a Tartar general named Mooko. If we are to believe some of the Japanese annalists the fleet consisted of 4,000 sail, and the number of men embarked amounted to 240,000. But other and rather more credible accounts diminish the number of the ships, and bring down the combatants to 100,000. Again the Japanese were found well prepared

---

* "Travels of Marco Polo," edited by William Marsden, p. 569 to p. 571.

for defence. But this time also the elements fought for them. The gods of the country, and protectors of the empire, say their writers, were so incensed at the insult offered them by the Tartars, that they excited a dreadful tempest, which destroyed all this reputed Invincible Armada. Mooko himself perished in the waves, and but few of his men escaped. This was a catastrophe very likely to befall Chinese junks in so stormy a sea, and on a coast so completely rock-bound. But it is reported that the invaders did not all find so easy a death as that of drowning; that many thousands escaped from the storm by landing on the coast, and that they were there massacred in cold blood by the Japanese, who spared only three of the number, in order that they might go back to China, and report to Kublai Khan the fate of his vast armament. For the sake of striking terror, the Japanese government and its writers may have exaggerated numbers; but it will remain an historical fact that, in the time of Kublai Khan, a fearful loss was twice sustained by an invading force.

For the space of nearly a hundred years, during which the Mongols held dominion in China and the adjacent states, the Japanese would have no intercourse with any of them, enforcing the law of proscription and death which they had pronounced to the envoys of Kublai; but when, in 1366, the Chinese dynasty of Ming expelled the Mongols, and re-established the ancient government, communications were reopened both with China and Corea, and a commercial intercourse was renewed upon the old cautious conditions. It appears, however, that the number of annual junks from those countries was strictly limited, that every vessel on her arrival in a Japanese port was subjected to a most rigid search, and that the foreigners were placed under strict surveillance during all the time that they remained in the country.

We trace in another succession of voluntary or forced abdications of the spiritual imperial crown, the growing prepotency of the Ziogune, who were then very efficient and active rulers, and not the secluded inactive princes they now appear to be. Ever since the time of Joritomo, these high functionaries had, as we have noted, virtually held the sovereign power. At last they possessed themselves of the name as well as the substance. The disturbed state of the country again called for a man of action,—a man of the sword. This was found in the celebrated Taiko-Sama, a soldier of fortune, who is said to have raised himself merely by his courage and merit. The spiritual emperor invented new titles for him, and intrusted him not only with the supreme command of all the troops, but also with the management of all the secular affairs of the empire. About the year 1585, this Taiko-Sama took to himself the title of *Koboe*, or lay emperor. He is considered as the first absolute secular monarch of Japan, that is, the first who assumed to himself the absolute government of the empire, whereof the ecclesiastical hereditary emperors had, till then preserved some share.* Ever since that time the Koboe, or secular monarch, has continued almost entirely independent of the ecclesiastical emperor, except in matters spiritual. We know of no other example of so singular a division of power. To this day, the Daïri and Koboe reign simul-

* The word Koboe does not strictly mean emperor; and it appears that the Japanese angrily deny that there is any other emperor than the Mikado, or Daïri. The power, however, of the Koboe is decidedly imperial, and far greater than that of the Daïri. See Titsingh, "Illustrations of Japan."

taneously and conjointly, and Japan has two emperors! Yet the evils which might have been expected from such a state of things do not appear to have arisen. A judicious English writer, to whose remarks we have been much indebted, says,—"From the close of the sixteenth century, when the Japanese *Maire du Palais*, Taiko Sama, separated the empire into its two lay and spiritual divisions, civil war has ceased, the pageant of government has been played on, without interruption, by the two principal actors and their subordinates, and the operations of the real executive have been continued with all the regularity and precision of machinery. The founder of these institutions must, surely, have been no ordinary legislator. The sceptre, which he wielded has, indeed, become a bauble in the hands of his descendants, for the Koboe, or lay emperor, equally with his spiritual counterpart, wears out his life in one long dream of ideal sovereignty; and so profound and subtle is the spell of habit, custom and etiquette, which wraps them in that charmed sleep, that it is impossible to anticipate the period of its dissolution, or the process by which it can be broken."*

Taiko Sama,† the most celebrated character in the an-

---

* "Quartely Review," vol. lii., 1834.

† *Taiko Sama* was known by various names, viz.:—1. *Toyotomo;* 2. *Toquixero;* 3. *Cicuquidono;* 4. *Faxiba;* "dont la signification," Charlevoix observes, "faisoit allusion aux armes ou quelque devise du Roi de Nanguto," who had been in rebellion, and was reduced to submission by Faxiba, on whom the Ziogun, Nobounanga, conferred the title. 5. Quabaucondono, which, by some writers, is said to mean "*The Lord of the Treasure.*" Captain Cock states (East-India House *MSS.*), it is equivalent to the "*Cæsar*" of the Romans. 6. *Taiko Sama*, which signifies "*The Most High and Sovereign Lord.*"—Rundall's "Memorials."

nals of Japan is represented to have been ill-favored, if not absolutely ugly and repulsive in person. He was below the average height, and corpulent to excess; but, withal, endowed with immense strength, extraordinary activity, and a spirit of daring beyond conception. On one hand he had six fingers; his eyes were so prominent that they seemed ready to start from their sockets; his chin was destitute of the appendage of a beard; and his features, altogether, were of so singular a mould, that he obtained the unenviable cognomen of "The Ape."* Yet these disadvantages were overcome by the high qualities of his mind. He commenced his career as a hewer and carrier of wood. From this menial occupation he was taken into the service of an officer attached to the court of Nobounanga, the Ziogun. In the capacity of a private soldier, he attracted the attention of the Ziogun, who had the reputation of being a shrewd judge of men. His advancement was rapid. At length he obtained a separate command, and in a short space of time was recognized as one of the most skilful generals of the empire. His patron, the Ziogun, now reaped the fruits of his discernment; and Taiko zealously strove to repay to his sovereign the favors he had received from him. It was owing to his skill and valor, that the cause of Nobounanga was maintained against a host of powerful opponents. But, though powerful against hosts, Taiko was unable to restrain private malice. Nobounanga fell beneath the sabre or dagger of an assassin; leaving, as his successor, a grandson, a youth possessed of little influence or talent.

Presently, on the death of Nobounanga, the most disaffected, turbulent, and ambitious of the princes and nobles

* According to Charlevoix. Titsingh says, *Sarout Soma*, or "*Monkey Face.*"

of the land, flew to arms, contending among themselves for the seat of power. For a time anarchy reigned; but, at length, Taiko, who had been fighting the battles of his late sovereign in a distant part of the land, arrived, by a succession of rapid marches, at the scene of action; and, falling suddenly on the contending parties, put their forces to the rout. The leader of a numerous and well-disciplined army, Taiko felt his power, and installed himself the successor of Nobounanga.

The superiority of the Mikado was at first acknowledged by the new Ziogun. After a few months, he declared himself independent and absolute. Irresistible in might and skill, he crushed every attempt at opposition; and, ruling the princes and nobles with a rod of iron, he reduced them to a state of abject submission. Adding policy to force, he declared war against Corea, which, in the lapse of ages had regained its independence, and despatched a force of 200,000 men for the conquest of that country.

In this army the most dangerous characters of the empire were absorbed. Few of the leaders returned to their native land, and the few who did return were not in a condition to excite any apprehension for the peace of the country. So far successful, he proceeded to devise means by which the restless spirits in the realm might be permanently kept in subjection. The measures he adopted remain part of the policy of Japan to the present day, and have proved efficient.

As a legislator, as well as warrior and politician, Taiko distinguished himself. He introduced laws which bear the impress of great severity, but they were necessary to meet the exigencies of the times, and were adapted to the temper of the people; which, at that period, whatever it may be now, is represented to have been "no less fiery and changeable, than the neighboring sea is stormy and tempestuous."—(Kämpfer.)

Magnificence and profusion were two of the leading habits of this Ziogun; but, as he taxed the aristocracy, and left the people unburthened with imposts, the plebeian part of his subjects were well content.

The renown of Taiko was not confined within the limits of the empire. It extended to China, and was acknowledged in Europe. His alliance was courted both by the Emperor of the Celestials, and by the King of Spain.

In reply to the overtures of an Ambassador despatched by the Viceroy of the Spanish Indies, the Ziogun gave the following brief account of his career:—"The kingdom of Japan," he said, "containeth above sixty states, or jurisdictions, which, from long time, had been sorely afflicted with internal broils and civil wars; by reason that wicked men, traitors to their country, did conspire to deny obedience to their sovereign lord. Even in my youth did this matter grieve my spirit, and from early days I took counsel with myself how this people might best be made subject to order, and how peace might be restored to the kingdom. That so mighty a work might be brought about, I especially essayed to practise these three virtues which follow:—Therefore I strove to render myself affable to all men, thereby to gain their good will: I spared no pains to judge all things with prudence, and to comport myself with discretion: nothing did I omit to do that might make men esteem me for valor of heart and fortitude of mind. Now, by these means, have I gained the end I sought. All the kingdom is become as one, and is subject to my sole rule. I govern with mildness, that yields only to my energy as a conqueror. Most especially do I view with favor the tillers of the ground ; they it is by whom my kingdom is filled with abundance.

"Severe as I may be deemed, my severity is visited alone on those who stray into the ways of wickedness. Thus hath it come to pass, that at this present time, peace universal reigns in the empire ; and in this tranquillity consisteth the strength of the realm. Like to a rock, which may not be shaken by any power of the adversary, is the condition of this vast monarchy under my rule."

Testimony to the merits of Taiko Sama is borne by Charlevoix; and he derived his information entirely from Roman Catholic sources. In a style of admirable candor, the learned Jesuit gives the following review of this Ziogun's reign:—"Never," he says, "was Japan better ruled than under Taiko ; and the condition of the country at that period affords a proof that the Japanese, as well as most other nations, only require to be subject to a man who knows how to govern, to conduct themselves peaceably and obediently. Vice was punished, virtue was rewarded, merit was acknowledged, and occupation was found for the restless, or they were coerced into quietness. Excepting the persecution of the Christians, in which, however, the emperor exhibited a degree of moderation hardly to be expected from a man of his character, no just complaint can be urged against his government. It is true he was not an object of affection ; but he was feared and admired. Moreover, the traditions of the country seldom fail to do justice to the memory of a sovereign, whether meriting applause or approbation. To the present day, the name of Taiko Sama is revered throughout Japan ; and his actions continue to be the theme of admiration."*

The Lutheran Kämpfer is equally warm in his praise

* Charlevoix. "Nipon o Daï," by Titsingh and Klaproth.

of this rare man,—a warrior and a statesman suited to his country and to the times in which he lived.*

There have been some civil wars since this division of authority, but, on the whole, Japan has enjoyed more tranquillity than ever it did before, and certainly more internal peace, and more uniformity of government than has been known by any European nation during the nearly three hundred years which have elapsed since 1585. One of the very latest of the Dutch writers conjectures that by a quarrel between the Koboe and the Daïri, and by such an event alone, can any innovation or revolution ever take place in the existing political institutions of Japan.† He does not indicate the nature of the contingency which could produce the collision between the two rulers; but it is not difficult to conjecture various means by which such a collision might be brought about. The very peculiar system is indeed fenced in with innumerable laws, regulations, and precautions; but these may all be taken as indications of doubt and apprehension, if not as something very like proofs, that the Japanese grandees, governing under the emperors, are oppressed with a conviction of the frailty of the institutions. Suspicion and distrust prevail through every link of the social chain, and the precautions against foreigners are said to be equalled by those adopted against innovation or disturbance within. Japan is a country filled with spies. A system of espionage extends itself

---

* In this account of Taiko Sama we have been greatly indebted to Mr. Rundall's valuable "Memorials of the Empire of Japan, in the 16th and 17th centuries," published by the Hakluyt Society. London. 1850. We have compared Mr. Rundall's text with most of his original authorities, and have never found him incorrect.

† J. F. Fischer.

throughout the empire, embracing not only every public functionary—including the Daïri and the Koboe themselves—but every component part of society.

Taiko Sama, who is still considered by the Japanese as one of their greatest heroes, is said to have contemplated the conquest of China, when his brilliant career, in 1598, was arrested by death. His son and successor highly favored the Japanese Christians and their teachers, and was strenuously supported by the Jesuits in his contentions and wars with some refractory native princes and provincial chiefs. It was fully expected that the young man would openly profess Christianity; but he was supplanted in the Ziogunship by a near relative, from whom is lineally descended the emperor who now occupies the lay throne.

This brief sketch brings down the history of Japan beyond the period of the Portuguese settlement in the islands. All the subsequent interesting events, or all that the European reader will care for, have been given, in a condensed shape, in our first chapter. The Japanese annalists mention the volcanic birth of another island, which rose suddenly out of the sea, in the form of a great mountain; at the early part of the seventeenth century, a Chinese embassy sent to compliment their secular emperor; a rain which brought down with it from the heavens a prodigious quantity of *hair;* a comet such as had never been seen before; sundry earthquakes, and terrible conflagrations. Fires do, indeed, appear to be as great a curse in this country as in Turkey. In the year 1657, a dreadful one broke out at Jeddo, the residence of the Koboe, and, continuing to burn with great violence for three days, it laid the greatest part of that immense city in ashes. M. Wagenaar, who was at Jeddo at the time, with the annual mission, saw this conflagration, and wrote an account of it, which may be compared with the account of another fire at the same city in 1806, as given by M. Doeff.*

* The description of the fire at Jeddo, 1657, is inserted in the curious compilation of Arnold Montanus, Amsterdam. 1670. See Appendix C.

PART OF JEDDO.

BUDDHIST TEMPLE.

BOOK IV.

RELIGION—GOVERNMENT—LEGISLATION.

An old Dutchman says, with the brevity and directness of a sailor, "There are twelve several religions in Japan, and eleven of them are forbidden to eat meat." If sects be counted, the number will greatly exceed twelve, or even twenty. Liberty of conscience, so far as it did not interfere with the interests of government, or affect the peace and tranquillity of the empire, was for a long time, allowed in Japan, and (exception being had to Christianity) may be said still to obtain to a very remarkable degree.

There were, no doubt, preceding and ruder forms of faith; but what is now considered the original, national religion of Japan, is called *Sinsyn;* from the words *Sin* (the gods), and *Syn* (faith); and its votaries are denominated *Sintoos.**

All primitive mythologies are coupled with, and made to rise out of, cosmogony. The cosmogony of the Japanese is of the wildest sort. From primæval chaos, there sprung a self-created, supreme God, who fixed his

* Dr. Von Siebold, however, says that the proper native name of this religion is *Kami-no-Mitsi*, signifying "the way of the Kami," or gods; that the Chinese translated this compound word into *Shin-Tao*, and that the Japanese adopted the Chinese term, and according to the genius of their language, softened it into *Sintoo.*

abode in the highest heaven, and could not have his tranquillity disturbed by any cares. Next there arose two plastic, creative gods, who framed the universe out of chaos. The universe was then governed, for myriads of years, by seven gods in succession. They are called the Celestial Gods. The last of them was the only one that had a wife, and to him the earth we inhabit owes its existence. Once upon a time he said to his wife, "There should be, somewhere, a habitable earth. Let us seek it under the waters that are seething beneath us." He plunged his spear into the water, and as he withdrew it, the turbid drops that trickled from the weapon, congealed and formed a great island. This island was Kewsew, the largest of the eight which then constituted the world—for Japan was then all the world. Eight millions of gods were then called into existence, and the ten thousand things necessary to mankind were created. The plastic divinity then committed the government of the whole to his favorite daughter, Ten-sio-dai-zin, the Sun Goddess, whose reign was shortened to the space of 250,000 years. She was succeeded by four other gods, who altogether reigned two million and odd years. These are the Terrestrial Gods. The last of them, having married a terrestrial wife, left a mortal son upon the earth, named Zin-mu-ten-wou, the ancestor and progenitor of every Daïri or Mikado that has ruled in Japan.

Of all these gods of Sintoo mythology, none seem to be objects of great worship except the Sun Goddess; and she is too great to be addressed in prayer, except through the mediation of the inferior Kami or of her lineal descendant, the Mikado. The Kami consists of 492 born gods, and 2,640 canonized or deified mortals. All these are mediatory spirits, and have temples dedicated to them.

We speak doubtingly of this ancient faith, for it has evidently been mixed up with other worships and superstitions, and the amount of the foreign admixture seems very much to vary in different parts of the country. In all probability the Sintoos have nowhere preserved its original simplicity. The only decorations of the old temples consisted of a mirror, the emblem of the soul's purity, and a *gohei*, which is formed of many strips of white, spotless paper, another emblem of purity. The temples now possess images of the Kami to whom they are dedicated; but it is assumed that these idols are not set up to be worshipped, that they are kept in secret recesses, and exhibited only upon particular festivals. Private families are said to keep images of their patron Kami, in shrines and chapels. Meylan asserts, that every Mya, or temple, was originally dedicated to one supreme divinity. We much question this pure theism in such a state of society as that of the early Japanese. Siebold considers every idol or image as a corrupt foreign innovation. He is of opinion, that, originally, the Sun Goddess alone was worshipped, that the Kami are analogous to Roman Catholic saints, and that no images of them existed prior to the introduction of the Buddhist idolatory. To us it appears, that the Sintoo worship is now thoroughly permeated with Buddhism. Religious festivals and holidays appear to be as numerous among the Japanese as among any other people in the world.

According to Dr. Siebold, the Sintoos have some vague notion of the immortality of the soul, of a future state of existence, of rewards and punishments, of a paradise, and of a hell. "Celestial judges call every one to his account. To the good is allotted paradise, and they enter the realms of the Kami; the wicked are condemned, and thrust into hell." The duties enjoined by this ancient religion are:—1. Preservation of pure fire, as the emblem of purity, and means of purification. 2. Purity of soul, heart, and body. The purity of the soul is to be preserved by a strict obedience to reason and the law; the purity of the body, by abstaining from everything that defiles. 3. An exact observance of festival days. 4. Pilgrimage. 5. The worship of the Kami, both in the temples and at home.

External purity is most rigidly enforced; and, in too many cases, stands in lieu of everything else. Impurity is contracted in various ways: by associating with the impure, by listening to impure language, by eating certain meats, by coming in contact with death or with blood. Whosoever is stained with his own, or with the blood of another man, is *fusio* for seven days; that is, *impure*, and unfit to approach holy places. If, in building a temple, a workman should happen to cut or hurt himself so as to bleed, it is reckoned a very great calamity, and the man is thereby rendered altogether incapable of working for the future on that sacred edifice. If the same accident should happen in building or repairing any of the temples of the Sun Goddess, at the holy town of Isye, the misfortune does not affect the workmen alone, but the temple itself must pe pulled down and built anew. With this inculcated abhorrence of blood, it is curious to see the Japannese government so much addicted to blood-shedding, as it indisputably is. Whosoever eats the flesh of any four-footed beast, deer only excepted, is *fusio* for the term of thirty days. On the contrary, whoever eats a fowl, wild or tame (water-fowls, pheasants, and cranes, excepted), is *fusio* for only one Japanese hour, which is about equal to two of ours. Whoever kills a beast, or is present at an execution, or attends a dying person, or comes into a house where a dead body lies, is *fusio* that day. But, of all the things which make us impure, none is reckoned so contagious as the death of parents and near relations. The nearer you are related to the dead person, so much the greater the impurity is. All ceremonies which are to be observed on this occasion, the time of mourning and the like, are determined by this rule. By not observing these precepts, people make themselves guilty of external impurity, which is detested by the gods, and they become unfit to approach their temples.* In serious cases of impurity, the *fusio* is not to be removed without a long course of purification, consisting of fasting, prayer, and the solitary study of devotional books. All the period appointed for mourning on the death of a relation, is supposed to be thus spent. When purified, they throw aside their mourning dress, which is not black, but white, and return to society in festal garments.

The religious observances on festival days appear to be very simple, and very short. The worshipper, clad in his best clothes, approaches the temple, performs his ablutions at a tank, kneels in the veranda opposite a grated window, through which he can fix his eyes on the mirror ; he then offers up his prayers, and a sacrifice of rice, fruit, tea, sackee, or the like ; deposits a little money in a box, and takes his departure, to spend the rest of the day in sports and pastimes, or in the manner he thinks best. According to Kämpfer, they conclude their ceremonies at the temple, by striking three times upon a bell, which is

* Kämpfer. Dr. Von Siebold, M. Fischer, and other recent writers appear to agree very closely with, and not unfrequently to follow, this excellent old observer.

hung over the door, believing the gods to be highly delighted with the sound of musical instruments. "All this being done, they retire, to divert themselves the remaining part of the day with walking, exercises, sports, eating and drinking, and treating one another to good things." The temple must not be approached with a downcast spirit or a sorrowful countenance: for that might disturb the placid beatitude of the Kami. This ancient religious rule appears to have had an effect on the national character. The early Dutch writers observed that the Japanese hardly ever betrayed any outward emotion of sorrow or grief; that they had a wonderful degree of resignation under misfortune; that they were hardly ever heard to murmur or complain, and that they went even to execution and a horrible death, with placid and even cheerful countenances.*

At home in every Sintoo house, each meal is preceded by a short prayer, and in nearly every garden or court-yard attached to such house, there is a miniature mya, or temple. The Sintoo priests are called *Kami-Nusi*, or the hosts or landlords of the gods; they dwell in houses built within the grounds attached to the temples. The money deposited by the worshippers goes into their purse, and the oblations of rice, fruit, tea, and the rest, go to their kitchen and table. They have thus the means of hospitality, and are said to exercise it liberally to strangers. The Dutch, however, always found, that in their case, a return in solid cash was expected, and that these temple-visits were very expensive. Celibacy is no tenet

* Arnold Montanus. "Remarkable Embassies of the East-India Company of the United Netherlands to several Emperors of Japan," &c. Amsterdam. 1670.

of the Sintoos: the Kami-Nusi marry, and their wives are priestesses, to whom specific rites and duties are allotted. It appears that they act as godmothers-general to all the female children of their sect that are born in Japan, giving them their names, sprinkling them with water, and performing other ceremonies.*

But pilgrimage is the grand and most sanctifying act of Sintoo devotion. There are no fewer than twenty-two shrines in different parts of the empire, which are frequented annually, or more frequently by the devout. The most conspicuous, and most honored of all—the very Loreto of the Japanese—is Isye, with its ancient temple of Ten-sio-dai-zin, or the Sun Goddess. The principal temple is surrounded by nearly a hundred small ones, which have little else of a temple than the mere shape, being, for the most part, so low and narrow, that a man can scarcely stand up in them. Each of these temples, or little chapels is attended by a priest. Near to them live multitudes of priests and functionaries, who call themselves the messengers of the gods, and who keep houses and lodgings to accommodate travellers and pilgrims. Not far off lies a considerable town, which bears the same name (Isye) as the temple, and is inhabited by inn-keepers, paper-makers, printers, book-binders, turners, cabinet-makers, and such other artisans, whose business is in any way connected with the holy trade carried on at the place. [This is very like Loreto, the principal trade of which is carried on with pilgrims.] The principal temple itself is a very plain, unpretending edifice, and evidently of great antiquity, though not quite so old as the priests and devotees pretend. According to the latter, the Sun Goddess

* Siebold.

was born in it, and dwelt in it, and on that account it has never been enlarged, improved, or in any way altered. Among the priestesses of the temple, there is almost always a daughter of a spiritual emperor.

"Orthodox Sintonists," says Kämpfer, "go in pilgrimage to Isye once a year, or at the very least once in their lifetime; nay, it is thought a duty incumbent on every true patriot, whatever sect or religion he otherwise adheres to, and a public mark of respect and gratitude which every one ought to pay to the Sun Goddess, as to the protectress, founder, and first parent of the Japanese nation. . . . This pilgrimage is made at all times of the year; but the greatest concourse of people is in their three first months, March, April, and May, when the season of the year and the good weather make the journey very agreeable and pleasant. Persons of all ranks and qualities, rich and poor, old and young, men and women, resort thither; the lords only of the highest quality, and the most potent princes of the empire excepted, who seldom appear there in person.

"An embassy from the emperor is sent there once every year, in the first month, at which time also another with rich presents goes to Miaco with presents to the ecclesiastical hereditary monarch. Most of the princes of the empire follow the emperor's example. As to the pilgrims, who go there in person, every one is at liberty to make the journey in what manner he pleases. Able people do it at their own expense in litters, with a retinue suitable to their quality. Poor people go on foot, living upon charity, which they beg upon the road. They carry their beds along with them on their backs, being a straw mat rolled up, and have a pilgrim's staff in their hands, and a pail hung by their girdle, out of which they drink, and wherein they receive people's charity, pulling off their hats much after the European manner. Their hats are very large, twisted of split reeds. Generally speaking, their names, birth, and the place from whence they come, are writ upon their hats and pails, that in case sudden death or any other accident should befal them upon the road, it might be known who they are, and to whom they belong. Those that can afford it, wear a short white coat without sleeves over their usual dress, with their names stitched upon it before the breast and on the back. Multitudes of these pilgrims are seen daily on the road. It is scarce credible what numbers set out only from the capital city of Jeddo, and from the large province Osju. It is no uncommon thing at Jeddo for children to run away from their parents, in order to go in pilgrimage to Isye. The like attempt would be more difficult in other places, where a traveller that is not provided with the necessary passports, would expose himself to no small trouble. As to those that return to Isye, they have the privilege, that the ofarria which they bring from thence, is allowed everywhere as a good passport."

This ofarria, or "capital purification," is considered equivalent to the absolution and remission of their sins, and is given to the pilgrims by the priest "for a small consideration." It appears to be nothing more (in its cheap or ordinary shape) but a scrap of paper with a few Japanese characters written upon it,—not unlike the things which are sold by the wandering dervishes in Turkey and Persia, and the fakirs in India. But the superstitious believe that, coupled with the pilgrimage they have performed, these vouchers secure them health, prosperity, and children in this world, and a happy state in the world to come. The priests drive a great trade in the article.

As there are very many who stay at home, and think it sufficient for the ease of their consience to purchase these indulgences, great quantities of ofarrias are sent every year from Isye to all parts of the empire.

The Mikado, or Daïri, did not always get the pilgrimage performed vicariously. At one period both he and the lay emperor went in person to the shrine, at least once or twice during their lives. Motives of economy are thought to have put an end to those journeys, and to those of the great lords and princes, from whom great donations were expected; but it is probable that the disuse has in part arisen from a decline in Sintoo piety, or from an addiction to other forms of worship.

Anchorites and hermits are numerous, but they appear to hold rather loosely to the ancient Sintoo creed. One set, called *Jammabos*, or "mountain soldiers," lead a very secluded, austere life, spending most of their time in going up and down holy mountains, and washing themselves in cold springs or rivers. The poorer sort of them go strolling and begging about the country. The order is said to have been founded more than 1,200 years ago, by a strange adventurous man, who consumed nearly all his days in wandering through deserts, mountains, and wild uninhabited places, which, in the end, proved of considerable service to his country, as he thereby discovered the situation and nature of such places, which nobody before him had ventured to visit, and thus found out new, easier, and shorter roads from district to district, to the great advantage of travellers. We believe also, at this day, that the houses or cells of many of these hermits are very useful to wayfarers in the remote and rugged parts of the islands, particularly when the mountains are covered with snow. They may be said, in this manner, to represent the monks of St. Bernard, the Camaldolenses, and other monastic orders of Europe, who affect wild countries and lonely places. As everything in Japan seems to have a tendency to split into two, so this order divided itself into two, each of which has its general or superior, residing in considerable pomp at Miaco, near the palace of the spiritual emperor. These hermits are mostly married like the priests, they pretend to practise magic, to influence rain, snow, thunder, and lightning, to control the winds, to foretell future events, to discover thieves and recover stolen property, to explain dreams, and to cure desperate distempers.* They admit the worship of a number of foreign idols.

There are many other religious orders and societies established in the country. The most interesting of these are the two associations of the blind,—ancient and numerous bodies, composed of persons of all ranks and professions. Originally, they made up but one society. In process of time, however, they too split into two separate bodies, one of which is called Bussets-Sado, or the blind Bussets, and the other Feki-Sado, or the blind Fekis.

The original founder of this "Order of the Blind" was the son of an emperor who reigned in very remote ages. This young prince, say the Japanese historians, wept himself blind for the loss of his beautiful beloved princess; and thereupon, with his father's leave, and under an imperial charter, he erected a society, wherein none were ever to be admitted but such as had the misfortune

* The passion of the Japanese for these pretended magical arts, is in itself a proof of their Mongol origin. Wherever that race has extended itself, from Lapland with its witches and drums, to the centre of Asia, and to the extremity of the Japan Islands, there we are sure to find hosts of magicians or conjurers.

to be blind. The society prospered exceedingly, and was held in great repute at court, and all over the empire, for many centuries.

The native annalists relate a characteristic, thoroughly Japanese legend to account for the rise of the Feki-Sado. During the dreadful civil wars between the great families of the Feki and Gendzi, Kakekiko, a very renowned general of the Feki party, was defeated and made prisoner by the celebrated Joritomo, who had slain the generous prince to whom Kakekiko had been devotedly attached. Instead of putting his prisoner to death, according to the usual practice in those times, Jeritomo treated him with the greatest kindness, allowed him much liberty, and endeavored to persuade him to enter into his service. One day, when he was pressing him in this manner, and offering him whatever conditions he might please to demand, the captive general said, "I was once a faithful servant to a kind master. He is dead, and none other shall ever have my faith and friendship. You have laid me under obligations; I owe to you my life; yet can I never set my eyes on you without a design of avenging my dear dead master by slaying you. These, therefore, these designing instruments of mischief, I will offer up to you, as the only acknowledgment for your generous behavior towards me, that my unhappy condition allows me to give." And having thus said, he plucked out both his eyes, and presented them on a plate to Joritomo, who, astonished at so much magnanimity and resolution, forthwith set him at full liberty. The dramas of the Japanese seem chiefly made up of incidents like these, in which the passion of revenge stands out most prominently. The blind general retired into a distant province, where he learned to play upon the bywa, or Japanese lute, and gave birth to the society of the Feki blind, of which he himself was the first head. These Feki do not live upon charity, but make a shift to get a livelihood for themselves and contribute to the maintenance of their convents, by following various professions or callings not altogether inconsistent with their unhappy condition of total blindness. The greater number of them apply themselves to music, and find employment in the houses of princes and great men, as also at weddings, festivals, processions, and all public solemnities. It appears that the orchestras of all the theatres in the empire are filled by members of the Feki society. At least, travellers tell us that all the musicians they saw in the theatres were blind men.

Mention is made of nunneries, and of an order called by Europeans, Mendicant Nuns. But the members of this society appear to be of no particular faith, and of very doubtful morality. On one of his journeys Kämpfer fell in with them several times.

"Among the pilgrims we met there was a woman well dressed in silk, with her face well painted, leading a blind old man, and begging before him, which we thought a very extraordinary sight. We also met several young Bikunis, a sort of begging nuns, who accost travellers for their charity, singing songs to divert them, though upon a strange wild sort of tune. They will stay with travellers as long as they may wish for a small matter. Most of them are daughters of the Jammabos, or mountain priests, and are consecrated as sisters of this holy begging order, by having their heads shaved. They go neatly and well clad, wearing a black silk hood upon their shaven heads, and a light hat over it to defend their faces from the heat of the sun. Their behavior is, to all appearance, free, yet modest, neither too bold and loose, nor too dejected and mean. As to their persons, they are as great beauties as one shall see in this country. In short, the whole scene is more like a pretty stage comedy than the begging of indigent poor people. It is true, indeed, their fathers could not send out, upon the begging errand, persons more fit for it, since they know not only how to come at travellers' purses, but have charms and beauties enough to oblige them to farther good services. For distinction sake, from other begging nuns, they are called Komano Bikuni, because they go always two and two, and have their stations assigned to them only upon the roads hereabouts. They are obliged to bring so much a year, of what they get by begging, to the temple of the Sun Goddess at Isye, by way of tribute."*

There are numerous nunneries or societies of females, who appear to follow the Buddhist religion, without any intermixture of the Sintoo, or old national faith.

Buddhism, the most widely diffused of all Eastern creeds,† seems, from all accounts we have read, to be, at present, the prevalent faith in Japan. Yet it cannot be called *dominant*, and it may be doubted whether it exists anywhere in the remoter parts of the country without an admixture of the old Sintoo.

It is not necessary to our present purpose to give any

---

* In another place our learned old German doctor says, that the Bikuni were certainly the handsomest girls he saw in Japan; that the daughters of poor parents, if they be handsome and agreeable, easily obtain the privilege of begging in the habit of nuns; and that they particularly watch along the roads for gentlemen of rank and fashion.

† It has been calculated that there are in the world 252,000,000 Mahometans, 111,000,000 followers of Brahma, and 315,000,000 of Buddhists.

detailed account of doctrines so well known (particularly through our connection with India) as those of Buddhism. Some excellent recent notices of the religion as it exists among the Chinese, Tartars, and Thibetans, will be found in that most amusing of books, "Huck's Travels in Tartary, etc.," and in the recent work of Mr. T. Prinsep.* It will be enough for the reader to remember here, that the leading dogma of Buddhism is the metempsychosis; from which belief arises the prohibition to take animal life; that the Buddhist believes that man, after going through a variety of animal forms, as an elephant, a dog, a horse, or so on, will in the end, when purged of all his sins upon earth, be absorbed into the divine essence; that they worship a countless number of uncouth idols; that they have the notion that the Delhi Lama, or high-priest-king, never dies; that their priests form a distinct order in the state, and are bound to celibacy. There is a difference of opinion as to the dates of the introduction and establishment of Buddhism in Japan; but the probability is, that the faith was first brought into the country from India or from Corea, at the close of the sixth century of our era.† The government appears to have tolerated it from the beginning; but the people several times rose in tumult, killed the bonzes, burned their idols, and levelled their temples with the ground. But as this spontaneous popular persecution passed away, and as Buddhism gradually blended itself with some of the old national faiths, it became

* "Tartary and Thibet," 1 vol. 8vo. London. 1851.

† Those who are curious on this subject may be referred to the publications of Klaproth and Von Siebold, who both give their statements upon the authority of Japanese writers. Yet the same two learned Europeans differ as to the dates.

an established religion, and gained innumerable converts. It should seem that at least in the maritime parts of the empire, there are twenty Buddhist to one Sintoo temple. In Japan, as in every other country where it exists, Buddhism is divided into a high, pure, mystic creed for the learned, and a gross idolatry for the unlearned and common people.

We believe that none of these creeds have now any great hold on the popular mind, and that what has been said by an able writer of the Chinese may, with equal justice, be said of the Japanese.

"It is rather extraordinary that foreigners, though conversant with every part of Chinese literature, know so little about their religious writings. One reason may be found in their being written in a style almost unintelligible to the common reader. The Buddhist works are full of expressions from the Pàli, of which the sound is clumsily imitated in Chinese characters. Even few priests of that sect know the true meaning, and the same set of phrases are chanted by the votaries, over and over, for ages, without a single thought being bestowed upon their import. The religion of Taou, which is a national superstition, has clothed its votaries in mysterious laconism; many sentences admit five or six different versions, and when the student imagines that he has caught the real signification, he finds himself puzzled by a new maze of vagaries. Only truth can show her face unveiled, error requires the fanciful and dark envelope of unmeaning language, for, if seen in its nakedness, it would be loathsome. The religious works of the literati are mere treatises on ceremony, dry and uninteresting to the general reader, and only of value to the master of rites to exercise himself in the prescribed prostrations, genuflexions, and bows. The work before us* is intended as a comprehensive statistical account of the gods, including all the fables that have been propagated about them, and describing their various offices and functions, nature, attributes, etc., without regard to connection and system. The author first treats upon that large class of beings known under the name of genii, who are the special objects of adoration amongst the Taou sect. He then expatiates upon Buddha and his fellows, and finally treats upon the sages and worthies that claim the veneration of scholars. It is a very pantheon—a labyrinth through which, even with the clue of Ariadne, it is difficult to thread our way.

"To understand the book thoroughly, one ought to be intimately acquainted with the absurdities suggested by a disordered fancy, one ought to study the deviations from common sense, and hear patiently the ravings of a diseased mind.

"We frankly confess that we have not yet come to a satisfactory conclusion regarding the religious opinions of the Chinese as a nation.

"The general division of their creed into the sects of Taou and Buddha, and the religion of the state, holds only true regarding the initiated, the priests, and their immediate adherents, whilst the mass of the people, devoid of religious instruction, combine all in one, and individuals are either entirely indifferent towards all superstitions, or each cherishes his own peculiar tenets. All religious persons are stigmatized with popular contempt, and viewed in no other light but as mountebanks and quacks,

* "Shin Seën Tungkeen," a general account of the gods and genii; in twenty-two Chinese volumes.

who practice their unhallowed arts in order to gain a scanty livelihood. Under such circumstances, it is extraordinary to see so many temples and shrines, some of them richly endowed. But it ought never to be forgotten, that the Chinaman loves show, and that he must have a public house, where he may occasionally spend an idle hour, consult his destiny, burn incense and offer sacrifices, upon which he afterwards may feast. We do not think that many of these edifices were erected from religious motives, but are mere matters of convenience, and are always viewed in that light.

"But there is none so poor that he fits not up a little shrine, or corner, with an inscription, or a bit of an idol, before which he every day burns incense.

"You may find these in the very sheds of beggars, and the small boats of Tauka-women are never without this appendage. It must be confessed, on the other hand, that the majority of the people view these images in no other light than as a child its doll, which old custom has taught them to have always at hand. We have never yet heard a pagan Chinese pray; he considers it is the business of the priest to rattle off a few unmeaning sentences, and that it is quite sufficient that he should just utter a few pious ejaculations. If you discourse with him about his religious opinions, he will always come forward with Heaven and Earth, the two grand objects of his veneration. There is no work exclusively on religion to which he may refer. If he consult the classics, he will be told that filial piety and loyalty constitute true religion; but no hint is given him that there is an omnipotent Creator and Preserver, to whom he owes his first and most sacred duty. It has again and again been asserted, without a shadow of truth, that the Chinese acknowledge one Supreme Being; if such a confession is ever made, it is by men who have come in contact with foreigners, and are anxious to avoid the ridicule which attaches to a votary of idols. Nor are the impressions of polytheism so very easily removed from the mind; and though the absurdity may be fully admitted, the son of Han cleaves tenaciously to his ancient superstition. God alone can change this state of things, and open the heart of their understanding to perceive the truth."*

Suto, meaning "the way of philosophers," is always called another leading Japanese religion, although it is, in reality, much rather a philosophic school or sect, inculcating no particular faith, and being compatible with almost any faith, whether true or false. It is evidently an importation from China, consisting almost entirely of the moral doctrines taught by Confucius, and of some high Buddhist mystic notions concerning the final condition of the human soul. It is totally unconnected with any mythology, and it has no religious rites or ceremonies. We believe that *Sintoo* never made much progress among the vulgar, but that it is very generally followed by the nobility and all the educated classes, who may therefore be described as men of no religion. This *philosophy*, as Kämpfer correctly calls it, may be reduced to five points, which they call *Dsin*, *Gi*, *Re*, *Tsi*, and *Sin*. *Dsin* teaches them to live virtuously; *Gi*, to do right and act justly with everybody; *Re*, to be civil and polite; *Tsi* sets forth the rules for a good and prudent government; and *Sin* treats of a free conscience and uprightness of heart. They have no metempsychosis, but, although they do not admit the transmigration of souls into mortal bodies, they

---

* "Chinese Repository," vol. vii. p. 505. Canton. 1839.

believe in a universal soul, spirit, power, or real essence, which is diffused throughout the universe, which animates all things, which re-assumes the departing souls of men, as the ocean receives the rivers and waters that flow into it from all parts of the globe. This universal spirit is not our Supreme being, but what we may call Nature. They thank Nature for the food on their tables, and for all the necessaries and blessings of life. Kämpfer, whose account of this sect has never been improved, says:—

"Some among them, whom I conversed withal, admitted an intellectual, or incorporeal being, but only as governor and director, not as the author of nature; nay, they pretended, that it is an effect of nature produced by *In* and *Jo*,—heaven and earth, one active, the other passive; one the principle of generation, the other of corruption: after the same manner, also, they explained some other active powers of nature to be spiritual beings. They make the world eternal, and suppose men and animals to have been produced by *In* and *Jo*,—the heaven and five terrestial elements. Admitting no gods, they have no temples, no forms of worship. Thus far, however, they conform themselves to the general custom of the country, in that they celebrate the memory of their deceased parents and relations, which is done by putting all sorts of victuals, raw and dressed, on a *Biosju*, as they call it, or table purposely made with this view; by burning candles before them; by bowing down to the ground, as if they were yet alive; by monthly or anniversary dinners, whereto are invited the deceased's family and friends, who appear all in the best clothes, and wash and clean themselves by way of preparation, for three days before, during which time they abstain from all impure things; and by many other tokens of respect and gratitude. As to the burial of their dead, they do not burn them, but keep the corpse three days, and then lay it on the back in a coffin, after the European manner, with the head raised. Sometimes the coffin is filled with spices and sweet scented herbs, to preserve the body from corruption, and when everything is ready, they accompany it to the grave, and bury it without any further ceremony.

"These philosophers do not only admit of *self-murder*, but look upon it as an heroic and highly commendable action, and the only honorable means to avoid a shameful death, or to prevent falling into the hands of a victorious enemy. They celebrate no festivals, nor will they pay any respect to the gods of the country, any more than common civility and good manners require. The practice of virtue, a free conscience, and a good and honest life, is all that they aim at. They were even suspected of secretly favoring the Christian religion, for which reason, after the said religion had been entirely abolished by cross and fire, and violent means taken to prevent its ever reviving again, they also were commanded to have each an idol, or, at least, the name of one of the gods worshipped in the country, put up in their houses, in a conspicuous and honorable place, with a flower-pot and incensory before them."*

Nearly all our early writers assert that by far the greater part of the Japanese men of learning follow this doctrine; and that, notwithstanding the infinity and variety of gods or idols introduced into the country, most of the grandees are either free-thinkers or downright atheists.

An industrious and accurate writer sets down the number of religions or sects, quite distinct from Buddhism,

* "History of Japan."

at *thirty-four.** It would be difficult to find in any other country (not England or the United States of America) such striking instances of religious toleration. As far as regards the State, all these sects indulge their several opinions without restraint. The fact is, the Japanese government exhibited a rare and wonderful indifference to mere matters of doctrine, so long as they did not interfere with the public tranquillity. When the bonzes of all the sects concurred in a petition to the emperor Nobunanga that he would expel the Jesuits and all the Romish monks from Japan, that prince, annoyed by their importunities, inquired how many different religions there were in Japan? "Thirty-five," said the bonzes. "Well," said the emperor, "where thirty-five religions can be tolerated, we can easily bear with thirty-six: leave the strangers in peace."†

In emoluments and dignities, all sects are pretty nearly on an equality. On these points, causes for dissension cannot often arise. Occasionally (but not recently), when disputes on doctrinal points were running rather high, the government decided them in a summary manner, whipping, and even beheading, some of the fiercest of the controversialists. Even in the time of the tolerant emperor Nobunanga, a terrible controversy was settled quite in the manner of our Henry VIII. in the last years of his reign. But this was not until the peace of the country

---

* T. Rundall, Esq. "Memorials of the Empire of Japan," etc.

† "Summary of the Journal of Don Rodrigo de Viveroy Velasco," in Asiatic Journal, July, 1830.

This Don Rodrigo, a favorite of one of the wives of Philip II., was governor of the Philippine Islands, and was shipwrecked upon the coast of Japan in the year 1608. The account of his journey to Jeddo is exceedingly interesting.

had been seriously disturbed. "Never," says Mr. Meylan, "do we hear of any religious dispute among the Japanese, much less discover that they bear each other any hate on religious grounds. They esteem it, on the contrary, an act of courtesy, to visit, from time to time, each other's gods, and do them reverence. While the Koboe sends an embassy to the Sintoo temple at Isye, to offer prayers in his name, he assigns, at the same time, a sum for the erection of temples to Confucius; and the spiritual emperor allows strange gods, imported from Siam or China, to be placed (for the convenience of those who may feel a call to worship them) in the same temples with the Japanese. If it be asked whence this tolerance originates, and by what it is maintained, I reply from this, that worshippers of all persuasions in Japan acknowledge and obey one superior, namely the Daïri, or spiritual emperor. As the representative and lineal descendant of God on earth, he is himself an object of worship, and as such, he protects equally all whose object it is to venerate the Deity; the mode of their so doing being indifferent to him. Let it not be thought that I prize this tolerance too high, nor let the cruel persecutions of the Christians in Japan be objected to me: I ask whether this toleration was not one of the causes which so far facilitated the introduction of Christianity there? But that which with me is conclusive is, that could the preachers of the gospel in Japan have been tolerant as the Japanese,—had they not mocked and despised the gods of the country,—could it have been possible that the bishops chosen from the first missionaries should have receded from insisting on their right of total independence, and could they have been contented to place themselves under the protection of God's representative on earth, which the Japanese acknowledge in their

Daïri,—lastly, could they have forborne to meddle in affairs of politics and government, then would no persecution of Christianity, in all human probability, have taken place, and perhaps, at this moment, the doctrine of Jesus would have been triumphant over that of Confucius."

Thunberg, Golownin, Fischer, Siebold, and all the recent writers about the country, are agreed as to this easy toleration. Every Japanese citizen has a right to profess whatever faith he pleases—provided only it be not Christianity,—and to change it as often as he may think fit. Nobody concerns himself whether he does so out of conviction, or out of regard to his wordly interests. It is said to happen frequently, that the members of one family follow different faiths or sects, and that the difference of belief does not disturb the family harmony.

FAMILY WORSHIP.

From all we can collect on this subject, we are inclined

to believe that if the government could only be relieved of its prejudices and implacable animosity against the Romanists, or thoroughly convinced of the difference between the church of Rome and the reformed churches, that a troop of reformed missionaries might have a better chance of success than a powerful fleet and a great army of soldiers. But the missionary ought to be kept apart from every political scheme, and from every display of military force. Should the Japanese government suspect the Americans of any extensive design of occupation, conquest, or annexation, its hatred of the religion they profess will, no doubt, become quite as inveterate as that which has for more than two centuries been nourished against the Portuguese and the church of Rome.

A VASSAL PRINCE.

BOOK V.

GOVERNMENT—LEGISLATION—POLICE.

THE government of Japan is an absolute despotism, yet far from being altogether arbitrary. Everything and everybody are under a system of ancient, unchanging laws. No individual in the whole empire, however elevated in rank, is above the law. Both sovereigns, the spiritual and the temporal, are as completely enthralled by Japanese despotism as the meanest of their subjects, if not more so. This despotism is in the law and custom of the land, and operates by and through them. Law and custom press upon all with the same tyrannous weight. Scarcely an action of life is exempt from their rigid and inflexible control; but he who complies with the dictates of law, and with the established usages, seems rarely to have cause to apprehend any other arbitrary power or capricious tyranny.* In times of successful usurpation, some of the laws have been set at nought, and occasionally the court and great Council of State, who, in reality, administer the government, have been irregular and arbitrary; but the number of these exceptional cases is said to be inconsiderable.

---

* "Manners and Customs of the Japanese." New edition. London. 1852.

We have already dwelt upon the remarkable anomaly presented by Japan of two co-existing sovereigns, each maintaining a state independent of the other, both being the objects of homage on the part of the people, and neither of them, as far as can be seen, betraying any dissatisfaction at the amount of allegiance that is tendered to him. One of the sovereigns,—the Mikado, or Daïri-Sama,—rules by "right divine," or by virtue of his attributed descent from the gods. The other sovereign,—the Ziogun, or Koboe-Sama,—rules by the "right of might," or by virtue of his ability to maintain the power wrested by his predecessors from the Mikado. Sovereign *de jure*, the Mikado is supreme in rank, but according to all appearances, quite insignificant in political importance:* the veneration which is paid to him, falls little short of the honors which are paid to the gods themselves; yet he is little more than a prisoner; for he is brought into the world, and he lives and dies within the precincts of his court. The Koboe-Sama, sovereign *de facto*, is inferior in station, but uncontrolled, except by law and usage, in political authority.

The numbers of the grand Council of State, or of those who govern in the emperor's name, are variously given by different writers; but the best, or the latest, authority makes them thirteen: to wit, five councillors of the first class, selected from the princes of the empire; and eight of the second class, selected from the old nobility.† There appears good reason to doubt whether all these high offices are not hereditary; in which case there can

---

* Rundall, "Memorials."

† Siebold. Kämpfer gives a different number; but there may have been some slight change since his time

be no selection or election. Under these, in regular, and apparently interminable gradations, are other state functionaries; as lords or guardians of the temples, commissioners of foreign affairs, ministers of police, superintendents of agriculture, etc. etc. It appears that all the offices of government are filled, not by the relatives of the spiritual, but by those of the temporal sovereign. Personal interviews happen very rarely between the two potentates: the Ziogun is now said to visit the Mikado only once in seven years. It appears, however, that the temporal emperor frequently sends embassies and rich presents to the holy court at Miako, in return for which the spiritual emperor sends back his blessing and prayers. This, it has been observed, is no more than an equitable arrangement: for the temporal emperor has the revenues of the whole country in his hands, whereas the spiritual emperor must be content with the revenues of his limited principality of Kioto. There he governs, or is governed for, as an independent prince, or Damjo, as the Japanese call them, only with this difference, that the princes, or Damjos, maintain their military at their own expense, while the Mikado, or god-descended Daïri, is not allowed to have any soldiers.*

The dignity of each of the emperors is inherited by the eldest of their male descendants. In default of male issue, they adopt the eldest son of some prince of the empire, who is nearest to them in blood. There appears to be a head councillor of state, with functions and powers corresponding to those of the grand vizier in Turkey. He is called the "governor of the empire," and all the other councillors are strictly subordinate to him. No public

* Golownin, "Recollections of Japan."

affair of any consequence can be undertaken without him. The councillor of state, as we have said, transacts the business of the whole government; decides upon every measure; sanctions or reverses every sentence of death, wherever it may be pronounced; appoints to all offices and employments, and corresponds with all the chief authorities of the empire. Whenever law or usage is not perfectly clear, he must be consulted before anything is done. The council, collectively, have the power of dethroning the lay emperor. When they adopt any important resolution, it is laid before the emperor for his approval. This is usually given as a matter of course, without any delay, or any inquiry into the matter. But if, by any extraordinary accident, he should trouble himself about the concerns of his empire, attempt to examine for himself, and then withhold the expected fiat, the measure is referred to the arbitration of three princes of the blood, the nearest kinsmen of the monarch, and their decision is final, and very often attended with melancholy and fatal circumstances. Should their verdict coincide with the sentiments of the council, the Ziogun must forthwith abdicate in favor of his son, or other legal heir. This despotic sovereign, as Europeans have considered him, has not, in these State cases, the liberty of retracting an opinion.

On the other hand, should the three arbitrating princes pronounce the monarch to be in the right, and the council in the wrong, the consequences are still more serious. The minister who proposed the obnoxious act must die the death; the ministers who most warmly seconded him must frequently die also, and, occasionally, all the members of the council, with the vizier or governor of the empire, at their head, must rip open their bowels. Under such responsibility, men must be little disposed to attempt new laws, or any sort of innovation. When to this we add, that the whole council, collectively and individually, is perpetually surrounded by spies (some known, and some unknown), employed by superiors, inferiors, rivals, and by themselves, the one against the other, it will be evident, that these seemingly absolute ministers cannot venture upon the slightest infraction of the law without fear and trembling.

If we turn to the vassal princes of the empire we find that they are the objects of as much caution as the members of the supreme council. It is, indeed, against these princes, that the jealousy of the Ziogun and council is chiefly directed.

There were, originally, sixty-six or sixty-eight principalities, which had previously been so many independent kingdoms. As principalities, they were hereditary, but subject to forfeiture in case of rebellion or other treason. As many of the princes incurred this penalty of forfeiture, advantage was taken of the circumstance, by splitting the forfeited principalities into many fragments; and instead of sixty-six or sixty-eight, there are now said to be six hundred, and four distinct administrations, including great and small principalities, lordships, imperial provinces, and imperial towns.

The vassal princes still govern with all the outward forms and appearances of actual sovereignty, and each, by means of the nobles who are his vassals, keeps up his own army. But this sovereignty is little more than an appearance: the princes can do nothing, can propose nothing, without the consent and concurrence of the Ziogun and his council; they are entangled in a most intricate web of policy and state craft, they are kept under the perpetual surveillance of spies and informers, who watch their private and domestic, as well as their political or public conduct. The real administration of every principality is conducted, not by the prince himself, or by ministers of his own choice, but by two secretaries, appointed by the supreme council. Of these two secretaries one resides in the principality, and the other at Jeddo, where the family of the absent secretary is detained in hostage for his fidelity. We have before noted the strong tendency of the Japanese to duality. These double appointments extend to all high provincial posts, and it is only by the annual alteration of the situation of two official colleagues, that men holding such posts ever see their families; for, the functionary on duty for the year in the provinces must leave his family in the capital, and when, at the expiration of the term, he returns thither, his colleague must go to the provinces and leave his family behind him.

Each alternate year the vassal princes are allowed, or rather compelled to reside at Jeddo, near the Ziogun's palace. They are then reunited to their families, but continue under the same surveillance as ever. In fact, so long as they retain their principalities, their life is one of constant inquietude and restraint. Hence the very prevalent practice among them of abdicating in favor of a son or other lawful heir. It has been remarked, that a reigning prince, of advanced age, is rarely seen in Japan. They vacate the throne, or they die prematurely upon it, of grief or ennui. Whatever it may be for the governed, the Japanese system seems to be a wretched one for the governors. Spiritual emperor or lay emperor, vizier or vassal prince, supreme council or provincial secretary, all are "cabined, cribbed, confined," and condemned to a state of existence, which would be, to a European, about as insupportable as that of a galley slave.

The government of the lordships (which are merely small inferior principalities) is managed and controlled upon the same jealous system as that of the principalities themselves; and the same may be said of the provinces and cities called Imperial, and which have been retained as imperial domains. To the government of each of them) two governors are appointed, who live alternately at their posts and at the capital, where their wives and children must always be in hostage. These governors of imperial provinces, or imperial cities, are not named by hereditary right, but are selected from among the nobility by the Jeddo vizier and council, who appoint their secretaries, sub-secretaries, police-officers, spies, and all their official establishment. At Nagasaki, where European observations have been most frequently made, only the treasurer, the military commandant, and the inferior police officers are allowed to have their families with them. All the rest, so long as they are in the service of government, must leave their wives and children either at Jeddo or at the capital of the province or principality, in which they are stationed. Whether at Nagasaki, or in any other place, the functionaries who are allowed the comforts of domestic life, are perpetually surrounded by spies—one spy watching another, one delator informing against another. It may well be called "a government of spies."

These spies are said to be of every rank in life, from the lowest to the highest, beneath that of a prince. The proudest of the nobility have been known to undertake the office, either out of the ambitious hope of succeeding to the places and emoluments of those whom he might denounce, or in dread of the consequences of a refusal.

Where a man, if nominated, must be a spy, or rip open his own bowels, it is not wonderful that there should be so many spies, of all classes, ages and conditions.

Complaints of the governor of Matsmai were remitted to the court at Jeddo, where the counsel resorted to its usual method for ascertaining the truth. The obnoxious governor was soon displaced, but it was not without astonishment that the people recognized, in his successor, a journeyman tobacco-cutter, who, a short time before, had suddenly disappeared from his master's shop. The journeyman tobacco-cutter had been personated, for the nonce, by a noble of the land, who had assumed that disguise in order to perform the office of a spy, for which he had been sent to Matsmai by the court.*

Yet, living under so detestable a governmental system, the people of Japan are, almost always, described as frank in their manners, free and open in speech, and most sensitively alive to the point of honor. We should have much difficulty in believing the fact if we had not, ourselves, seen precisely the same thing in the Ottoman empire. There, nearly every Turk unconnected with government may be described as a frank, honest, truth-loving, honorable man; while every Turk at all connected with government (with remarkably few exceptions) may be, with equal safety, set down as the very reverse—as a man capable of playing the spy, or of resorting to any other iniquity or baseness. And, let the most honest-hearted Turk, by ambition or by accident, or by the caprice of some great man, only once get involved in the governmental meshes, and, at once, his nature is changed. With our experience of this seeming anomaly, we can

* Meylan.

give credit to the favorable reports of the character of the Japanese people.

Savary, and Fouché himself, might have taken lessons from the Japanese in that art of mystery and spying.

"Not only," says M. Meylan, "is the head of every family answerable for his children, his servants, and the strangers within his gates, but the city being divided into collections of five families, every member of such division is responsible for the conduct of the others, and, in consequence, that which, according to European ideas, would be the height of indiscretion, becomes here the duty of every man; for every extraordinary occurrence which falls out in a household is reported by four several witnesses to the members of the civil administration. House arrest is usually the penalty of the irregularities thus reported; and a severe one it is. The doors and windows of the offender's house are closed, generally for a hundred days; his employments are suspended; salary, if any, stopped; and the friend and barber alike forbidden entrance.* Every household is held bound to produce a man capable of bearing arms; a division of five constitutes a company; twenty-five such companies are arrayed under an officer, and constitutes a brigade of six or seven thousand men; and tnus the force of the city, apart from the regular military or police, can be presently mustered.

---

* This system of house arrest is very common among the Turks. In Constantinople, in 1828, and again in 1848, we frequently saw a house having all its windows blocked up with deal boards, roughly nailed on the outside. It was the konak or town residence of some pasha, bey, or other official, who had fallen into disgrace. So long as those boards remain up, the man is cut off from all society. If his nearest relative has courage enough to visit him, he does so under cover of night, and by stealing in at the back door.

Guard-houses are established in every street, in which a guard is on duty every night, and on occasions of festivity, or other cause of popular concourse, by day. Each street has a rail or barrier at its issues, and can consequently be cut off from communication with the rest of the city at a moment's notice."

No one can change his residence without obtaining a certificate of good conduct from the neighbours he is about to leave, and permission from those among whom he wishes to go. The result of this minutely ramified organization is said to be, that the whole empire affording no hiding-place for a criminal, there is no country in the world where so few robberies are committed. It is even said that, with valuable property within, the doors of the house may be left open all night with impunity.

Although not divided, like the Hindoos and other Oriental peoples, into castes, the Japanese may be said to be nearly, if not strictly, divided into hereditary classes. To be respected, every man must remain through life in the class in which he was born, unless exalted by some very rare merit, or very peculiar circumstance. Generally, the Japanese abhor *parvenus*. But it is very discreditable to sink below one's original class. These classes are eight in number.

Class I. is that of the hereditary vassal princes.

Class II. consists of the hereditary nobility under the rank of princes. These nobles hold their lands in fief, by military service, due to these several princes, or, in the imperial provinces, to the Ziogun. The number of fighting men to be furnished by each lord is regulated by the size and value of the estate he holds. Each lord has generally sub-vassals under him, who are bound to furnish their quotas. This closely resembles our old feudal system; but assuredly the condition of a feudal lord in England or in Normandy was one of independence, freedom, and happiness, compared with that of the Japanese prince or noble. It is from this second class that the officers of state, governors, generals, and the like, are selected. Wherever they may be employed, they are all subjected to long separations from their families. They are also compelled to live a part of their time in the capital, and there to incur heavy expenses, it being the policy of this suspicious government to keep all its officers and servants out of the way of accumulating wealth;—for wealth is power as well in Japan as elsewhere.

Class III. comprises the priests (apparently indiscriminately) of all the religions and sects that flourish in the empire.

Class IV. consists of the military, or the vassals furnished as soldiers by the nobility.

All these four classes, who constitute the higher orders of Japanese society, enjoy the envied privilege of carrying two swords, and of wearing a sort of loose petticoat trouser, which none beneath them dare ever put on. Thus, unless he be disguised to do spy work, the way to tell whether a man belongs to the upper classes, is to look at his sword-belt and breeches.

Class V. appears to comprehend what we call the upper portion of the middle classes; consisting of medical men, government clerks, and other professionals, and employés.

Class VI. consists of the more considerable shopkeepers and of merchants, who, whatever may be their wealth or intelligence, are held at a very low price by the Japanese. According to Kämpfer, the very gods they worship are rated as sordid, inferior divinities. The gentleman, or even the common soldier, that should engage in any trade or traffic, would be thereby disgraced for ever. Yet among these trading classes are to be found the only very rich men in the country. Speaking of his residence at Jeddo, M. Doeff says, "There is here an extensive dealer in silks, by name Itsigoja, who has large establishments besides in all the other great cities of the empire. Any customer who conveys his purchase to another of these cities, Nagasaki, for example, and there tires of his acquisition, may give it back and receive the price in full. The wealth of this man must be enormous, as the following will show:—During my residence at Jeddo, there occurred a vast fire, which consumed everything within a space three leagues in length and a mile and a half in breadth; among the rest, our lodging. Itsigoja lost his entire shop, and a warehouse containing more than a hundred thousand bales of silk thread; which loss was unmitigated; for the Japanese knew nothing of insurance. He, nevertheless, sent to our assistance forty of his servants, who stood us in great stead; and on the second day he was already actively engaged in rebuilding his premises, paying every carpenter six florins per diem."*

Nor is such a case of commercial wealth by any means rare in the great cities of the empire. A merchant, or an aspiring shopkeeper of London, Paris, or other European capital, may spend his money as he gets it,—or faster than that,—by taking a house in a fashionable quarter, by setting up fashionable equipages, by giving costly entertainments, and by imitating, in all things, the style and magnificence of the wealthiest and most profuse nobleman. But the Japanese merchant can do nothing of the sort: his style of living is strictly regulated by sumptuary laws, which he dare not infringe. He cannot even have the

* "Recollections of Japan."

satisfaction of wearing the single sword, unless he attach himself in a menial capacity to the household of some great lord. It appears, however, that not a few of them take this degrading course, and that the impoverished nobility are generally very ready to swell the number of their nominal retainers upon considerations given and paid.* But no amount of money or patronage can procure for the merchant the inestimable honor of wearing petticoat trousers.

Class VII. is composed of retail dealers, little shop-keepers, pedlars, mechanics, and artisans of all descriptions. It also includes painters and other artists, who might have been expected to occupy a somewhat higher grade in the social scale.

Class VIII. consists of the peasantry, agricultural laborers, and day-laborers of all kinds. The mass of the peasantry are said to be little better than the serfs, or villeins, attached to the soil, and the property of the landholder. There is, however, a class who hire and cultivate land on the *metayer* system, so common in many parts of the European continent,—that is, they divide the produce of the estate and farm with the landed proprietor, according to certain proportions previously agreed upon

* Something like the system obtained in England down to "the happy days of good Queen Bess." The retainers of the Earl of Leicester, as painted by Sir Walter Scott, in his "Kenilworth," were living realities. The practice continued in the reign of Charles I., and many traces of it are found in the reign of Charles II., and down to the Revolution of 1688.

It appears, however, that though these Japanese sometimes pay for the privilege of wearing a sword, they rarely use the weapon; that they are not brawlers and fighters, as the retainers of our nobility, in the olden time, were wont to be.

between them. Unfortunately, it is added, that the Japanese landlords take the lion's share, and leave so little to the farmers, that they are generally found as indigent as the serfs.

There is another class, which is held to be so vile, that it is not even enumerated or set down in the list. They are the very *pariahs* of Japan. All tanners, curriers, leather-cutters, and, in fact, every man connected in any way with the preparation of leather, or the leather trade, lie under ban and interdict. They are not permitted to dwell in any town or village with other classes of men; but they live in detached huts, or in hamlets exclusively their own. They are not even numbered in the census of the population, which appears to be taken, with considerable care, at certain intervals. They may not enter an inn, public-house, tea-house, or any place of public entertainment. If they are travelling, and in want of food or drink, they must wait humbly outside the wall, and be there served in their own bowl or platter; for no one but a man or woman of their own class would ever use the vessel out of which they have eaten or drunk. They are the public executioners and gaolers in most parts of the empire. It is conjectured that this banning of a whole class originated in the Sintoo doctrine of defilement by contact with any dead body.*

Although the Japanese have been so long at peace, internally as well as externally, and although they govern rather by spies, policemen, and other civilians, than by soldiers, it should appear, from all accounts, that a very considerable standing army is kept up in the empire. It is, however, very difficult, from the data before us, to

---

* Meylan, Siebold, Kämpfer. See Appendix E.

come to any conclusion as to the actual number of this force. It is divided into two classes: 1. The imperial guards, or the troops of the Ziogun. 2. The vassal soldiers of the nobility. It has been asserted that the first of these amount to 100,000 foot, and 20,000 horse; but this appears to be exaggerated.

As, by the military tenure, every prince, sub-prince, or lord, must furnish his full contingent of able-bodied men whenever called upon, by the lay emperor, so to do, we might form some estimate of the number of combatants that could be brought into the field, if we only knew the total amount of the population of the empire. But although the census is taken, it is kept a state secret, and, as we have stated, there is a great difference of opinion on the question of population. The Ziogun's own troops are far superior in appearance to those furnished by the vassal princes and lords. The fact is mentioned in one of the early Dutch accounts. This old writer, after speaking of the military tenure, and of so many armed men being raised and maintained for so much land, praises the order, *discipline*, dress, and *silence* of the imperial guards, and concludes by calling them "all chosen, brave fellows, clad in rich black silks."* Golownin, at first, mistook all the privates for officers. In ancient times they were highly esteemed for their valor in actual combat, for their celerity on the march, and for their perseverance and cheerfulness under fatigue and privation; and, with a very few exceptions, they may probably be found, at this day, the bravest of Asiatic nations.

Anterior to 1615, Japanese served as soldiers of fortune in many of the neighboring countries, and were highly

---

* "A Collection of Voyages, &c." 6 vols. folio. London. 1732.

esteemed by the princes who retained them. On more than one occasion they fought side by side with Spanish and Portuguese troops, at that time as good soldiers as any in the world. As for *discipline*, as we now understand that word, we should be inclined, with due deference to the old Hollander sea-captain, who wrote his account 200 years ago, that they have none of it. Their formations, their manœuvres, their tactics, would no doubt excite the derision of the least martial of European nations. Apparently they know next to nothing of military architecture, or of the art of defending or attacking fortresses or fortified positions. Their gunnery appears to be of the very worst sort, although their guns are beautifully made. Their portable fire-arm is the old, long, slow matchlock, which from prejudice, they will not change for our modern muskets and rifles, with which they are well acquainted, and with which they could be well supplied by their own native artisans. But even the matchlock appears to have a very confined range; for bows and arrows, awkward spears, long and weak in the shaft; javelins, and even wooden clubs, are often mentioned as common Japanese arms. Their sword-blades, however, are of admirable temper, and many of the Ziogun's picked men are said to be expert swordsmen. But, in modern battles, the *armes blanches* of chivalry really count for little.

In the old times, the Japanese made use of curious chain armor, and, occasionally, their officers are still seen wearing these coats of mail over their silk jerkins, having below their jerkins the wide silk petticoat or petticoat-trousers.

Notwithstanding the 200 years of profound peace (which *may* have deteriorated the military virtues of the nation), the military profession is held in great honor. In conversation, the common people, and even the rich merchants, give the common soldier the title of *Sama*, or my lord, and address him with all possible respect. To turn a soldier out of his profession is considered the greatest punishment that can be inflicted on him. Every soldier, whatever may be his rank, has the right to wear two swords, or a sabre and dagger, like the first lord of the empire. It is said that the common men have such a keen sense of the point of honor, that they frequently resent affronts by fighting duels with one another, or by ripping themselves up, in order to show that they prefer death to dishonor.* If they really retain this mettle, they are troops that will assuredly stand and fight. Beaten they must be by men such as those who marched from the United States into Mexico; but we cannot, without emotion, think of the numbers that may be slaughtered before any surrender, capitulation, or military or political settlement whatsoever can take place.

The severity of the Japanese laws are Draconic. They may really be said to be written in blood, as death is the allotted punishment for every offence, and, not unfrequently, whole families are involved in the fate of a single offender. Death, by decapitation at the hands of the common executioner, or by instant self-murder—and nothing short of death is considered an atonement of the slightest breach of the law or of public tranquillity, or of disobedience to any order or instruction of government. Imprisonment, exile, or relegation in distant, cold, and desolate islands appear to have fallen out of use since the troubles of the seventeenth century. In the rare occasions,

* Golownin. "Recollections of Japan."

on which they are now resorted to, they seem to be extended not only to the offender, but to his wife and children, however innocent, and however young.

Apparently they have no condensed, written Code of Laws. Their laws consist of edicts issued in the name of the emperor from time to time. They are said to be exceedingly simple in their construction, and to possess the somewhat rare merit of being intelligible to the commonest capacity. On the issue of every new edict, the magistrates, in the first instance, assemble the people, and proclaim, by word of mouth, the will of the emperor. Next, the edict is extensively circulated in a printed form, and, as nearly every man and woman in the empire is said to be able to read, the law must thus become well known. But they have yet another method of giving it publicity: the edict is placarded, for a permanency, in a public hall or place appropriated to the purpose, in every city, town, and village, throughout the empire.

"I have often admired," says Kämpfer, "while traveling through this country, the shortness and laconism of these tables, which are hung up on the roads, in places especially appointed for the purpose, to notify to the public the emperor's pleasure, and to make known the laws of the country; for it is mentioned, in as few words as possible, what the emperor commands to be done or omitted by his subjects. There is no reason given how it came about that such and such a law was made; no mention of the law-giver's views and intention; nor is there any certain determined penalty put upon transgression thereof. Such conciseness is thought becoming the majesty of so powerful a monarch."*

* "History of Japan." Appendix E.

The Japanese have laws, and lawgivers, but no professional practising barristers or lawyers of any kind. Every man is considered competent to be his own lawyer or pleader. We will here quote from the most recent English writer on the subject of Japan, to whom we have repeatedly acknowledged our obligations. Mr. Thomas Rundall, who has consulted and condensed all the best authorities, says:—

" *The proceedings under the laws* are as simple as the laws themselves.

" The Japanese system does not admit any technical and complicated forms; and, consequently, there is no professional class required to elucidate, or, as the case may be, further to perplex what is already obscure. In the empire, a party feeling himself aggrieved, appeals direct to the magistrate. The case is stated in presence of the accused, and he is heard in reply. Witnesses are examined. Sentence is then passed, and generally carried into execution *instanter*. In trivial cases, the parties are usually ordered to retire and settle the difference, either between themselves, or with the assistance of mutual friends; and the matter may be considered to be adjusted.

" It is perfectly well understood, that persisting in the dispute would lead to unpleasant consequences. Should both parties appear to be blameable, the judge makes his award accordingly, and neither escapes without censure. When false accusations are preferred, the false accuser is punished; and should malice be apparent, the punishment is augmented in proportion.

" In cases of great importance, the magistrate has the option of referring the matter to the Chief Justice at Miaco, or to the Emperor in Council; but when a decision is once given, there is no appeal.* Towards the conclusion of the seventeenth century, Kämpfer makes the following remarks on the Japanese system of administering justice. He says:—"Some will observe, that the Japanese are wanting in a competent knowledge of the law. . . . . But I would not have the reader imagine that the Japanese live entirely without laws. Far from it. Their laws and constitutions are excellent, and strictly observed."

"Coming down to the present century, competent authorities concur in bearing testimony to the purity with which justice is administered in the empire: to the great solemnity and strict decorum with which the proceedings are conducted before the tribunals: to the ardent desire manifested by the magistrates to elicit the truth; and to the remarkable acumen they display in detecting falsehood."† If the representations on the subject be not overcharged, the judicial institutions of the empire appear to realize, in a great degree, the maxim propounded by one of our most profound thinkers, that "*Truth is but justice in our knowledge, and justice is but truth in our practice.*"‡

"In the theory of PUNISHMENT, it is not considered

---

* No superior court hath it in its power to mitigate the sentence pronounced in another, though inferior. . . Although it cannot be denied but this short way of proceeding is liable to some errors and mistakes in particular cases, yet I dare affirm that, in the main, it would be found abundantly less detrimental to the parties concerned, than the tedious and expensive lawsuits in Europe.—(Kämpfer, Appendix, vol. ii. p. 64.)

† Doeff, Fischer, Siebold, etc.; quoted in 'Manners and Customs of the Japanese in the 19th century."

‡ Milton, "Answer to Eikon Basilike."

'*qu'un homme pendu est un homme perdu.*'* As a principle, *death* is the punishment for all offences.

"It does not, however, appear to have been adopted either from caprice, or through wanton disregard of human life; but may be traced rather to an erroneous conception of the means of doing equal justice. It is maintained, that justice would be violated, unless all persons, whatever their ranks, guilty of similar offences, were punished in an equal manner; and it is conceived that death is the only penalty that affects alike prince and peasant. 'Justice,' says William Adams, 'is very severe, having no respect to persons.' Accordingly, the only favor exhibited in regard to the man of rank, is that of his being permitted to anticipate the act of the executioner by the commission of suicide.

"But though sanguinary in principle, the laws are greatly modified in practice.

"The power of inflicting death appears to be permissive, not compulsory, on the magistrate; and accordingly, a very wide discretion is exercised. From this discretion murder alone is excepted, including homicide of any kind, even in its least aggravated form. This appears to have arisen from the disposition of the population, represented to have been originally, but probably now tempered by altered circumstances, 'no less fiery and changeable than the neighboring sea is stormy and tempestuous.' On the principle of equal justice, *pecuniary fines* are not tolerated. Recourse is had to *imprisonment* as a punishment, which is rendered more or less severe according to the place in which incarceration takes place. One description of prison is called *raya* or *cage*. Here due provision is made

* "Voltaire, "L'Homme aux Quarante Ecus."

for cleanliness and ventilation, and a fair proportion of wholesome food is provided. The other description of prison is denominated *gokuya*, or *hell.* It is a dungeon, generally within the walls of the governor's house, into which from fifteen to twenty persons are usually thrust, or at least more, ordinarily, than the place can conveniently accommodate. The door is never opened but for the admission or release of a prisoner. A hole in the wall serves as the means of ejecting the filth, and of receiving food. Except from a small grated window at the top, there is neither light nor ventilation. Books, pipes, all kinds of recreation are prohibited. No beds are allowed, and, as a mark of disgrace which is acutely felt, the prisoners are deprived of their silk or linen waist girdles, for which bands of straw are substituted. A singular regulation is connected with these hells. The diet is limited in quantity, and execrable in quality; but on a certain condition, prisoners who have the means, or who have friends willing to assist them, are allowed to be provided with good and sufficient food. *The condition on which this indulgence is granted, is, that it shall be shared equally by all the inmates of the dungeon.* It is utterly repugnant to the Japanese notions of justice, that a criminal of wealth, or influence, should fare better than those who may be destitute. *Banishment* seems not to extend beyond the persons of the nobles attached to the imperial court, with some political offenders of high rank. These parties are deported to certain barren islands, from whence escape is impracticable. Food is provided for them, but they must work for their living. Their usual employment is the manufacture of silk goods, which are represented to be of an exceedingly fine description, and to be highly prized.

"*Corporal punishment* is inflicted frequently, and with great severity. *Torture* is resorted to but rarely, principally in cases of religious apostasy or political delinquency.

"The substance of the following proceeding, derived by Titsingh from a native source, is given in his 'Illustrations of Japan,' and will afford an idea of the manner in which the discretionary power, vested in the magistrate, may be exercised.

"A man was charged by his master, a trader in Osacca, with having robbed him of five hundred kobans, equivalent in sterling value to about £700. The charge was made before the governor. The accused solemnly protested his innocence; and the accuser, supported by the testimony of other servants, as solemnly maintained the truth of the charge. Circumstances were against the prisoner; but the evidence was of that doubtful nature, that the magistrate did not feel himself warranted in convicting or discharging the man. He, therefore, to use a familiar phrase, remanded him. At the end of some days, the magistrate called the parties before him again; and he remonstrated with the accuser, but ineffectually. At length he required the charge, and the demand of the accuser, to be submitted to him in writing. This was done in the following terms:—'Tchoudjet, servant to Tomoya, has robbed his master of five hundred kobans. This we attest by this writing, and we demand, that by way of example, he be punished with death.' 'We, the servants and relatives of Tomoya-Kiougero, have confirmed this writing, by affixing our signatures and our seals, the second month of the first year *Geu-boun* (1736).' The governor, Kavatche-no-kami by name, read the paper attentively, and then said to Tomoya: 'Good. Now am I absolved from responsibility. Depart. Be assured justice shall be done.' So Tomoya and his party went away rejoicing. A short time afterwards a convicted felon confessed himself guilty of the robbery with which Tchoudjet had been charged; and Tomoya, with all his people were straightway summoned into the presence of the governor. 'What is this thing ye have done?' said the governor, addressing the party sternly; 'Know ye not, that your false accusation hath tended to cause the death of an innocent man? Know ye not the law, that ye have put your own lives in jeopardy? that thou, thyself, Tomoya, thy wife, and thy people, may be delivered over to the executioner? And behold me, should I not die the death, because I have not looked with greater care into this matter. Prepare for doom.' Thunderstruck, the terrified wretches threw themselves on their knees and implored for mercy. The magistrate beheld their abject state for some time in silence. He kept them in agonizing suspense, willing to give them a lesson they should not speedily forget. At length he exclaimed:—'Be of good cheer. The man is not dead. I doubted his guilt, and I have kept him in concealment, hoping that, in process of time, his innocence might be brought to light. Most sincerely do I rejoice that my precaution hath proved of avail. Let Tchoudjet be brought in.' The order was obeyed, and the governor, resuming his address, said: 'Tomoya, behold an innocent man, who might have fallen a victim to thy unjust accusation. A grievous injury hast thou inflicted on him. Thy life I spare, because his has not been taken; but for what he has suffered through thy injustice, thou owest him reparation. Pay unto him, then, the sum of five hundred kobans, and thenceforth cherish him as a faithful servant. Go thy ways. Justice is now done.' In due course, this proceeding was reported to the Emperor. What had been done by Kavatche was approved, and he was in a short space of time appointed to the lucrative and high posts of Inspector of the Chamber of Accounts, and Governor at Nagasaki, where his good qualities endeared him to the people, his memory being held in reverence in the time of the European narrator of the transaction."*

According to some writers, torture is very common where the crime is heinous, or where the evidence is deficient; but we are disposed to believe with Mr. Rundall, that it is now but rarely resorted to. We have also our doubts as to some other horrible, revolting stories which have been told by travelers, and which seem to be opposed to the character given to the Japanese by these very travelers themselves. It has been said, for example, that public executions, not by one merciful stroke, but by slow torture, are by no means unfrequent; that the young nobles are accustomed to lend their swords to the torturing executioner, in order that the edge and temper of the blade may be tried; that they take great delight in witnessing tortures, particularly when the criminal is enveloped in a thick close-fitting garment or shirt made of reeds, and to which fire is applied; that they laugh and applaud, as at a dance in the theatre, when the poor victim feels the flames, and runs and leaps about in his agony, and that this they call by the pleasant name of the "Death-dance."

Several executions witnessed by the Dutch near Nagasaki were conducted with decency and humanity. The

* "Memorials of the Empire of Japan," etc. Printed for the Hakluyt Society. London. 1850.

prisoner was carried to the place of execution—a large open field outside the town—on a horse, his legs and arms being bound with cords. On his way thither any person might give him refreshment. At the appointed spot were the judges, with their assistants and insignia of office. Here the victim to the laws received from the executioner a cup of cheering sackee, with its usual accompaniments, dried fish, fruit and pastry, which he was allowed to share with his relatives and friends. He was then seated upon a straw mat between two heaps of sand, and his head was struck off with a sharp sword. The severed head was set upon a stake, to which was affixed a placard, indicating the crime for which he had died. At the end of three days, the relations were allowed to take down the head, and bury it and the body in their own way.

It is stated, though not upon the very best authority, that in certain cases, involving the honor of wives or daughters, the Japanese may take the law into their own hands, and that fathers have the power of life and death over their refractory, wicked children. Although the contrary has been stated, it does not appear,—except in very peculiar cases,—that the lord has the power of life and death over his serf. We have somewhere seen it stated that he cannot inflict any severe punishment, unless he previously take the serf before a magistrate.

To return from criminal to civil jurisprudence, or practice, it is stated that the law of primogeniture is so thoroughly recognized and established, that family disputes about property very rarely occur. The younger sons have small portions, regulated according to usage, and of which, if old enough, they are put in possession during their father's lifetime. If of noble birth, they are regarded

THE PORT OF SIMONESEKE.

with respect, however poor they may be. The pride of birth seems to be very strong among all the upper classes. As a general rule, the daughters even of the high nobility have no fortunes or dowry on marriage. On the contrary, if they are considered very handsome, amiable in temper, and very accomplished, the parents expect the bridegroom to pay down to them a handsome sum of money, or to make over to them some other valuable property.

Whatever may be the extent of his harem, the Japanese can have only one lawful wife at a time; and she must be of the same rank as her husband. Her issue alone can inherit family property, titles, and honors. It appears, however, to be very easy for a man to put away his wife and take another,—at least, as far as any law exists to the contrary. But this tendency to divorce is said to be checked by serious financial considerations. If he sends one wife back to her home, he does not recover the money he paid for her; and if he gains the evil reputation of being a capricious, inconstant husband, the price in the matrimonial market is raised upon him, and he must disburse largely before he can get another wife.

These are, of course, some lingering remains of the old Mongol barbarism; but, whether it be by law or by usage, by the edicts of emperors, or by a natural gallantry in the people, the position of women in Japan is far higher and better than in any other essentially Asiatic country. A lady at Jeddo enjoys a hundred times more real liberty, and is treated with immeasurably more respect, than a Turkish lady at Constantinople,—and this, after all the reforms or innovations of Sultans Mahmoud and Abdul-Medjid.

THE KIRISIMA JAMMA.

BOOK VI.

MINERAL WEALTH, PEARLS, PRECIOUS STONES.

"THESE islands," says a Spanish writer of the seventeenth century, "are excessively rich in gold and silver. The abundance of these metals is scarcely credible. In Jeddo, the capital, not only the palace of the emperor, but also many houses of great lords, are covered with rich plates of gold."* "The greatest riches of the Japanese soil," says the careful and accurate Kämpfer, "and those

* Don Pedro Hurtado de Mendoza, "Espejo Geographico."

wherein this empire exceeds most known countries, consist in all sorts of minerals and metals, particularly in gold, silver, and copper."* On this point, all the old writers are agreed.

Gold is dug out of the mines in many provinces. The greatest quantity of it is melted out of its own ore. Some is washed out of gold sand, and small quantities are said to be contained in the copper. The richest gold ore, and that which contains the finest gold is mined in one of the northern districts of the great island Niphon. There is also a very rich gold sand in the same part of the island. But gold ore, or gold in dust, appears to be found in innumerable parts of the Japanese Archipelago.† Deterred by superstitious fears, the native miners have seldom penetrated far into the earth, but have rested satisfied with the gold found near the surface.

In a memorandum laid before the Dutch governor-general at Batavia, in 1744, is a calculation, showing that in the beginning of the seventeenth century, when the trade with Japan was an open one, the export of gold and silver was ten millions of Dutch florins, or about £840,000 per annum. This export was first contracted, and in 1680, entirely forbidden. The same calculation goes on to prove that, in the course of sixty years, the export of gold and silver must have amounted to the enormous value of from twenty-five to fifty millions sterling.

In a good many old accounts of India (both French and

* "History of Japan."

† We have seen some gold articles of Japanese manufacture, in which the precious metal was uncommonly pure and beautiful,—thoroughly virgin gold. The same may be said of some of their silver, which we have examined.

English), we find frequent mention made of "the gold lingots of Japan." About the middle of the seventeenth century, these lingots appear to have abounded in Bengal. But at an earlier period, or between 1545 and 1615, it is notorious that the Portuguese obtained in Japan, in exchange for merchandize, enormous quantities of the precious metals.*

Silver-mines are described as being quite as numerous as the gold mines, and their produce as excellent in quality. In one year we find the Portuguese exporting 2,350 chests of this fine silver, valued, in round numbers, at £587,500 sterling. To the east of Japan lie two islands, called, *par excellence*, the "gold and silver islands." These have never been touched by Europeans.

Copper abounds all through the group, and some is said to be the finest in the world. It is refined and cast into small cylinders about a foot long and an inch thick. It was formerly one of the chief commodities purchased in Japan by the Dutch, who brought it into Europe, and carried on a great trade in it. There is also a coarser kind of copper, which is cast into large roundish lumps or cakes.

The Dutch have in some years carried off from thirty to forty thousand pekuls of this copper, each pekul being about 133 pounds weight English. Alarmed at the amount, the Japanese government decreed that instead of two yearly ships, only one should be allowed to carry off copper, but, in 1820, the restriction was mitigated, and the number of vessels and amount of copper were again increased. It may be said that all the Japanese metals are everywhere esteemed for their high degree of purity. If

* T. Rundall, "Memorials."

they nave exhausted their old copper mines, there can be little doubt that new ones would easily be found, if the restrictive and tyrannical government did not interfere with, and almost entirely check, private enterprises.

Both lead and quicksilver are said to be abundant.

Tin, so fine and white, that it almost comes up to silver, is found in small quantities. As this metal is not much used or prized by the natives, it has probably not been much sought after.

Iron is dug up only in three of the provinces, although it may very likely exist in many other parts of the islands. The Japanese smelt it on the spot, and cast it into small bars or cylinders. It is of admirable quality, as is also the steel which they make from it. Although they have great ingenuity in smelting and refining metals, and in working them, there can be little doubt that modern European science would turn all these mines to an incomparably greater account.

Coal, which gives wings and life to steam navigation, and so tends to unite together all portions of the globe, is the mineral for which the Americans profess to have the greatest desire. Indeed, they declare that their main object in fitting out their Japan expedition is to obtain from the emperor permission to purchase from his subjects the supplies of coal which their steamers in their out and inward voyages may require.* "They have no want of coals in Japan," says Kämpfer, "they being dug up in great quantities in the province of Sikusen, and in most of the northern provinces." Von Siebold speaks of coal as being in common use in the country. At Koyanose, in very

* See instructions to Commander Aulick, as given in the *Times* newspaper, of May 12th, 1852.

cold weather, he found a comfortable coal fire. At Wu-ku-moto he visited a coal mine, and although he was not permitted to descend quite to the bottom of the shaft, he saw enough to convince him that the mine was skillfully worked. The upper strata were only a few inches thick, but he was told that the lower beds measured many feet, and he saw some very thick blocks which had been brought up. It appears that, for domestic uses, the natives convert this coal, which is very bituminous, into coke. The value of these beds can scarcely be over estimated. They will contribute wonderfully to the interests of commerce, and may, indeed, be considered "a gift of Providence, deposited by the Creator of all things in the depth of the Japanese islands for the benefit of the human family."* Without free access to this coal, the chain of steam navigation must remain broken. In this sense, it is to be considered of more value than all the mines of gold, silver, and copper, that the islands may contain.

Pearls are fished up on nearly all parts of these coasts, and they are frequently of great size and beauty. The native Japanese put little or no value upon them, till they found that the Chinese were ready to pay high prices for those of the finest qualities. Mother-of-pearl, of great size, transparent and beautiful, is found in abundance, as are also corals, corallines, sea-fans, and other submarine productions. Naphtha, ambergris, and sulphur (the last in inexhaustible quantities) are to be numbered among the exports of the islands, which abound in volcanos, extinct or in action. Fine pure native sulphur is found at many of these volcanos, in broad deep beds,

---

* Mr. Webster's Letter of Instruction to the Commodore of the American Expedition.

and may be dug up and removed with as much ease as sand. One small volcanic island renders, or rendered, by its sulphur, a considerable annual revenue to the government.

We have mentioned in our historical sketch how, at comparatively recent dates, volcanic islands have been projected from the depths of the sea. It should seem that some of these have disappeared, like the volcanic island which rose so suddenly off the coast of Sicily some twenty years ago; but others have not only remained, but have gradually increased in size. Adjoining to the department of Satsuma is an island covered with sulphur. Kämpfer states that the Japanese did not venture there more than a hundred years before his time. "The island was thought to be wholly inaccessible, and by reason of the thick smoke which was observed continually to rise from it, and of the several spectres and other frightful apparitions which people fancied to see there, chiefly by night, it was believed to be a dwelling-place of devils; but, at last, a resolute man obtained permission to go and examine it. He chose fifty bold fellows for this expedition; upon going on the shore they found neither hell nor devils, but a large flat piece of ground at the top of the island (the crater originally), which was so strongly covered with sulphur that wherever they walked a thick smoke issued from under their feet. Ever since that time this island brings in, to the prince of Satsuma, about twenty chests of silver per annum."

Agates, cornelians, jaspers, fine variegated marbles, and other precious or valuable stones are brought down from many of the mountains. Some of the agates are uncommonly fine, of a bluish color, and not unlike sapphires. Of diamonds we find no mention. It is rather singular in a people so keenly alive to all that is rich and beautiful, that the Japànese have entirely neglected the arts of the lapidary, and hold jewels in hardly any esteem. All the precious stones of which travellers speak, appear to have been found by them in the rough, unpolished, uncut state. It is conjectured that some properly skilled men might drive a very profitable trade in this line.

We have the testimony of Tavernier to the size, purity, and value of the pearls of Japan, and we could hardly look for a better authority on such a point, as Tavernier was a thorough proficient, and gained a great estate by trading in gems and jewels.*

---

* "Travels in the East," etc. The first edition of this valuable work appeared at Paris, in 1676. The author of it, a traveller of the right stamp, and one who, according to Gibbon, united the soul of a philosopher with the pursuits of a jeweller, died, on his way to Moscow, in July, 1689, in the 84th year of his age.

The reader may also be referred to Captain Alexander Hamilton:—"A New Account of the East Indies," etc., etc., 2 vols. 8vo. Edinburgh. 1727. This Hamilton spent his time from the year 1688 to 1723 in trading, and travelling by sea and land, in most of the countries between the Cape of Good Hope and the islands of Japan. On matters of trade his book is worthy of consultation. It has been republished in Pinkerton's Collection of Voyages and Travels. See, also, Appendix F.

JAPANESE GARDEN.

BOOK VII.

SYLVA—FOREST TREES—FRUIT TREES—PLANTS—FLOWERS.

THOUGH, to some extent, rocky or mountainous, the islands may be described as well-wooded and shaded. Firs and cypresses are the most common trees in their woods and forests. Of both there are several different sorts. In the plains, the natives who, like the Chinese, make the most of every inch of ground, take care to plant them in barren and sandy soils, which are fit for nothing else. For the sake of ornament and shade, they are, however, planted in rows along the roads, and over the ridges of hills. This gives great beauty to the country, and renders travelling in warm weather very pleasant.

A noble Spaniard, who was shipwrecked on the coast, and made a journey to the emperor's court in the year 1608, says:—"On whichever side the traveller turns his eye he perceives a pleasant concourse of people, passing to and fro, as in the most populous cities of Europe; the roads are lined on both sides with superb pine trees, which keep off the sun; the distances are marked by little eminences planted with two trees."*

* "Journal of Don Rodrigo de Vivero y Velasco."—*Asiatic Journal*, July, 1830. The whole of this paper is in the highest degree interesting.

No firs nor cypress-trees are allowed to be cut down without permission of the local magistrate, and for every full-grown tree that is felled, a young one must be planted. From remote time the Japanese appear to have bestowed an exceedingly great care on the growth and preservation of their timber-trees, thus shaming some nations of Europe, who pretend to more wisdom and civilization than they.

Cedars of great size and beauty, and compared with those that once flourished so luxuriantly on Mount Lebanon, are very frequently met with. A Portuguese missionary, who was in the country in 1565, vividly describes the approach to one of the temples, which was through an avenue of pines and cedars intermixed, the trees uniting over head, so as entirely to exclude the heat and glare of the hot summer sun. Some of the cedars he measured were more than eighteen feet in girth. The roof of the temple was supported by ninety columns of cedar, of prodigious height, regular in the stem, and perfectly round.*

The Jesuit Charlevoix was much struck with one particular camphor-tree. One hundred and thirty-five years after his time, Von Siebold visited the same tree, and found it still healthy and rich in foliage. It had attained to the circumference of fifty feet. Captain Sir Edward Belcher, being in want of some small spars, was supplied with a quantity at Nagasaki. They were all cedar, and measured about ninety-six feet in length.

The views of Japanese scenery, published in the works of M. Fischer and Von Siebold, convey the idea of a superb sylva, and of a luxuriantly wooded country. It should appear that all the temples, of any size or consideration,

* P. Almeyda, as quoted by Mr. Rundall, "Memorials."

are approached through an avenue of evergreen trees. The cedar timber would, no doubt, prove a valuable article of export.

The oak flourishes in two varieties, both of which are very different from any that grow in Europe. The acorns of the larger oak are boiled and eaten by the common people, and are said to be nutritious and not unpalatable.

The mulberry-tree grows in most parts of Japan, but in greatest plenty in the provinces of the north, where many towns and villages subsist almost entirely upon the silk manufactures. But the silk of Japan is coarse, and very inferior to that of China, a circumstance which arises from the natives allowing their mulberry-trees to grow to age and size, instead of keeping up a constant supply of young dwarf trees. The coarseness of the leaves of the old tree imparts its quality to the silk. Wherever fine silk is produced, the worms are fed on the leaves of saplings. The Japanese mulberry-tree grows with surprising quickness, and spreads its branches to a great extent. It is found in its wild state in the country, but, on account of its great usefulness, the people transplant it and cultivate it. From its bark they make much of their curious paper, as also ropes, matches, coarse stuffs for dresses, and several other things.

The *urusi* or varnish-tree, of which they make so extensive a use, is a noble tree when grown to its full size. On incision it yields a rich, milky, glutinous juice, out of which the Japanese make the celebrated varnish, known in Europe by the name of *Japan*. With this varnish they cover and coat all their household furniture, all their dishes and plates, and all their drinking vessels, whether made of wood or of paper. The use of plate, or porcelain or glass, appears to be very limited, and is probably interdicted by some rule of nationality or religion: from the emperor down to the meanest peasant, all make use of the light varnished or japanned cups and dishes, the inner substance of which is wood or paper, or what we term papier-maché.

Another tree, called *forasi*, renders a varnish of an inferior quality.

The camphor-tree exists in many parts, and bears black and purple berries which are pleasant to the sight. The country people make the camphor by a simple decoction of the stem and roots cut into small pieces. The tea-plant, which was long believed to be peculiar to China, thrives luxuriantly, and the Japanese are great tea-drinkers. The pepper-tree, or a tree which supplies the place of pepper, is common. They have three different sorts of fig-trees, one of which, introduced by the Portuguese, produces a fruit larger and of better flavor than any in Europe. The chestnut-tree is still more plentiful, and the fruit of it excellent. The walnut-tree flourishes, but chiefly in the northern provinces. In the same provinces is a tree called by the natives *kaja*, which produces an oblong nut, inclosed in a pulp, and not unlike, in size and shape, to the areca nut. The oil compressed out of these nuts is very sweet and agreeable, resembling the taste of the oil of sweet almonds. It is much commended for its medicinal virtues. They make much use of it in dressing their food. The condensed smoke and soot produced by the burning of the shells of these nuts is the chief ingredient of the best and blackest Japanese ink, much of which is sold in Europe under the name of Indian ink. Another sort of nuts grow very plentifully almost everywhere, on a fine tall tree, with large, beautiful leaves. The nuts yield plenty of oil, which is also much commended for several valuable properties. The orange-tree and the lemon-tree grow very plentifully, and are of several sorts. The juice of a very small but delicious lemon is commonly used in cookery. The plum-tree, the cherry-tree, and the apricot, are cultivated. But the cherry-tree and the plum are valued chiefly not for their fruit but for their flowers. The people improve them so much by a peculiar culture, that the flowers become as large as roses,* and, in the season when they are in full blossom, these trees afford a delightful sight, about their temples, in their gardens, and public walks. The vine is not much grown.

They take great delight, and have extraordinary skill as well in enlarging as in dwarfing all manner of plants. The branches of some of their trees, springing at the height of seven or eight feet from the ground, are occasionally led out across ponds, and supported on props, so as to afford a shade and covering of 300 feet in circumference.

There are various other trees, not easy to describe, which appear to be peculiar to Japan and the neighboring islands.

"Assuredly," says an old Neapolitan monk and missionary, "this is a right pleasant land, and abundantly supplied with fair, tall trees." Nobody that has ever been in the East can forget the soft, fascinating, poetical odor emanating from groves of cypress and clumps of cedar. It is a natural, living, growing incense, offered up to heaven at all seasons of the year, at all times of both

---

* Kämpfer saw cherry-blossoms, on the common cherry-tree, as large as roses. Meylan observed plum blossoms four times the size of our cabbage roses.

night and day, and the man has no poetry nor devotion in him, if he fail to be soothed and enchanted by it.

The noble Spaniard whom we have repeatedly quoted, felt the charms of these woods and groves as a man of taste and sentiment ought; and he was so pleased with the whole aspect of Japan that he declared, "if he could have prevailed upon himself to renounce his God and his king, he should have preferred that country to his own."*

The bamboo, which is applied to many purposes, and so extensively used throughout India and all the eastern countries, is very common in Japan. It supplies materials for almost everything, from the partition walls of their houses and the fences of their gardens to the sails of their boats and junks. The fine sort of bamboo, which the Dutch exported by the name of rattan, and sold for walking-canes, was a Japanese production and preparation. Both firs and bamboos are highly prized among the natives, for their constant verdure, and from a superstitious belief that they have an influence over the happy occurrences of human life. The approaches of their temples and other holy places, are fringed with them; and they make frequent allusions to them in their poetical writings, particularly in congratulatory poems, for they believe that the fir and the bamboo, if respected by the elements and not disturbed by man, will live and flourish for an almost indefinite period of time. Thus, "May you live as long as the bamboo," is considered no bad compliment.

The *jusnoki* is a species of iron-wood which also is very much used in building.

---

* Don Rodrigo de Vivero y Velasco.

The country abounds in flowers and flowering shrubs. The *subacki* is a pretty large shrub, growing in woods and hedges, and bearing flowers not unlike roses. There is a vast variety, the Japanese in their copious language, giving 900 names to the different sorts of *subacki*. The *satsuki* is another shrub bearing flowers like the lily, and offering many varieties. The two sorts which grow wild, one with purple, the other with scarlet flowers, are a great ornament to the hills and fields in the proper season, "affording," says the old German traveler, "a sight pleasing beyond expression." The *momidsi* is a kind oι maple, having leaves of a beautiful purple color. Our bulb-lily, narcissus, and gilliflower, are both cultivated and found growing in the wild state. There are other flowers, peculiar to the country, too numerous to be named, and all said to be superior to ours in brilliancy of color, but inferior in odor. "Indeed," says Kämpfer, "I think that Japan may vie with most if not all known countries, for a great variety of beautiful plants and flowers wherewith kind nature had most liberally and curiously adorned its fields, hills, woods and forests. Some of these they transplant into gardens, and improve by assiduity and culture to the utmost, and indeed to a surprising degree of perfection."

This love of flowers is one of the most pleasing features in the character of these most singular people. Nearly every house has its little garden in its rear, and a few flowering shrubs in its front. The garden is commonly square, and very neatly walled in. "It cannot be denied," adds Kämpfer, "that the great number of beautiful incarnate, and double flowers, which they bear in the proper season, are a surprisingly curious ornament to the back part of the house. In some small houses and inns of less note, where there is not room enough either for a garden, or for a large flowering tree, they place in the back window one or two flower pots, or some dwarf trees, or some little plants which will grow easily upon pumice, or other porous stone, without any earth at all, provided the roots be supplied with water; and they generally add to these a small vessel full of water, with a few gold or silver fish in it." The gardens attached to the better sort of houses are kept with uncommon care and neatness, and, though somewhat artificial in their arrangement, are described as being very delightful. They are laid out by professional gardeners, who do no other work, and who proceed upon certain established and ancient rules. In such a garden there must be a small rivulet falling over rocks, or tinkling among stones.

As florists and gardeners they are indeed conspicuous, and the beauty of a production of the soil in this department is seen in the Camelia Japonica, now found in every English greenhouse. Like the Chinese, they possess the singular art of producing miniature samples of the larger products of vegetation, an art scarcely known in Europe, and only to be admired as a curiosity. A box was offered for sale to the Dutch governor of Nagasaki, in which were flourishing a fir-tree, a bamboo, and a plum-tree, the latter in blossom, and the box was only three inches long and one inch wide. The account is given by an eye-witness, who adds that the price demanded for so great a curiosity was 1,200 florins.* Another very small box is

* "Account of Japan," by Door G. F. Meijlan. Amsterdam, 1830, as quoted in the "Quarterly Review," vol. lii.

The Chinese method of producing these miniature plants is given in G. Bennett's "Wandering in New South Wales," etc. More informa-

mentioned as having contained miniature specimens of every tree that grows on the islands.

The great industry, and even the skill of the Japanese, as agriculturists, have been praised by all the travelers who have visited and written about their country. Kämpfer says they are perhaps as good husbandmen as any in the world. This he attributes not only to the extreme populousness of the country, but chiefly to the circumstance that the natives, being denied commerce and communication with foreigners, must, of necessity, support themselves by what they can produce by their own labor and industry on their own soil. Hence, the laws on this head are very particular and severe, the state making it its business to see not only that the lands are cultivated, but also that they are cultivated in the best manner, or, at least, according to the best rules of such agricultural science as the country possesses. Not only the fields and flat country, which are seldom or never turned into meadows, or kept for pasture, but likewise the hills and mountains, are made to produce corn, rice, pease, pulse, and numerous edible plants. Every inch of ground is improved to the best advantage; and it was not without astonishment that Kämpfer and his traveling companions, on their journeys to and from the imperial court, beheld mountains inaccessible to cattle, cultivated up to their very tops. This is managed by a succession of walls and terraces, rising above each other, and by the people ploughing or hoeing without the help of oxen. The same system obtains in many

---

tion will be found in a recent French work, Le Baron Leon de Saint Denys' "Recherches sur l'Agriculture et l'Horticulture des Chinois." Paris. 1850.

parts of China, and in not a few parts of Europe. The Japanese are skillful in manuring their grounds, and use a variety of substances for manures. Their rice,—their main food,—grown in the low country, is said to be the best of all Asia. It is perfectly white, and so nourishing and substantial, that foreigners, not used to it, can eat but little of it at a time. The rice-fields are cut through and through by little canals, and irrigated in the most careful manner. The rice grown in the upper grounds, where irrigation is difficult, is of an inferior quality. From rice they brew a sort of strong thick beer called *sackee*. Among their many laws relating to agriculture, there is one by virtue of which whosoever leaves his ground uncultivated for the term of one year forfeits his title and possession. All lands must be surveyed every year by certain officers who are called *Kemme*, and who are held in such repute that they have the privilege of wearing two swords, which is otherwise allowed to none but the nobility and soldiers.

Maize, or Indian corn, millet, and, in general, all sorts of grain are said to grow well in most of the islands. Turnips are exceedingly plentiful and of very large size. They have pease, horseradishes, carrots, fennel, lettuces, cucumbers, gourds, and good melons. The natives also derive sustenance from a variety of wild plants and roots, as well as from the leaves of certain trees, and from the flowers and berries of certain shrubs. They possess the art of depriving poisonous plants of their noxious qualities, and rendering them edible. The mushroom, under several varieties, is found everywhere. Both hemp and flax thrive well under Japanese management, and the people, being great smokers, grow vast quantities of tobacco. In fact, through the goodness of the soil and the skill and care of the natives, all the most valuable of the productions of the earth are brought to great perfection.

If we assume the perfection of the arts of tillage and manufacture as a test of civilization. Japan may, at least, compete with any Oriental nation. M. Meijlan places it higher than any. The same recent Dutch observer bestows an amount of praise on their field cultivation which could not be justly applied to many European nations.*

* "Account of Japan." Quarterly Review, vol. lii.

OLD CAMPHOR-TREE.

A JAPANESE FISHING FAMILY.

BOOK VIII.

ANIMALS.—REPTILES.—BIRDS.—FISHES.

THOUGH abundantly stocked with pictures and carvings, with chimeræ and all other sorts of monsters, borrowed from the Chinese, the Japanese empire is but sparingly provided with four-footed beasts, wild or tame. The country is too much cultivated and peopled to afford cover to the wild quadrupeds, and the tame are bred only for carriage and agriculture. The use of animal food is interdicted by the national religion, and they have not left pasture enough to support many sheep and oxen. The horses are generally small, but there is a breed said to be not inferior to that imported into India from the Persian Gulf. But the horses of this kind now appear to be rare. In the time of old Captain Saris they were common enough. "Their horses are not tall, but of the size of our middling nags, short, and well trussed, small headed, and full of mettle, in my opinion far excelling the Spanish jennet in pride and stomach."* The Japanese relate most marvellous stories of the performance of some of their steeds. There is also a breed of ponies, which, though small, has been much admired. Oxen and cows are kept only for ploughing and for carriage. Of milk and butter the Japanese know nothing. They have a large humped buffalo, sometimes of a monster size, which they train to draw carts or to carry heavy goods on their backs. The elephant, the camel, and the ass, are unknown animals. Sheep and goats were kept formerly at the Dutch settlements, in the neighborhood, of which some few may yet be found. They may be bred in the country to great advantage, if the natives were permitted to eat the flesh, or knew how to manage or manufacture the wool. They have a few swine, which were brought over from China, and which some of the country people near the coast still keep, not, indeed, for their own use, but to sell to certain Chinese junks which are allowed to come over to trade, most of the Chinese mariners being addicted to pork. Captain Sir Edward Belcher was supplied with some hogs that were overwhelmed with their own fat, and weighed about 150 lbs.

Dogs or common curs they have,—and in superfluous

* Saris's "Narrative in Purchas."

numbers. These dogs are as much the pest of the towns of Japan as they are of Constantinople and the other foul cities and towns of the Ottoman empire. This vast increase of the canine species, and the encouragement and immunity accorded to it, arose (according to the popular account), out of a curious superstition and an extravagant imperial decree. An emperor who reigned at the close of the eighteenth century chanced to be born under the Sign of the Dog, the Dog being one of the twelve celestial signs of the Japanese. For this reason, the emperor had as great an esteem for dogs as the Roman emperor Augustus is reported to have entertained for rams. When he ascended the throne, he willed and ordained that dogs should be held as sacred animals; and, from that time, more puppies saw the light and were permitted to live in Japan than in any other country on the face of the earth, Turkey, perhaps, excepted. These dogs have no masters, but lie and prowl about the streets, to the exceeding great annoyance of passengers, especially if they happen to be foreign travellers, or Christians in Christian dresses. If they come round you in packs, barking, snarling, and showing their teeth,—nay, even if they fall upon you and bite you, you must on no account take the law into your own hands, and beat them off or shoot them. To kill one of them is a capital crime, whatever mischief the brute may have done you. In every town there are Guardians of the Dogs, and to these officers notice must be given in case of any canine misdemeanor, these guardians alone being empowered to punish the dogs. Every street must keep a certain number of these animals, or at least provide them with victuals; huts, or dog-hospitals stand in all parts of the town, and to these the animals, in case of sickness, must be carefully conveyed by the inhabitants.

The dogs that die must be carried up to the tops of mountains and hills, the usual burying places of men and women, and there be very decently interred. Old Kämpfer says:—"The natives tell a pleasant tale on this head. A Japanese, as he was carrying the carcase of a dead dog to the top of a steep mountain, grew impatient, grumbled, and cursed the emperor's birth-day and whimsical command. His companion bid him hold his tongue and be quiet, and, instead of swearing, return thanks to the gods that the emperor was not born under the Sign of the Horse, for, in that case, the load would have been heavier."

We give the pleasant tale as we find it, but we do not believe that it points to the real origin of the superstitious regard for dogs, which many of the Mongol race share with the Japanese and Turks. That superstition had its origin in the wilds of Tartary, or in whatever other part of the world it was that served as the cradle and great starting point of the wide-spread Mongol race. The dog must have been in a manner deified, when they first put him among their celestial signs.

Among some of the Mongolian tribes, the dog is the indicator of fate, the harbinger of death; and among others, the dog is an object either of dread or devotion.*

But our learned German is not always so facetious about this monstrous annoyance of street dogs. On reaching Nagasaki, he says, "The street dogs also deserve to be noticed among the inhabitants of this city, they being full as well, nay, better maintained and taken care of than many of the people, and although the imperial orders on this head are not regarded and complied with at Nagasaki, with that strictness as they must be in other parts of the

* Appendix G.

empire, which are not so remote from court, yet the streets be full of these animals, leading a most easy and independent life, giving way neither to men nor horses. The town is never without a great deal of noise from these animals."*

The Japanese have no dogs of superior breed, but they have cats of a peculiarly beautiful kind. These are of a whitish color, with large yellow and black spots, and a very short tail: the ladies carry them about as lap-dogs.

In the islands are found deer, wild boars, and hares, but apparently in no great numbers. There are also monkeys, wild dogs, foxes, some curious animals that look like a cross between the fox and the wolf, and a few small bears in the secluded parts of the northern provinces. The fox bears not the very best of characters among the Japanese; the peasantry believe him to be in league with all evil spirits or devils, and to be himself the very incarnation of craft, malice, and wickedness; "but," says old Kämpfer, "the fox-hunters are expert in conjuring and stripping this animated devil, his hair and wool being much coveted for writing and painting pencils." The weasel and ferret are found. Rats and mice swarm throughout the country, for the beautiful cats, being pets, have no turn for mousing. The rats are tamed by the natives, and taught to perform several tricks, and form a common diversion for the poorer people. We find mention made of two small animals of a red color, that live

* The nocturnal noise made by the dogs of Constantinople can never be forgotten by those who have heard it. Such as have had the felicity of passing a long dreary winter in that comfortless city, are apt to have their dreams disturbed, years after, by the yelling of dogs, and the nightly cry of *yang-in war!* fire! fire!

under the roofs of the houses, and are very tame. They are called the *itutz* and the *tin.*

The destructive white ant, that great annoyance of most parts of the East Indies, is very common. The Japanese call them *do toos* or piercers, a name they well merit, for they perforate whatever they meet, stones and metals only excepted, and when once they get into a merchant's warehouse, they in a very short compass of time can destroy or ruin an amazing quantity of his best goods. Nothing has been yet found that will keep them off, except salt laid under the goods and spread about them. The common European ants are their mortal enemies, and wherever these have been introduced, the *do toos* have rapidly disappeared, like the original English rat before the invasion of the Norwegian.

The islands, however, may be said to be remarkably free from insects and obnoxious reptiles. There are but few snakes, and hardly any of them appear to be venomous. One of these is of a beautiful green color, with a very flat head. Japanese soldiers cook it and eat its flesh, in the belief that it imparts courage and audacity. The natives also calcine the flesh in an earthen pot hermetically sealed, and derive from it a powder, which they believe to possess the most extraordinary medicinal virtues.* There is a water snake of monstrous size, and another very large snake, of black color, but quite inoffensive, is found in the mountains. Both are very scarce, and when taken are shown about for money.

Birds are rather numerous. Of tame poultry they keep only fowls and ducks. They sell them sometimes to

* The bite of this snake is, however, considered very dangerous.

foreigners, but never eat them. Cocks are highly prized by the religious orders, because they mark the time, and foretell changes of the weather. Indeed, they are chiefly kept up as *time keepers.*

The crane is the chief of the wild birds of the country; but like the heron, and the stork, which also abound, they can scarcely be called wild, for they are held as sacred birds, and nobody must injure or molest them. They thus become quite familiar, and mix with the people, and throng the market places, just as the storks do in all towns, villages, and bazaars in Turkey, where they are equally objects of affection and veneration. No doubt this feeling also had its rise in the Tartarian regions. When the conquering Turks first came into Europe, they were accustomed to say that the stork had a singular affection for their race, and that whithersoever they might carry their victorious arms, the stork would follow them and live with them. In Japan the country people never call the crane by any other name than that of *O Tsurisama*, "My great lord crane." There are two sorts of them: one white as snow, and the other gray. They portend good fortune, and long life. For this reason the imperial apartments, the walls of temples, and other happy places, are commonly adorned with figures of them. Cranes are also painted on dishes and drinking cups, and reproduced on articles of domestic furniture. We have seen native paintings of these birds that are exquisitely beautiful, as true and correct in drawing as beautiful in finish and coloring. They are among the very best specimens of Japanese art.

The tortoise is another happy and sacred creature, and is represented on walls, and reproduced in the same manner.

Wild geese and wild ducks are very abundant, and

very tame. There are several species of both. One kind of duck is of immense size and of wonderfully brilliant and beautiful plumage. Pheasants, wild pigeons, and woodcocks, are very common birds. Hawks also are common. Ravens are scarce. Our common European crows, as also parrots, and other Indian birds, are never to be met with.

Of singing birds, Kämpfer mentions only larks and nightingales; but he says that both of these sing more sweetly than with us. The natives highly prize the nightingale, and large sums are paid for a caged one, with a good voice.

They have plenty of bees, and, consequently, honey and wax are produced.

The shrill cicala, or winged-grasshopper, peoples the pines, and fills the woods and mountains with its incessant song. Butterflies and beetles are numerous and diversified, some of both kinds being very beautiful. Among the night-moths there is one sort which the Japanese ladies keep* in little cages, as pets and curiosities. This moth is about four inches long, slender, round-bodied, with four wings, two of which are transparent, and concealed under the other pair of wings, which shine like polished metal, and are most curiously and beautifully adorned with blue and gold lines and spots. The following graceful fable owes its origin to the matchless beauty of this moth. All other night-flies fall in love with it; and to get rid of their importunities it maliciously bids them, as a trial of their devotion and constancy, to go and fetch it fire. The blind lovers, obedient to command, fly to the nearest lamp or candle, and never fail to get burned to death.

The sea all about Japan is plentifully stocked with all

sorts of fish, and the natives are very expert fishermen. In the time of Charlevoix and Kämpfer, and earlier travellers, the whale fishery was carried on to a great extent, particularly in the sea which washes the southern coasts of the great island, Niphon. The common way of catching them was by harpooning, in the manner of our Greenland fishermen; but the Japanese boats seemed to be fitter for the purpose than ours, being small, narrow, tapering at each end into a sharp point, and rowing with incredible swiftness. "About 1680 a rich fisherman, in the province of Omura, found out a new way of catching whales with nets made of strong ropes, about two inches thick. This method was afterwards followed with good success by another man of the country. They say that, as soon as the whale finds its head entangled in a net, he cannot, without great difficulty, swim away or dive, and may be very easily killed with the harpoon in the common manner. The reason why this new method hath not been universally received is, because it requires a greater and much more expensive set of tackle than common fishermen can afford."*

They enumerate six kinds of whales, differing in name, form, and size. Of all these several kinds nothing was thrown away by the Japanese as useless. They boiled the fat or blubber into train oil; they pickled, boiled, roasted, or fried the flesh, and ate it; they even reduced the cartilaginous bones into food; they made cords, ropes, and strings for their musical instruments out of the nerves and tendons; they made a great use of the fins; and out of the jaw-bones, and other solid bones, they manufac-

* Kämpfer.

tured numerous articles, particularly their fine steelyards for weighing their gold and silver.

The Japanese fishermen attribute to the flesh of the whale their favorite food, their strength and hardihood, and their extraordinary capability of enduring exposure to cold and foul weather.

It was in pursuing the whale to the coasts of Japan that the American ships met with those disasters, and that inhospitable treatment, which first made the government of the United States turn its attention in this direction.

Turtles of enormous size are said to abound on the southern or eastern coasts. Salmon, soles, turbot, a sort of cod, smelts, and other delicious sea fish, together with all sorts of lobsters, crabs, shrimps, oysters, muscles, &c., are taken in surprising abundance; and there are other fish of species unknown to us, and of which, some are said to be delicious. It is fortunate for the natives that their prejudices and superstitions allow them to eat fish. In the larger islands every part of the coast is thickly strewed with buildings, and at every second or third mile are populous villages, from which extensive fisheries are carried on.* In fact, the Japanese are essentially *ichthyophagi.* Aided by a good growth of potatoes, or an adequate supply of rice, the sea alone would support a vast population.

Without going into further detail, enough has been said

* Golownin.—As this Russian captain and fellow-captives were conveyed along the coast, they were fed with rice and broiled fish, the natives putting the food into their mouths with their little sticks, which are like the chop-sticks of the Chinese.

JAPANESE FISHERMEN.

to convey to the reader an adequate notion of the natural riches and ample resources of this beautiful and healthy country.

ORNAMENTAL VASES.

BOOK IX.

ARTS—MANUFACTURES—SHIPPING, NAVIGATION, ETC.

THERE is but one opinion as to the industry, ingenuity, and manual dexterity of the Japanese. These people, to use the words of an old Italian missionary, work admirably well in iron, silver, gold, and all metals; also in wood and bamboo, and in all such materials as they possess in that fair country. They also have the art of making good use of many materials which by us are thrown away as of no value.

"Arts and manufactures," says Thunberg, "are carried on in every part of the country, and some of them are brought to such a degree of perfection, as even to surpass those of Europe; whilst some, on the other hand, fall short of European excellence. They work extremely well in iron and copper, and their silk and cotton manufactures equal, and sometimes even excel, the productions of other eastern countries. Their lacquering in wood, especially their ancient workmanship, surpasses every attempt which has been made in this department by other nations. They work likewise with great skill in *sowas*, which is a mixture of gold and copper, which they understand how to color blue or black with their tousche, or ink, by a method hitherto unknown to us. They are likewise acquainted with the art of making glass, and can manufacture it for any purpose, both colored and uncolored. But window-glass, which is flat, they could not fabricate formerly. This art they have lately learned from the Europeans, as likewise to make watches, which they sometimes use in their houses. In like manner, they understand the art of glass-grinding, and to form telescopes with it, for which purpose they purchase mirror-glasses of the Dutch. In the working of steel, they are perfect masters, of which their incomparable swords afford the most evident proof. Paper is likewise manufactured in great abundance in this country, as well for writing and printing as for tapestry, handkerchiefs, cloths for packing of goods, &c., and is of various sizes and qualities. They prepare it from the bark of a species of mulberry-tree,—*Morus papyrifera.* The method is as follows: After the tree has shed its leaves, in the month of December, they cut off the branches about three feet in length, which they tie up in bundles, and boil in a ley of ashes, standing inverted in a covered kettle, till such time as the bark is so shrunk, that half an inch of the woody part is seen bare at the ends. They are then taken out and left in the open air to cool, cut up lengthwise, and the bark is stripped off. Upon this the bark is again soaked, three or four hours, in water, and when it is become soft, they scrape off the fine black skin with a knife. The next thing to be done is, to separate the coarse bark from the fine, which produces the whitest paper. The older the branches are, the coarser is the paper. The bark is now boiled again in fresh ley, and the whole continually stirred with a stick, and fresh water added to it. A nice and delicate operation is then performed in a brook, by means of a sieve, by stirring the bark incessantly about till the whole is reduced to the consistence of a fine pap, and, thrown into the water, separates in the form of meal. It is then further mixed in a small vessel with decoction of rice and the *Hibiscus-manibot*, and stirred well about, till it has attained a tolerable consistence. After this it is poured into a wider vessel, from whence the sheets are taken and put into proper forms, made of grass straw, and laid one upon another in heaps, with straw between, that they may be easily lifted up. They are further covered with a board, and pressed, at first lightly, but afterwards, and gradually, harder, till the water is separated. When this is done, they lay the sheets upon a board, dry them, in the sun, and then gather them into bundles for sale and use. An inferior kind of paper is likewise manufactured from the *Morus Indica.*

" The *lacquered* wood-work, which is executed in Japan, excels the Chinese, the Siamese, and, indeed, that of all other nations in the world. For this purpose they make choice of the finest sort of firs and cedars, and cover them with the very best varnish, which they prepare from the *Rhus vernix*, a tree that grows in great abundance in many parts of the country. This varnish, which oozes out of the tree on its being wounded, is procured from stems that are three years old, and is received in some proper vessel. When first caught, it is of a lightish color, and of the consistence of cream; but grows thicker and black on being exposed to the air. It is of so transparent a nature, that when it is laid, pure and unmixed, upon boxes and other pieces of furniture, every vein of the wood may be clearly seen. For the most part a dark ground is spread underneath it, which causes it to reflect like a looking-glass; and for this purpose recourse is frequently had to the fine sludge which is caught in the trough under a grinding-stone. At other times, ground charcoal is used, and occasionally some blacker substance is mixed with the varnish, and sometimes leaf-gold, ground very fine, when it is called *Salplicat.* This lacquered-work is afterwards, for the most part, embellished with gold and silver flowers and figures laid on upon the varnish, which, however, are liable to wear off in time."*

Fashion, that most absolute of all tyrants, has almost entirely exiled these beautiful Japanned wares from our houses; but we are old enough to remember the time when nearly every respectable drawing-room, dining-room, and boudoir, presented specimens of them, in the shape of screens, desks, cabinets, caskets, or other objects

ORNAMENTAL CANDLESTICKS.

of ornament and utility. They were rather more numerous in Scotch than in English houses, and this from the

* "Travels in Europe, Africa, and Asia, made between the years 1770 and 1779." Four vols. 8vo.

very obvious reason that, mainly in grace of the patronage of hearty Henry Dundas, Lord Melville, so many Scotchmen sought and found fortune in the East. Many of these articles were most admirable specimens of the arts of the cabinet-maker, japanner, and gold-embosser. It is said, however, that the finest specimens were never allowed to be exported out of Japan. The finest collections existing in Europe are those of Von Siebold and His Majesty the King of the Netherlands, at the Hague.

Generally, Japanese workmanship has more strength, solidity, and real finish than that of the Chinese. They seem to have a contempt for all that is flimsy. Their common packing-cases are nearly always strong and finished specimens of materials and workmanship. There may be said to be about the same difference between Chinese and Japanese work that there is between French and English; but, if the French, in most things, can claim, over us, a superiority in taste of design, no such superiority can be claimed by the Chinese over the workmen of Japan.

In the art of making and tempering steel, they must possess some valuable secret or most extraordinary skill. The finest blade we ever handled was an indisputable old blade of Japanese make. It beat all the Damascus blades and Adrea-Ferraras we ever saw. It is mentioned, as a notorious fact, that a sword of this sort would, at a blow, cut a man's body in two.

"With respect to steel manufactures," says Golownin, "the Japanese sabres and daggers surpass all others in the world, those of Damascus, perhaps, excepted. They bear extraordinary trials. The edge of the sabre is kept as sharp as that of a razor. The Japanese are extremely skilful in polishing steel, and all other metals. They make metal mirrors, which, for their object, are scarcely inferior to our looking-glasses. We often saw carpenters' and cabinet-makers' tools, made in Japan, which may be compared with the English. Their saws are so good that the thinnest boards may be sawed out of the hardest wood."*

In cotton fabrics they appear to have little skill. They use a coarse, thick spongy paper, made from a tree, for pocket-handkerchiefs, for napkins, and for other purposes in which we employ calico, silk, or muslin.

We have mentioned the inferiority of the native silk; but rich and beautiful articles are manufactured out of silk imported from China. These valuable silk goods are said to be produced only by unfortunate noblemen and gentlemen, who are exiled to a lonely island, and compelled to work for their own livelihood.

Both in carving and in die-sinking, the Japanese are very skilful. Their copper coinage is stamped, and very good.† The metal, that pure, matchless copper of Japan, after being roasted and smelted at various smelting-houses, is always refined and manufactured at Miako, where also all the coin is struck and stamped.‡

The Japanese understand the art of casting metal statues, and abundant employment is found for artisans of this class in furnishing temples, joss-houses, and dwelling-houses with idols, large and small.

Some of the trades are followed up in a grand, whole-

---

* "Recollections of Japan."

† It appears that this is their only coinage, gold and silver being cut and weighed, as among the Chinese.

‡ We give this last fact, with some doubt, on the authority of old writers. We have heard, or somewhere read, that, since the decline of the power of the spiritual emperor, the mint has been transferred from his residence, Miako, to Jeddo, the residence of the lay emperor.

sale way. Among these are their iron-works, tobacco-manufactories, breweries, and distilleries. Some of the last are said to be very extensive. Many thousands are constantly employed in the manufacture of straw shoes, straw hats, and mats. The consumption of this straw, made out of a native grass, must be truly prodigious.

"When on a journey," says Thunberg, "all the Japanese wear a conical hat, made of a species of grass, platted, and tied with a string." He also observed, that all the fishermen wore hats of the same material and shape. But, in addition to this extensive use, the Japanese hardly ever wear any shoes or slippers but such as are made of platted straw. "This," remarks the same excellent traveller, "is the most shabby and indifferent part of their dress, and yet in equal use with the high and the low, the rich and the poor. They are made of rice-straw platted, and by no means strong." They cost, however, a mere trifle; they are found exposed for sale in every town, and in every village, and the pedestrian supplies himself with new shoes as he goes along, while the more provident man always carries two or three pair with him for use, throwing them away as they wear out. "Old worn-out shoes of this description are found lying everywhere by the sides of the roads, especially near rivulets, where travellers, on changing their shoes, have an opportunity, at the same time, of washing their feet."* In very wet weather they use wooden clogs, which are attached to their straw-platted shoes by ties also made of straw-plat. People of very high rank sometimes wear slippers made of fine slips of rattan neatly platted.

It is said that the common people count the length of a

* "Thunberg's Travels," vol. iii.

journey by the number of these straw shoes that they wear out in making it.

"The Japanese have little furniture in their houses, beyond the apparatus for their kitchen and what they use at their meals. Of these, however, as likewise of clothes and other necessaries, one sees such an incredible quantity exposed for sale in the shops of their tradesmen, both in town and country, that one is led to wonder where they can find purchasers, and would be apt to suppose, that they kept magazines here to supply the whole world. the native may select, according to his varying taste and fancy, all his clothes ready made, and may be furnished with shoes, umbrellas, lacquered ware, porcelain, and a thousand other articles, without having occasion to bespeak anything beforehand."*

In their great fondness for dishes and vessels of light lacquered ware, they rather neglect the porcelain fabrics; but they are said to produce, in this line, some articles that far exceed the finest Chinese.

Nothing can well be more light, neat, and graceful, than the superior kinds of their lacquered cups. They are generally painted in a very pretty style, and are so exceedingly light as scarcely to be felt in the hand through their weight.

Although these various manufactories are spread all over the empire, the principal ones are said to be confined to the cities of Miako, Jeddo, and Osacca.†

As no Japanese is allowed to leave his native land, the long voyages which the people of this nation formerly undertook in their own vessels to Corea, China, Java, Formosa, and other places, can be no longer performed,

---

* Thunberg. Kämpfer. † Golownin.

and the art of navigation must of course be upon the decline. This, however, does not prevent them from making short voyages among the rocks, with an inconceivable number of trading vessels, of different sizes, as likewise with fishing-smacks. They seldom venture out far enough at sea to lose sight of land, and always take care to have it in their power to run every evening into some port, or else to come into some other place of safety, in case of sudden storms. Yet they are provided with a compass, which is not divided into so many points as those which the Europeans make use of; but their vessels are open at the stern, so that they cannot weather the open sea; and their rudders are large and inconvenient.*

This is but a landsman's account, and it explains very little. We, therefore, subjoin some sketches given by an American seaman, who went to Japan and the Loo-Choo Islands in the ship "Morrison," with Mr. King.

"In the afternoon one of the Japanese junks left the harbor, laden with upwards of 200 peculs of sugar, bound for Satzuma, a port in Japan, lying about 400 miles N.N.E. from Loo-Choo. In coming out, she struck on a reef, but was soon got off without apparent damage, and as she passed the ship, we went in the gig to examine her. The hull was made of pine, and, in its general form, resembled a Chinese fast boat; the bow was sharp,. without bowsprit; but, instead, there was a high beak, like that of an ancient galley, with a fender, in case she should run stem on. The solitary mast was about forty feet high, and supported by a huge forestay, under which hung a yard, in form like two cones united at their bases; this was raised by halliards passing over the top of the mast,

---

* Thunberg.

aft, to the quarters, where they went over a sort of windlass, and then round a capstan, below deck. The sail was made of very coarse heavy cotton, and the bolts were loosely laced together with cords, each being four or five inches apart, giving the sail a singular appearance; at the bottom, several ropes secured it in its proper place. There was no sternpost, and the open work permitted us to look directly into the cabin, where, at this time, the crew were hoisting sails with loud cries. The rudder was about fifteen feet long and eight broad, with a tiller like a spanker-boom, reaching forward nearly to the mast. The long-boat was lashed athwart the vessel, near the bow, the ends projecting over each side about five feet, placed, one would suppose, in a very hazardous manner. Three or four grapplings lay on the bows attached to large hawsers; and a double-headed one was placed athwart the vessel near the mast, with the flukes outside, for the purpose of strengthening the sides. The stern was high out of the water, as in the junks of China, and upon it was her name, *Hozammah*, painted in large Chinese characters; upon the bow was a bird rudely carved, and the character *pin*, 'ashore,' all neatly ornamented with copper, which here, as in other parts of the vessel, was laid on profusely. The capstan stood in the cabin, which, like every other part of the vessel, was kept very clean; her sides fell in above the water-mark, and she was rudely, though strongly built. The crew numbered about fifteen, one or two of whom wore the singular leggings seen in Japanese pictures; but most of them were scantily clad."*

* "Narrative of a Voyage of the ship 'Morrison,'" etc. By S Wells Williams. Not possessing this work, we are indebted for our extracts to the "Chinese Repository," vol. vi. Canton. 1838.

On making the Bay of Jeddo, the same writer says:— "As the ship approached the land, the number of junks and boats in sight increased; at one time we counted between forty and fifty; most of them bound westward, right before the wind. Iwakitchi, who was pretty good authority in such matters, having been at Jeddo upwards of twenty times, according to his own account, said that the fleet had probably been wind-bound, and prevented coming out of the bay,—not an unusual occurrence. There were boats and junks of many sizes, from a fishing-smack up to a junk of 200 or 300 tons, all in their general form and rigging resembling those at Napa Keäng. The single mast was supported by a large forestay and by several backstays, passing to the sides of the vessel. Off the wind, they sailed with a rolling motion; and when close-hauled, made much leeway, being, like the Chinese vessels, without keels.

"They neither avoided nor sought us, though their proximity to the shore prevented our speaking or approaching any of them.

"Towards evening their number decreased, and by nightfall, whatever may have been the reason, there was not one to be seen, except a few at anchor in an inlet. Ginsabaru, who appears to be well informed in naval affairs, says that the names of vessels are usually three Chinese characters, the last one of which is always *fan* (all), applied in this case to mean a vessel."*

This passage, in the correctness of which we have full confidence, invalidates the statement, which has been frequently made, that the size of the Japanese junks is strictly limited to about sixty tons. Here we see junks

---

* S. Wells Williams, "Narrative of a Voyage," etc.

of 300 tons. We believe, however, that the awkward rudder, the open stern-quarter, and other things about the craft, are prescribed by law, in the view of preventing the people from undertaking long voyages.

In another place the same writer says:—"The boats in which the natives came off were rudely, though strongly, built of pine; and most of them carried a sail of coarse cotton canvass, suspended from a single moveable mast. Their progress was accelerated by three or four large sculls attached to each side, near the stern, on pivots, and formed of two pieces lashed together like the Chinese; with this difference, that the loom was very broad at its lower end, in its general shape resembling a paddle; the upper surface was convex, and the rounded edges made the under somewhat concave: this form appeared to be for convenience in sculling. Some of the largest of the boats were thirty feet long and six wide, having the two ends open like a scow, and carrying between twenty and thirty men. In two or three were a few women, of whom we did not see much; for they were fully occupied in protecting themselves from the rain, piling bamboo cloaks and hats upon their persons, in a very singular manner, while they lay in the bottom of the boats."*

The number of these boats and junks was such as to denote a most active coasting trade; and, it seems, that we might exclaim now as honest old Kämpfer did more than a century and a half ago:—"How much commerce is carried on between the several provinces and parts of the empire! How busy and industrious the merchants everywhere are! How full their harbors of ships! How many rich and mercantile towns up and down the country!

* "Narrative of a Voyage of the ship 'Morrison,'" etc.

FLOWER BASKETS AND VASES.

There are such multitudes of people along the coasts and near the seaports, such a noise of oars and sails, such numbers of ships and boats, both for use and pleasure, that one would be apt to imagine that the whole nation had settled there, and that all the inland parts of the country were left quite empty and deserted."

Yet, according to every account that we have been able to procure, trade is as active in the interior of Niphon and the other great islands, as it is along the coasts. The roads appear to be excellent and admirably kept. They have not yet arrived at the art of tunnel-making. In the more rugged parts of the country, where high and very steep mountains are to be crossed, they carry their roads zig-zag, and cut the rocks into steps. Stables, inns, tea-shops, and other resting-places occur, at regular distances, in all parts of the country. But in many parts, town joins on to town, and village to village, for the extent of very many miles, and the road is like one continuous street. The noble Spaniard who travelled in 1608 says, that between Sorongo and Jeddo, a distance of 100 leagues, a large city, town, or village, occurred at every quarter of a league, with an average number of inhabitants for each place of 100,000; and that from Sorongo to Miako, also about 100 leagues, the inhabited places were equally numerous and populous. Abundance, he adds, reigned in them all, provisions being so cheap that the poorest could purchase them.* Captain Cock, who succeeded that

* Don Rodrigo de Vivero y Velasco.

This very attentive observer makes the following entries as to population:—

Miako	1,500,000
Jeddo	700,000
Sorongo	600,000

very great man, the general and ambassador Saris, in 1614, equally bears testimony to the denseness of the population, and the activity of trade in the interior. In the diaries of his journeys between Firando and Jeddo, he is constantly speaking of the great wealth of many of the traders. Kämpfer, who came nearly a century after Cock, says:—"The country is, indeed, populous beyond expression, and one would scarce think it possible, that, being no greater than it is, it should nevertheless maintain and support such a vast number of inhabitants. The highways are almost one continued line of villages and boroughs. You scarce come out of one, but you enter another; and you may travel many miles, as it were, in one street, without knowing it to be composed of many villages, save by the differing names that were formerly given them, and which they after retained though joined to one another. It hath many towns, the chief whereof may, of a certainty, vie with the most considerable in the world, for largeness, magnificence, and number of inhabitants." As to the extent of Jeddo, the same honest German says,—"Thus much I can affirm from my own certain knowledge, that we were one whole day, riding at a moderate pace, from Sinagawa, where the suburb begins, along the main street, which goes across, a little irregularly, indeed, to the end of the city." MM. Doeff, Meylan, Fischer, and Siebold all confirm these accounts of populousness and active trade.

As we have already mentioned, any theft or robbery is a most difficult matter in Japan. The roads are perfectly safe. The merchant loads his bullocks with the richest goods, or with gold and silver, and travels cheerily along without any fear of robbers. This result is not all produced by legislation, severe laws, and municipal and police regulations; the Japanese, as a proud people, have a contempt or abhorrence of cheating, pilfering, stealing, or robbing. In this respect they are most advantageously contrasted with the Chinese.

If a free intercourse could be established, there is no calculating to what an extent foreign trade might be carried in Japan.

JAPANESE MERCHANT.

JUGGLERS OR TUMBLERS.

BOOK X.

POPULAR AMUSEMENTS—DOMESTIC MANNERS—GENERAL CHARACTER.

THE Japanese are everywhere described as being essentially a social, pleasure-seeking people. They work hard the greater part of their time, but they must have their feasts and their frolics on the great holidays, which appear to occur rather frequently.

Music, dancing, and the theatre, are favorite amusements with all classes. Mummers and mountebanks parade the streets. Tumblers, conjurers, and all manner of jugglers exercise their callings to the great delight of the common people. We do not see any mention of Punch; but, as that mysterious personage,—that great universality,—flourishes in China, and has been traced in Tartary and all through the Asiatic continent to the Bosphorus and Constantinople, there can be little doubt that he has some modified form of existence in the islands of Japan. Besides thronging the public theatres, the Japanese very frequently get up plays and farces among themselves in their own houses. Private theatricals, indeed, seem to be even more fashionable with them than with us.

Fun and drollery appear to be very liberally diffused. Their beggars are merry rogues.

"The mendicants exhibit touches of humor; a troop apparently of 'halt, lame, and blind,' will one moment solicit alms in doleful strains, and the next, throwing off disguise, leap about, and chant merrily, in return for the guerdon that may have been bestowed on them; or, calculating that they are more likely to gain their object by mirth, than by persisting in the assumption of distress, the unreality of which can be easily detected. During fine weather, junketing parties into the country are universal. The more wealthy place themselves under the direction of the professional master of the ceremonies. He amuses the company by retailing the tattle of the town, by his 'quips and cranks,' and by a certain degree of buffoonery. Yet, should any of the party, in the exuberance of their spirits, encroach on decorum, he immediately interposes his authority, and is implicitly obeyed."*

Every writer who has treated of the subject, praises the great urbanity, mutual respect, and formal, but real politeness of the people.

Their theatrical entertainments are said to be far superior to those of the Chinese in respect to scenery, costume, and decoration. Their theatres have usually three tiers of boxes, in the front of which all the ladies who are young and pretty, or fancy themselves so, take care to show themselves. The milliners of London might derive great benefit if our *beau monde* would only adopt a Japanese fashion during the opera season. "The ladies," says M. Fischer, "who frequent the theatre make a point of changing their dress two or three times during the representation, in order to display the richness of their ward-

---

* T. Rundall, "Memorials of Japan," etc. Notes in Appendix.

robe; and they are always attended by servants who carry the necessary articles of dress for the purpose."

With these frequent transmutations, the dear creatures must afford as much amusement as the actors on the stage.

Play-bills, or printed programmes of the piece about to be represented, are always in circulation, and, no doubt, the playgoer at Miako or Jeddo is invited to "buy a bill of the play" just as if he were going to a London theatre.

The Dutch writer from whom we last quoted throws an air of poetry as well as truth over some of his descriptions of social enjoyments. We have before hinted, that Secretary Fischer had a lively eye for female beauty, and a susceptible heart. It will be as well to inform the reader that the passage of English verse is of his own quoting.

"In the great world the young ladies find delight, at their social meetings, in every description of fine work, the fabrication of pretty boxes, artificial flowers, painting,

LADY PAINTING.

of fans, birds, and animals, pocket-books, purses, plaiting thread for the head-dress, all for the favorite use of giving as presents. Such employments serve to while away the long winter evenings. In the spring, on the other hand, they participate with eagerness in all kinds of out-door and rural amusements. Of these the choicest are afforded by the pleasure-boats, which, adorned with the utmost cost and beauty, cover their lakes and rivers. In the enjoyment of society and music, they glide in these vessels from noon till late in the night, realizing the rapturous strain of the author of Lalla Rookh:—

> "O! best of delights, as it everywhere is,
> To be near the loved one! what a rapture is his,
> Who, by moonlight and music, thus idly may glide,
> O'er the Lake of Cashmeer with that one by his side!"

"This is an enjoyment which can only be shared under the advantages of such a climate and scenery; viz. the climate of Nice and the scenery of Lugano. Their lakes and rivers are, after sunset, one blaze or illumination, as it were, with the brightly-colored paper lanterns displayed in their vessels. They play meanwhile that game with the fingers, which has been perpetuated from classic times in Italy. A floating figure is also placed in a vase of water; as the water is stirred by the motion of the boat, the figure moves. The guests sing to the guitar the strain 'Anataya modamada,'—'He floats, he is not still,' till at last the puppet rests opposite some one of the party, whom it sentences to drain the sackee bowl, as the pleasing forfeit of the game. All this stands out in cheerful contrast to the dull debaucheries of the men, and the childish diversions of the women, among other oriental nations. The female sex, at least, have greatly the advantage over the scandal of the Turkish bath; and the man has, equally with the Turk, the resource of his pipe, in the intervals of those better enjoyments which the admission of the female sex into society affords him, and which are prohibited to the Mussulman."*

Assuredly, these are captivating, delicious pictures of life and manners.

I shall never forget the testimony borne to the charming manners of the Japanese ladies by the accomplished old friend whom I have named in my preface.† "They have a natural grace which cannot be described. The Japanese are the most facscinating, elegant ladies that I ever saw in any country in the world. Take away a few peculiarities, to which one soon gets accustomed by living among them, and they would, at their first debut, be admired at St. James's, or in any other court of Europe."

And he who bore this high testimony was a great traveller, who had been in nearly every country, and who had lived, in each of them, in the most refined, most accomplished circles of society. As these words were spoken many years ago, I need not now be much ashamed of confessing that it was they that first excited me to a deep and lively interest in the subject of Japan.

In manners it is woman that makes the man. Where the gentler sex are graceful, elegant, and refined, the other sex are never found to be coarse, ungainly, and vulgar. At least, such has been our own experience in all the countries we have visited. The Japanese gentleman is

---

* Fischer, "Japan."

† I cannot deny myself the pleasure of naming him once more—the late James Drummond, Esq., Commissary-General, Commissioner of Accounts at Paris, etc.

invariably described as a person of pleasing address and most polished manners. Even among the commonest people, brawlers, braggarts, loud-tongued disputants, dirty slovens, or men with coarse repulsive manners, are very seldom met with. The poorest laborer, toiling by the wayside for his daily bread, expects a civil question, and is always ready with a civil answer. In their most familiar intercourse with one another, they scrupulously observe the set forms of politeness. Unless it be some person in authority, they will not reply to the man that addresses them in an insolent or rough way. They will even refuse to work for a violent or coarse-tongued employer.

Thunberg says: "Although gravity forms the general character of the Japanese nation, this serious disposition does not prevent them from having their pleasures, their sports, and festivities. These are of two kinds—occasional or periodical—and constitute part of their worship. Their chief festivals of all are the '*Feast of Lanterns*,' and what is called the *Matsuri*.

"The Lantern Festival, or Feast of Lamps, is celebrated towards the end of August, and is called by the natives *Bong*. It lasts three days; but the second afternoon, with the following night, are kept with the greatest festivity. It was originally instituted in memory and honor of the dead, who, they believe, return annually to their kindred and friends on the first afternoon of these games, every one visiting his former house and family, where they remain till the second night, when they are to be sent away again. By way of welcoming them on their arrival, they plant stakes of bamboo near all the tombs, upon which they hang a great number of lanterns, with lights, and those so close to each other, that the whole mountain appears illuminated: these lanterns are kept alight till nine or ten o'clock at night. On the second evening, when the spirits of the defunct are, according to their tradition, to be sent away again, they fabricate a small vessel of straw, with lights and lanterns in it, which they carry, at midnight, in procession, with vocal and instrumental music, and loud cries, to the sea-shore, where it is launched into the water, and left to the wind and waves, till it either catches fire and is consumed or is swallowed up by the waves. Both of these illuminations, consisting of several thousand fires, exhibit to the eye an uncommonly grand and beautiful spectacle.*

"The feast of *Matsuri*," continues Thunberg, "is celebrated upon some certain festival-day, and in honor of some particular god. Thus, for instance, in the town of Nagasaki, where I was present at one of these festivals, it is celebrated in memory of *Suwa*, the tutelar deity of the town. It is celebrated on the ninth day of the ninth month, which is the day of the idol's nativity, with games, public dances, and dramatic representations. The festival commences on the seventh day, when the temples are frequented, sermons preached, prayers offered up, and public spectacles exhibited; but the ninth day excels all in pomp and expensive magnificence, which they vary every time in such a manner, that the entertainments of the present year bear no resemblance to those of the last; neither are the same arrangements made. The expenses are defrayed by the inhabitants of the town, in such manner, that certain streets exhibit and pay the expenses of certain pieces and parts of the entertainment. I, together with others of the Dutch, had an invitation sent me, to be

* Thunberg. Kämpfer.

a spectator of this festival, in 1776, which was celebrated in a large open spot in the town of Nagasaki. A capacious house, resembling a large booth, raised upon posts, and provided with a roof and benches, was erected on one side, for the convenience of the spectators. These consisted not only of the magistrates and ecclesiastics, but likewise of foreigners; and a guard was placed to keep off the crowd. First of all appeared the priests, carrying the image of the idol *Suwa;* and took their places, habited in black and white. A company of ten or twelve persons played upon instruments of music, and sang the exploits of their gods and heroes; in the mean time that a party of virgins dancing, displayed the most enchanting elegance in their gestures and deportment. The music consisted in a mere rattling noise, which might, perhaps, sound more grateful in the idol's than in human ears. A large parasol was next introduced, inscribed with the name of the street, and emblazoned with its coat of arms, followed by a band of musicians, in masks, with drums, flutes, bells, and vocal music. These were succeeded by the device itself, which was different for every street; then followed a band of actors; and, lastly, the inhabitants of the street, in solemn procession, with an innumerable and promiscuous crowd at their heels. This progressive march lasted nearly a whole hour, after which they marched back again in the same order, and a second procession succeeded in its place: this was followed by a third; and so on, during the whole forenoon. The inhabitants of each street vied with each other in magnificence and invention, with respect to the celebration of this festival, and in displaying, for the most part, such things as were characteristic of the various produce of the mines, mountains, forests, navigation, manufactures, and the like, of the province from which the street derived its name, and whence it had its inhabitants."*

Kämpfer enumerates three other great annual festivals. We cannot do better than give, at full length, his account of one of them, because it contains, in addition to some very agreeable pictures of festive life, a wild Japanese romance or legend. The passage may, therefore, be taken as a specimen of old native literature as well as an illustration of manners and customs:—

"The second *sekf*, or great yearly festival, is called *Sanguatz Sannitz*, because of its being celebrated on the third day of the third month. On this, also, after the usual compliments and visits, which friends and relations pay one to another, and inferiors to their superiors, every one diverts himself in the best manner he can. The season of the year—the beginning of the spring, the trees, chiefly plum, cherry, and apricot trees, which are then in full blossom, and loaded with numberless white and incarnate flowers, single and double, and no less remarkable for their largeness and plenty, than for their singular beauty, invite everybody to take the diversion of the country, and to behold nature in her new and inimitable dress. But this same festival is, besides, a day of pleasure and diversion for young girls, for whose sake a great entertainment is commonly prepared by their parents, whereto they invite their nearest relations and friends. A large and spacious apartment is curiously adorned with puppets to a considerable value, which are to represent the court of the Dairi, or ecclesiastical hereditary emperor, with the

* "Travels in Europe, Africa, and Asia, made between the years 1770 and 1779."

person of *Finakuge*. A table, with Japanese victuals, is placed before each puppet, and among other things cakes, made of rice and the leaves of young mugwort. These victuals and a dish of sackee the guests are presented with by the girls, for whose diversion the entertainment is intended; or if they be too young, by their parents.

"The following story gave birth to this custom:—A rich man, who lived near *Rinsagava*, which is as much as to say, the Bird River, had a daughter called *Bungjo*, who was married to one *Symmias Dai Miosin*. Not having any children by her husband for many years, she very earnestly addressed herself in her prayers to the Kamis or gods of the country, and this with so much success, that soon after she found herself big, and was brought to bed of 500 eggs. The poor woman, extremely surprised at this extraordinary accident, and full of fear that the eggs, if hatched, would produce monstrous animals, packed them all up in a box, and threw them into the river Rinsagava, with this precaution, however, that she wrote the word *fosjoroo* upon the box. Some time after an old fisherman, who lived a good way down the river, found this box floating, took it up, and having found it full of eggs, he carried them home to present them to his wife, who was of opinion that there could not be anything extraordinay in them, and that certainly they had been thrown into the water for some good reason; and therefore she advised him to carry them back where he found them. But the old man replied: 'We are both old, my dear, and just on the brink of the grave; it will be a matter of very little consequence to us, whatever comes out of the eggs, and therefore I have a mind to hatch them, and see what they will produce.' Accordingly he hatched them in an oven, in hot sand, and between cushions, as the way is in the

Indies, and having afterwards opened them, they found in every one a child. To keep such a number of children proved a very heavy burden for this old couple. However, they made a shift, and bred them up with mugwort-leaves minced, and boiled rice. But in time they grew so big, that the old man and his wife could not maintain them any longer, so that they were necessitated to shift for themselves, as well as they could, and took to robbing on the highway. Among other projects, it was proposed to them to go up the river to the house of a rich man, who was very famous for his great wealth in that part of the country. As good luck would have it, this house proved to be that of their mother.

"Upon application made at the door, one of the servants asked what their names were, to which they answered, that they had no names, that they were a brood of 500 eggs, that mere want and necessity had obliged them to call, and that they would go about their business if they would be so charitable as to give them some victuals. The servant having taken the message in to his lady, she sent him back to inquire whether there had not been something writ upon the box in which the eggs had been found, and having answered that the word *fosjoroo* was found writ upon it, she could then no longer doubt but that they were all her children, and, accordingly, acknowledged and received them as such, and made a great entertainment, whereat every one of the guests was presented with a dish of *sokana*, with cakes of mugwort and rice, and a branch of the apricot-tree. This is the reason they give, why, on this festival, branches of the apricot-tree are laid over the kettle, and cakes made of mugwort and rice, which they call *futsumotzi*, that is, *mugwort cakes*, and prepared after the following manner:—The mugwort-leaves are soaked in water over-night, then pressed, dried, and reduced to powder, afterwards mixed with rice, which hath been boiled in water, then again reduced to powder, and mixed with boiled rice and *adsuki*, or red beans, grossly powdered, and so baked into cakes. The mother of these children was afterwards translated among the goddesses of the country, by the name of Bensaitree. They believe that she is waited upon, in the happy regions of the gods, by her five hundred sons, and they worship her as the goddess of riches."*

At one of the five great annual festivals, in the midst of good eating and drinking, the school-boys erect poles or posts of bamboo, and tie to them verses of their own making. At another—"Joy, mirth, and hospitality are universal. Not even strangers are suffered to pass by without being invited to make merry with the company. In short, one would imagine that the Bacchanals of the Romans had been brought over into Japan and established there. All sorts of diversions and public shows, dancing, plays, processions, and the like, so greatly divert and amuse the people, that many choose rather to lose their dinners, than to give over sauntering and staring about the streets till late at night."†

In addition to these five great yearly festivals, there are many more holidays observed at different seasons of the year. Honest old Kämpfer found them so numerous, that "it would be almost endless to mention them all."‡

But, with all these holidays, and out-of-door pastimes,

---

* "History of Japan."

† Kämpfer.

‡ For further particulars of feasts, ceremonies, etc., the reader may be referred to the curious but somewhat tedious book of M. Titsingh, "Illustrations of Japan."

THE TEA PARTY.

the Japanese do not neglect in-door amusements and entertainments. Never did English dame or dowager, in the days of our good old great-grandmothers, or in those of the *Tatler* and *Spectator*, more rejoice in her tea-parties and their concomitants, than do the ladies of Jeddo and Miako at the present day. It is at these parties that they display their newest dresses, and discuss the latest bit of fashionable news. No doubt if we could have their tittle-tattle properly done into English, it would be found pretty much to resemble the gossip of some of our own soirées. To conduct a Japanese tea-party *comme il faut*, requires education and long training. Kämpfer says:—"It is a particular art to make the tea, and to serve it in company, which, however, consists more in certain decent and agreeable manners, than in any difficulty as to the boiling or preparation. This art is called *Sado* and *Tsianoi.* As there are people in Europe who teach to carve, to dance, to fence, and other things of the like nature, so there are masters in Japan who make it their business to teach children of both sexes, what they call Tsianoi, that is, to behave well when in company with tea-drinkers, and also to make the tea, and to present it in company, with a genteel, becoming, and graceful manner."

The rules and laws which govern these matters and numerous others contingent on them, are formed into a regular system, and printed and published in books, which must be diligently studied by every young lady at school.

There are various sorts of tea-parties, and various methods of making and serving out the beverage. At a very grand party the cups and bowls, and all the utensils or implements employed, must be ornamented, and of high price. Here the matron takes that pride in showing her lacquered ware that our grandmothers used to feel in displaying their rare and costly china. The silken napkins, the little stools, the trays, must all be of the very finest qualities. At these parties the best sorts of tea are ground to powder; a tea-spoonful of this powder is, with all the necessary graces, put into a richly ornamented bowl, boiling water is then poured upon the powder, and the whole is stirred or whipped with a piece of split bamboo, till it creams.

In a morning call, pipes and tea are as invariably brought in at Jeddo, as pipes and coffee at Constantinople. At the conclusion of such call, sweetmeats or other dainties, to be eaten with chopsticks, are served up on a sheet of paper, sometimes purely white, and sometimes ornamented with tinsel or bright colors. Pocketing is not a vulgarism, but a duty strictly imposed by etiquette. If the visitor cannot eat all the dainties, he must fold up the remainder in the sheet of paper, and deposit them in his wide sleeve, which serves as a pocket. At grand dinners, each guest is expected to take with him a servant or two, to carry off, in baskets, the remnants of the banquet. We are not told whether, at these social meetings, the ladies smoke, as well as the gentlemen, but we are afraid that they do.

A Japanese feast usually consists of seven or eight courses. During the several removes, the master of the house walks round, and drinks a cup of sackee with each guest. This is their way of hobnobbing, or "taking wine." The viands consist of game, venison, poultry, fish, and all kinds of vegetables, seaweeds not excepted. Fish is, however, the *pièce de résistance*, the standing dish, the roast beef of the Japanese. As we have already mentioned, they eat of all sorts, not excluding the whale, nor even the shark. Each guest is served with a portion of every dish in a small, light lacquered bowl. Another bowl of the same description is placed at his side, and kept constantly replenished with rice. As whets, servants, of both sexes, from time to time, hand round soy, other sauces, pickled or salted ginger, and small nicely-cut morsels of salted fish, which are all eaten with the Chinese chopstick. It is expected that the guests compliment the giver of the feast on the beauty of his lacquered ware, on the splendor of his bowls, and on the richness and beauty of his domestic utensils, and furnishing in general.

None but personages of high hereditary rank dare presume to give a feast of the first order. A wealthy merchant must on no account entertain his friends like a lord or prince. It is, however, believed, that when a wealthy trader can conciliate all the spies that are watching over him, by making them partakers of the banquet, he sometimes ventures to give, *sub rosâ*, as grand a "spread" as any of his betters.*

It appears that the feasts are generally enlivened by music, and followed by music and dancing, and copious libations of sackee and tea. Occasionally some new little play or interlude, analogous to the occasion, is introduced

---

* For further particulars, see Titsingh, "Cérémonies Usitées au Japon," etc. 8vo. Paris. 1819; "Manners and Customs of the Japanese," 8vo. New edition. London. 1852; Kämpfer, Golownin, Fischer, and the old compilation which goes under the name sometimes of T. Meurs, and sometimes under that of Arnold Montanus.

It appears that Meurs, who was an engraveras well as a bookseller, really compiled the work, and that the person designated on the title-page as Arnold Montanus, merely put in the learning, furnishing the classical allusions, Latin quotations, and the like. The engravings, which are very curious, and very full of character, appear all to have proceeded from the industrious hands of the engraver-bookseller Meurs.

and performed by amateur actors. According to honest Captain Cock, all the Japanese in his time were much addicted to the good old hospitable fashion of giving "house-warmings," and considered that no dwelling could be prosperous, or stand long on its foundations, that was not (on its being finished) opened with a banquet and a jovial carouse. But it was the custom, on every such occasion, for all the neighbors of the master of the new house to send him liberal presents of eatables and drinkables.*

The interior of the Japanese houses—even among those of the poorer classes,—are said to be remarkably clean, neat, and orderly, everything being in its place, and there being a place for everything,—a golden domestic rule, the more easily to be observed by them, as they do not crowd their apartments with cumbrous and useless furniture. The old friend, to whom we have more than once referred, spoke almost with rapture of some of the villas of the nobility.

Generally the Japanese seem to merit the praise of being a cleanly people. All classes of them make a very frequent use of the bath, and are scrupulous as to partial ablutions, at certain fixed periods of the day. This alone does not insure cleanliness. The Turks bathe, or rather stew themselves, as often as the Japanese; but the Turk puts on foul, unchanging clothes over a clean skin, and has gene-

---

* "Journal and Notes," as given by Mr. Rundall, "Memorials of the Empire of Japan."

In Cock's time no English or Dutch vessel was ever allowed to leave port for Batavia, or for Europe, without receiving presents, and holding a good drinking bout. The people went off to the ship, carrying with them good store of foreign wines, and of native potables, to drink success to the voyage. The Japanese, like our English tars of the old school, had no notion of "parting dry."

COUNTRY HOUSE.

rally a house encumbered with filth, and swarming with bugs, fleas, and other intolerable vermin; but the Japanese contrives usually to put clean clothes over his clean skin, and to be neat and tidy at home. Kämpfer observes:—"They are indeed very nice in keeping themselves, their clothes, and houses, clean and neat." To every house of any pretension to respectability, there is attached an apartment called a "*Fro*," which is fitted up with vapor-baths, and with warm and cold baths. One or the other of these the Japanese use every morning and every evening. The loose nature of their costume renders the operations of undressing and dressing very quick and easy. Unfasten the girdle that encircles the waist, and the whole of the simple habiliments drop at once to the ground. It is mainly to this practice of constant bathing that our learned German doctor attributes the generally robust health and longevity of the people in this empire.*

Both hunting and hawking are frequently mentioned by the early travellers as common pastimes of the nobility and gentry. Hawks of a wonderfully fine breed, and of admirable training, are not mentioned occasionally. It should appear, however, that these sports are not now very common, and that the Japanese grandees have quite lost their taste for equitation, although, when rich, they always keep a numerous, if not good stud in the stable, and are very rigorous with the grooms who neglect the feeding and proper cleaning of their horses. Some of these stables are said to be as neat as a drawing-room.

The rich Japanese make a great show with their equipages. The princes and most distinguished people have

---

* Kämpfer, in vol. ii. p. 424, of his excellent history, gives a minute description of the *fro*, or bath, with the process of heating it.

carriages which resemble our old-fashioned ones, and were introduced into Japan by the Dutch. They are often drawn by horses, but for the most part by oxen. But the grandees are more commonly carried in chairs, like the sedan-chairs of Europe. They also ride on horseback, but consider it as vulgar to hold the bridle themselves. The horse must be led.*

Golownin says: "We once saw the governor of Matsmai ride on horseback to a temple, where thanksgivings were to be celebrated, and where he must go once every year in spring. The high priest, the priests and officials, and officers who were obliged to be present, were gone there before. He rode alone, without ceremony; a small train attended him on foot. To the horse's bit there were fastened, instead of the bridle, two light blue girdles, which two grooms held fast on each side of the horse's mouth; the two ends of these girdles were held by two other grooms, who went at a little distance from the others; so that these four men occupied almost the whole road. The tail of the horse was covered with a light silk bag. The governor, dressed in his usual clothes, in which we had often seen him, sat without his hat, upon a magnificent saddle, and held his feet in wooden japanned stirrups, which resembled little boxes. The grooms who

* This is not unlike the style of riding now in fashion among the fat and dignified pashas and effendis of the Ottoman empire, where equestrianism and every other manly exercise, or manly virtue, seems dying out. The horse of the pasha is not led; the great man holds the reins himself, but two grooms walk on foot at the horse's head, while two other grooms, one on each side, walk on a line with the stirrup-irons, to prop up his greatness, by catching him under the arm-pits, in case the horse should fall or stumble,—no uncommon event where the roads are execrable, and good horses an exceeding great rarity.

AN EQUESTRIAN PARTY.

held the horse at the bit, continually cried: '*chai, chai,*' that is, softly, softly; however, they pushed on the horse, and made it jump and go quick; the governor therefore stooped and held fast to the saddle with both hands. At a short distance before him, went some soldiers in a row, with two serjeants, and though nobody was in the way, they continually cried, 'Make room! make room!' Behind the governor followed the armor-bearers, who carried all the insignia of his dignity in japan cases. This was to signify that the governor was *incognito.*"*

Incognito or not, this certainly looks very much like a decay in the noble art of horsemanship. Perhaps, however, it may be found that gentlemen, remote from court and great cities, and not puffed up with the pride of office, may still delight in the saddle, and ride like men, instead of being carried like bales of silk or satin. We hope that such may really prove to be the fact; for no nation that is not equestrian can pretend to be a nation of gentlemen.

As we have repeatedly stated, the condition of women —that real test of true civilization—is incomparably better and higher in Japan than in any other Oriental country. It may, indeed, be safely said, from all the evidence before us, that "Japanese women are subjected to no seclusion; they hold a fair station in society, and share in all the innocent recreations of their fathers and husbands. The fidelity of the wife and the purity of the maiden are committed wholly to their own sense of honor, somewhat quickened, perhaps, and invigorated, by the certainty that death would be the inevitable and immediate consequence of a detected lapse from chastity. And so well is this

* "Recollections of Japan."

confidence repaid, that a faithless wife is, we are universally assured, a phenomenon unknown in Japan."*

From the highest down to the very lowest, every Japanese is sent to school. It is said that there are more schools in the empire than in any other country in the world, and that all the peasants and poor people can, at least, read. This is surely a noticeable fact, and a most honorable distinction. The minds of the women are as carefully cultivated as those of the men. Hence, in the array of the most admired poets, historians, and other authors are found very many females.

Among the rich and great, the husband, in general, is very far from corresponding to the fidelity of the wife; and, among all classes, those pleasant vices that turn themselves into scourges to whip themselves, appear to be exceedingly prevalent. Incontinence is, in fact, as we have already declared, on many good current authorities, the great national vice of the Japanese. Yet the purity of mothers and wives remains an indisputable and striking fact. Innumerable native stories bear testimony to it, and innumerable incidents, related by different travellers and their own writers, prove the respect in which a married woman is invariably held by the men.

The women of Japan strongly resent dishonor; and there is more than one instance recorded of death having been inflicted on her dishonorer by the injured woman. As an evidence of determination of character, the following anecdote is related:—"A man of rank went on a journey, and a noble in authority made overtures to his wife. They were rejected with scorn and indignation,

---

* "Manners and Customs of the Japanese."

but the libertine, by force or fraud, accomplished his object. The husband returned, and was received by his wife with affection, but with a dignified reseve that excited his surprise. He sought explanations, but could not obtain them at once. His wife prayed him to restrain himself till the morrow, and then, before her relations and the chief people of the city, whom she had invited to an entertainment, his desire should be satisfied. The morrow came, and with it the guests, including the noble who had done the wrong. The entertainment was given in a manner not unusual in the country, on the terraced roof of the house. The repast was concluded, when the lady rose and made known the outrage to which she had been subjected, and passionately demanded that her husband should slay her as an unworthy object unfit to live. The guests, the husband foremost, besought her to be calm; they strove to impress her with the idea that she had done no wrong,—that she was an innocent victim, though the author of the outrage merited no less punishment than death. She thanked them all kindly. She wept on her husband's shoulder. She kissed him affectionately, then suddenly escaping from his embraces, rushed precipitately to the edge of the terrace and cast herself over the parapet. In the confusion that ensued, the author of the mischief still unsuspected, for the hapless creature had not indicated the offender, made his way down stairs. When the rest of the party arrived, he was found weltering in his blood by the corpse of his victim. He had expiated his crime by committing suicide in the national manner—by slashing himself across the abdomen with two slashes, in the form of a cross."*

* Rundall. "Memorials."

Incidents like these furnish the ground-work of many of their dramas and popular novels.

Other tales are told in honor of female presence of mind, courage, and fortitude.

A great lord, named Tchouya, with his friend named Ziositz, entered into an extensive conspiracy against the emperor. Tchouya had a wife who had been greatly celebrated as well for her beauty as for her wit and heroic constancy.

"An act of indiscretion on the part of Tchouya, after so many years (nearly fifty) of prudence, betrayed the conspiracy, and orders were issued for his arrest and that of Ziositz. It was deemed important to seize both, if possible, or at least Tchouya, who resided at Yeddo, alive, in the hope of extorting further disclosures. To effect this, it was indispensable to surprise him, and measures were taken accordingly. An alarm of fire was raised at Tchouya's door, and when he ran out to ascertain the degree of danger threatening his house, he was suddenly surrounded and attacked. He defended himself stoutly, cutting down two of his assailants, but, in the end, was overpowered by numbers and secured. His wife, meanwhile, had heard the sounds of conflict, and apprehending its cause, immediately caught up those of her husband's papers which would have revealed the names of his confederates (among whom were men of distinction and princes of the land), and burnt them. Her presence of mind remains even to this day a topic of admiration in Japan, where the highest panegyric for judgment and resolution that can be bestowed upon a woman is to compare her to the wife of Tchouya."*

* Rundall. "Memorials."

The love, obedience, and reverence manifested by children towards their parents are stated to be unbounded. On the other hand, it is said that the confidence placed by parents in their children is equally without limit. Parents frequently select their elder sons to be arbitrators in their disputes with others, and submit implicitly to their decisions. It is also a very common practice with parents to resign their property and state to a son who has attained a suitable age, remaining for the rest of life dependent on him for support; and it is added that any abuse of this trust is unknown in the country.

Next to the vices to which we have made allusion, the great defect of the national character—though coupled with a keen sense of the point of honor,—appears to be the thirst and madness of revenge. This passion, as we have intimated, also furnishes great staple materials for their dramatists and other writers; and it seems to be illustrated in numerous popular stories.

Some of these tales throw more light on the Japanese character than can be derived from any other source.

"Fakaki-fikoyemon, the governor of Nagasaki, having obtained permission of the Djogoun to wear two sabres, and to have a pike in his coat of arms, his people became in consequence so insolent that they treated every one with the utmost haughtiness and disdain.

"On the 20th of the 12th month of the 14th year Genrok (1701), they were carrying his daughter in a sedan-chair to the temple, to receive a name.* Heavy rains had rendered the road very muddy. Fokka-fouri-kouan-

* The children of persons of distinction receive a name the seventh day after their birth. Among the lower classes, boys are not named till the expiration of thirty days, and girls at thirty-one.

seïmon, that is, the governor of the village of Fokka-fouri, hastily passing by the chair, had the misfortune to splash it. Fikoyemon's people began to abuse him, and regardless of his excuses, fell upon and beat him, and then ran to his house in the street called Ouya-goto-matche, where they destroyed all the furniture.

"The servants of Kouanseïmon took a boat, and lost no time in carrying to him intelligence of what had happend. After deliberating on the means of revenging this insult, which could not be washed away but with blood, they returned to Nagasaki, with several of the inhabitants of Fokka-fouri, assembled to the number of more than two hundred before the residence of Fikoyemon, and as soon as the door was opened, rushed in and attacked the master and his people. Fikoyemon valiantly defended himself; but his foot having unfortunately slipped, his adversaries fell upon him and cut off his head, which they carried in triumph to Fokka-fouri, as a trophy of their vengeance.*

"It was conveyed to Nagasaki, and interred with the body near the temple of Fon-ren-si, together with a white dog, which had rushed among the assailants to defend his master, and been killed after wounding several of them.

"Two of Kouanseïmon's people ripped themselves up on the bridge, near the residence of Fikoyemon, calling loudly upon the people to witness the courage with which the inhabitants of Fokka-fouri suffer death in order to revenge injuries."†

* "While I was in Japan, a woman was still living at Nagasaki, who recollected seeing the murderers pass by, holding by the hair his head dripping blood." Titsingh.

† Titsingh. "Illustrations of Japan."

"M. Caron relates a remarkable instance, which occurred within his own knowledge. It appears that two high officers of the court met on the palace-stairs and jostled each other. One was an irascible man, and imme diately demanded satisfaction. The other, of a placable disposition, represented that the circumstance was accidental, and tendered an ample apology: representing that satisfaction could not reasonably be demanded. The irascible man, however, would not be appeased, and finding he could not provoke the other to a conflict, suddenly drew up his robes, unsheathed his cattan, and cut himself in the prescribed mode. As a point of honor, his adversary was under the necessity of following the example, and the irascible man, before he breathed his last, had the gratification of seeing the object of his passion dying by his side."*

"Having a keen sense of the slightest insult, which cannot be washed away but with blood, they are the more disposed to treat one another in their mutual intercourse with the highest respect."†

Whatever the people or the government may be, both are certainly raised far above the contempt with which Europeans usually regard Asiatics. We cannot find a single writer, whether of a remote or of a recent period, that gives other than a high, manly character to the Japanese. The reader will remember the opinions delivered by Adams the mariner, and Xavier the sainted missionary. Father Froes, after a residence of some years, eloquently defended the people against all detractors. "They are," said he, "as gifted a nation as any in Europe."

In another letter the same missionary says,—"That

---

* Rundall. "Memorials."

† Titsingh.

which is proper to give great consolation and joy, and Christian hope for the future, is the good natural disposition of these people: the young men we have in our seminary at Arima are so well conducted. They are nearly all of noble birth: they live like so many devout recluses; they are modest, quiet, and studious, friends of purity, most tractable and obedient, and quick at their studies. They literally adhere to the rules set down for them. Their hours are so distributed that they never lose any valuable time. They learn our languages and literature, as also music, both vocal and instrumental. In sooth, they are by nature docile and of a lively genius."*

Don Rodrigo, the noble viceroy, who suffered shipwreck on the coast, gives the people a very high character; but, like a sober Spaniard, he blames the men for being too fond of drink.

We need not repeat the many recent and favorable glimpses of character afforded by late voyagers and residents. On the whole, it appears to us that there is no disputing the short, general estimate presented by a very recent English writer, who had carefully collected and perused all accessible authorities.

"To sum up the character of the Japanese: They carry notions of honor to the verge of fanaticism; and they are haughty, vindictive, and licentious. On the other hand, brawlers, braggarts, and backbiters, are held in the most supreme contempt. The slightest infraction of truth is punished with severity; they are open-hearted, hospitable, and, as friends, faithful to death. It is represented that there is no peril a Japanese will not encounter to serve a friend; that no torture will compel him to betray

---

* "Nuovi Avvisi del Giapone." Venetia. 1586.

a trust; and that even the stranger who seeks aid will be protected to the last drop of blood. The nation, with all their faults and vices, evinced qualities that won the hearts and commanded the esteem of the missionaries."*

* Rundall. "Memorials."

JAPANESE WRESTLERS.

ENGRAVING BLOCKS FOR PRINTING.

BOOK XI.

LANGUAGE—LITERATURE—SCIENCE—MUSIC—PAINTING.

One of the old Jesuits felt quite certain that the language and the letters of the Japanese had been invented and rendered difficult by Satan himself, in order to perplex poor missionaries, and impede the progress of the true faith.

Although, as yet, very few Europeans have acquired anything like a perfect familiarity with this tongue, it appears to be less difficult than several other Oriental languages. Should friendly relations be established with the government, and a greater freedom of intercourse allowed, we, no doubt, shall soon have accomplished Japanese scholars among American citizens and British subjects. There are very strong incentives to the study, for the patented native interpreters, as Sir F. Davis has remarked, are not to be trusted in diplomacy, and without a knowledge of the tongue they speak, it will be found very difficult to make any progress with the people. There already exist, in different European languages, grammars, vocabularies, and other books, quite sufficient to teach the rudiments.

We are indebted to a kind friend—a learned and most ingenious philologist—for the remarks on language which immediately follow :—

"The Japanese language has been usually said to be unlike all the languages of the globe, and, in one point of view, the statement is true; but it is in its structure analogous to the languages of the Tartar or Scythic class; and although in the lexicographic portion of the language differs from all others of that class, so far as we know, this can hardly be a foundation for making a general distinction, because they differ very considerably from each other in this respect. It would seem as though languages less fully organized than those of the Indo-Germanic class, those which are merely pegged together and not dovetailed like the work of a cabinet-maker—to use Dr. Johnson's metaphor—do more readily change the form and meaning of their words; and that while Sanskrit and English, for instance, after a separation of half the age of the world, still retain very many roots perfectly alike, two tongues like the Mordwin and Cheremiss, spoken by neighboring tribes on the Volga, who were probably one not many centuries ago, have now distinct words in most cases for their most ordinary ideas. We may be theorizing too far, perhaps; much of the variation may have arisen from the fact that those languages have never been cultivated, and that the people who speak them are *nomad.*

The features of the Japanese language which coincide with those of the Tartar tongues are these:—the substantives have no gender; they form all their cases and other modifications by subsequent particles; and these particles are too numerous to come under our strict ideas of grammatical declension. As an instance, we take the word *fito*, man; *fito-bito*, *fito-dono*, *fito tato*, and some other expressions, signify men; *fito-no*, or *fito-ga*, of a man; *fito-ni*, or *fito-ye*, to a man; there is also *fito-wa*, *fito-wo*, *fito-yori*, &c., and these are not indiscriminately used, but they answer to what the Finnish grammarians call the predicative, factive, adessive, allative, and other cases, in addition to our well-known datives and accusatives.

"There is a very singular fact in relation to the pronoun, which we believe to be unknown to any other language: it is that the same word may be I, or thou, or he, according to circumstances: in fact, that the so-called personal pronoun is not personal at all, or that it belongs to any person. Landresse, in his Supplement to "Rodriguez' Japanese Grammar," Paris, 1826, 8vo., states that *Watakusi* is the pronoun of the first person, according to Rodriguez, and of the second according to Oyanguren; *waga* is made "thou" by Rodriguez, and "I" by Oyanguren. Rodriguez makes *konata*, thou and he, and Oyanguren makes the same word I and thou. Collado makes *konata*, I, thou, and he.

"In our ignorance of native Japanese works, it is difficult to find a way through this labyrinth, but in all probability there is in Japanese something like what we find in some European languages, in Italian for example, where *ella* means she and you; or in German, where the word *sie* is used for they and you, although grammatically distinct, and when *er* is used for he and you; these distinctions being determined by recognized modes of politeness, which may be still further extended in Japan.

"The verbs have their tenses produced by additions to, and not changes of, the root; the word *yo*, to read, may be an example. We have *yomi*, I read; *yoda*, I did read; *yomo*, *yomozu*, or *yomozuru*, I shall read; *yomokasi*, might I read; *gomeba*, when I read; *yomaba*, if I read, &c., &c., to a considerable extent; there is also, as in Turkish, a negative incorporated with the verb, as *Yomami*, I do not read: *Yomananda*, I did not read, &c., and through all the same variations as the affirmative verb.

"The Japanese say they have two languages—*Yomi* and *Koye*—but the fact is, that *Koye* is pure Chinese with a different pronunciation, though still monosyllabic. As the Japanese write the Chinese sounds with alphabetic symbols, these Japanese pronunciations may represent the sounds of the Chinese characters as they were fifteen or twenty centuries ago, for an alphabet, however imperfect, must contribute to retain more of the sounds than any ideographic character, and a study of these sounds might be useful in comparisons of tongues, and help to form a judgment upon the ethnographical position of the Chinese nation.

"Practically, the Japanese mix the Koye or Chinese with their own language to the best of their ability; the most learned inflicting such a mass of Chinese upon their readers, or hearers, as to be unintelligible to all but those as learned as themselves.

They speak of two kinds of styles—the mai-den, or the most learned or religious style, and the gheden, the secular; each of these has its subdivisions, but scarcely any is free from admixture with Chinese words. Japanese poetry is composed most commonly in yomi only, in feet of five or seven syllables: it is now and then mingled with prose, as is done by Persians and Turks, and even the prose has often a cadence or rhythm in imitation of poetry. The recitation is said to be very harmonious. The writer has heard the language recited by two Europeans who spoke the language, and can testify to its rather agreeable sound. The language is usually written with a syllabarium of forty-seven characters, each character representing a syllable. There are in fact two systems in use, one very easy, and the other extraordinarily difficult, and of course the latter is selected for general use, the easy one being employed only for notes, glosses, and interlineary versions. The latter, which is called katagana, is very simple, each sound having one invariable representative.—"The other style, called hiragana, employs at least six characters, radically different from each other, for each sound; varying each of these characters at the pleasure of the writer, and, notwithstanding this barren redundancy, employing, in addition, any Chinese character which the writer may choose to adopt, twisted into any cursive form he pleases, instead of using one of the characters more generally known.*

"The probability is, that it is this habit of adapting new Chinese characters which has caused the hiragana syllabarium to grow to its present incredible extent, and bids fair to render it at last utterly illegible. The extent of this system may be judged from the fact, that the Vienna printing office, in order to produce a copy of a Japanese novel with moveable types, was obliged to cast a fount of four hundred and eighty-one Japanese types for the ordinary syllabarium, and two hundred and twenty-seven more for the additional Chinese types which the writer chose to adopt; and the learned scholar, Pfitzmayer, who has, with much learning and incredible pains, edited the above novel with a translation, complains that the types are not nearly numerous enough to represent the variety of forms

---

* "In the early part of the eighth century, the syllabic systems, denominated *katagana* and *hiragana*, were invented and found completely adapted to the idiom of the country. The use of this species of writing is now almost universal in Japan; it is rare to find a person unable to read it." "Chinese Repository," vol. iii. p. 206. Canton. 1835. The authority quoted is that of the learned Orientalist, Klaproth.

used. All this is for an ordinary tale, intended to be intelligible to the many.

"The translation of the Gospel of St. John, which was, I believe, made by Gutzlaff, with the aid of a native, is printed very judiciously in the easy, or Katagana character.

"It must be admitted that a good proportion of this large number of types cast by the Vienna type-founders was unnecessary, many of them being required merely to imitate the irregular writing of the Japanese scribe."

But such errors have not often been committed, and the liberal and extraordinary efforts made by the imperial government of Austria (without any immediate view to self-interest) to promote Oriental learning, and facilitate the means of studying the languages of the East, entitle that government to the gratitude of the whole civilized world, and are deserving of far more praise than they seem hitherto to have obtained. Certain deep-rooted, ill-considered prejudices, arising chiefly out of political feelings, cool or entirely suppress European gratitude. It has been a fashion to consider the ancient house of Austria as an enemy rather than friend to letters, science, and art. Yet that house is now, and has long been, spending annually vast sums of money upon these objects, while, from our own constitutional and *liberal* government, it is always a most difficult task to procure a grant of a few hundred pounds for any such purpose. It will be found out some day,—perhaps, when too late,—that all things cannot be conducted by private enterprise, and upon purely commercial principles, and that the application of those principles is, in certain cases, detrimental to the national spirit, to real intellectual progress, and to the honor and even safety of the country.

Where is the enterprise among booksellers, where the commercial principle by which so elaborate and costly a work as the immense Japanese dictionary of Professor Pfitzmayer, now in course of printing at Vienna, could have been produced?* We may safely venture to say that by such means, the book could not have been brought out in any country in Europe. Yet no one will deny the value and importance of the work, or question the now increasing necessity of our possessing such a lexicon. Private speculation has its limits, and it is when it reaches them, and halts upon them, that the State ought to step in. Societies or learned associations may do a good deal, and some of them have done much, but it should seem that their resources are far too narrow, and the number of their subscribers too uncertain, to permit of their prosecuting any very extensive enterprises and labors. Where is now the Oriental Translation Fund attached to the Royal Asiatic Society of Great Britain? To retain its valuable vitality, it ought to have been nourished by an annual government grant.

But we must return to our own immediate subject.

"The Japanese alphabet," says another writer, "contains forty-eight letters, and is written in two different ways, somewhat analogous to the printed and written forms used in our own language.

"The first, which is called the *Katagana*, is the clearest and most definite, and is chiefly used in dictionaries and works of science; the other, called *Hiragana*, is more like a running hand, and is the character generally in use in all kinds of light reading, and in the transaction of the

* It is calculated that, if this dictionary be continued and concluded on its present ample scale, it will run to twenty volumes.

common business of life; it is also called the female character, from its being usually employed by the fair sex."*

It appears to us that what are here called letters are syllables, and that the Japanese have rather a syllabarium than an alphabet. They do not write, like us, across the page from the left hand to the right, nor, like the Persians, Arabs, Turks, and so many other eastern nations, from the right hand to the left; but, like the Chinese, they write, in lateral straight lines from the top of the page to the bottom. Some specimens of their writing and printing which have come under our observation are uncommonly neat and clear, but are quite crowded with Chinese characters.

Paper came into use in Japan as early as the beginning

---

* "Chinese Repository," vol. iii. The authority here followed is that of Mr. Medhurst, of Batavia, author of a Japanese vocabulary. The clearest and briefest Japanese grammar that we have examined is the following:—"Elémens de la Grammaire Japonaise; par le P. Rodriguez. Traduits du Portugais sur le Manuscrit de la Bibliothèque du Roi, et soigneusement collationnés avec la Grammaire publiée par le même auteur à Nagasaki, en 1604; par M. C. Landresse, Membre de la Société Asiatique; précédés d'une explication des syllabaires Japonais, et de deux planches contenant les signes de ces syllabaires; par M. Abel Remusat. Ouvrage publié par la Société Asiatique." Paris. 1825.

There is a supplement to this work also published by the Asiatic Society of France. "Supplément à la Grammaire Japonaise, du P. Rodriguez; ou, Remarques Additionnelles sur quelque points du système grammatical des Japonais, tirées de la Grammaire composée en Espagnol; Par le P. Oyanguren, et traduites par M. C. Landresse, Membre de la Société Asiatique; précédées d'une notice comparative des Grammaires Japonaises des P. P. Rodriguez et Oyanguren; par M. le Baron G. de Humboldt." Paris. 1826.

of the seventh century; and printing, from engraved wooden blocks, in the Chinese manner, was introduced A. D. 1206, about two hundred and fifty years before that invaluable art was invented in Europe.

From the moment the Japanese acquired a written language, their literature advanced rapidly, and it appears to have improved from age to age. Unfortunately, in Europe, it is scarcely known; but from the few Japanese books that have fallen into the hands of learned foreigners, and from the accounts left us by the missionaries and other travellers, it is evident that these people possess works of all kinds,—historical compositions, geographical and other scientific treatises, books on natural history, voyages and travels, moral philosophy, cyclopædias, dramas, romances, poems, and every component part of a very polite literature.

The wide diffusion of education, which has been more than once mentioned, is of no recent date. The first of all the missionaries who visited the country found schools established wherever they went. The sainted Xavier mentions the existence of four "Academies" in the vicinity of Miako, at each of which education was afforded to between three and four thousand pupils; adding, that considerable as these numbers were, they were quite insignificant in comparison with the numbers instructed at an institution near the city of Bandone; and that such institutions were universal throughout the empire.*

Nor does it appear that these institutions have decreased in modern days. Speaking of the early part of the present century, M. Meylan states that children of both sexes and of all ranks are invariably sent to rudimentary

* Charlevoix.

schools, where they learn to read and write, and are initiated into some knowledge of the history of their own country. To this extent, at least, it is considered necessary that the meanest peasant should be educated. Our officers, who visited the country as late as the year 1845, ascertained that there existed at Nagasaki, a college in which, additionally to the routine of native acquirements, foreign languages were taught. Among the visitors on board our ship, many spoke Dutch. Some understood a little French. One young student understood English slightly, could pronounce a few English words, caught readily at every English expression that struck him, and wrote it down in his note-book. They all seemed to be tolerably well acquainted with geography, and some of them appeared to have some acquaintance with guns, and the science of gunnery. The eagerness of all of them to acquire information greatly delighted our officers.*

The Japanese printers keep the market well supplied with cheap, easy books, intended for the instruction of children, or people of the poorer classes. The additions or impressions of books of the higher order appear to be uncommonly numerous. Most of these books are illustrated and explained with frequent woodcuts, which are engraved on the same wood-blocks with the type. Like the Chinese, they only print on one side of their thin paper. An imperial cyclopædia, printed at Miako, in the spiritual emperor's palace, is most copiously embellished with cuts.

All are agreed that reading is a favorite resource and recreation with both sexes, and that the Daïri, or court of the Mikado, is eminently a bookish, literary court.

---

* "Narrative of the Voyage of H. M. S. Samarang," vol. ii.

It is said that few sights are more common in Japan, during the sunny seasons of the year, than that of a group of ladies and gentlemen seated by a cool, running stream, or in a shady grove, each with a book in hand. Whatever their literature may be, it is evident that it delights them, and that it has polished their manners.

It is scarcely fair to judge of the literature of any country by mere translations. The difficulty of so judging is vastly increased when the language of the original writer and that of the translator differ so entirely as does the Japanese from Dutch, German, French, English, or any European dialect. Then again, we possess, as yet, but very few and fragmentary translations from the Japanese, of any kind. In this our uninformed condition, it appears to have been rather premature in any English writer to sit in judgment on the literature of these people. The few specimens of their histories or annals have been called jejune, trivial, and monotonous; the specimens of their geographical works, dry and dull. But in the multiplicity of native authors and books, the best may not have been chosen, or the very few Europeans who have tried their hands at the task may not have been the best of translators.

It is said that every Japanese is fond of quoting poetry, and enlivening his conversation with verse. So far, he seems to be a perfect Doctor Pangloss. But of the metre, or rhyme, or construction of Japanese poetry, we can scarcely be said to know anything. It appears pretty evident that their poets delight in point, antithesis, epigrammatic turns, and what we call *concetti*, or conceits.

Here are a few specimens, with the somewhat doubtful translations of M. Titsingh.

A princess, afflicted by the death of dear relatives, composed these lines:—

"Woudje kotowa
Tsoukouki ga fara na
Tsougou namida
Kousa na tomoto wa
Nava sigoure tsousou."

[Our misfortunes follow one another like the links of a chain. Though my garments are moistened with my tears, my eyes are incessantly filled afresh with them.]

Another princess, a daughter of the Daïra-Sama, or spiritual emperor, was married to the lay emperor, and carried from Miako to Jeddo. Living very unhappily with her husband, and regretting her native home, she thus gave vent to her feelings:—

"Omoï na ki,
Mini si nare domo
Faro sato no
Namo no tsouka siki
Miyako tori kana."

[Never did I conceive the idea of marrying the Ziogun. Since this union I am cut off from the privilege of going out into the world. Miako is ever present to my thoughts, and if I perceive any object that reminds me of it, my sorrows are aggravated.]

Another poet thus sings of happiness or longevity, and its popular emblem, the bamboo:—

"Take-no-kotoba no
Fodomo yokou
Tjiyo no fourou mitji
Fiki tarasou
Modita karikerou
Tokito kaya."

[The knots of bamboo are all at equal distances from one another: years and ages roll away without producing any alteration in this arrangement. Thus our happiness will be eternal.]

The next verses are interesting, as illustrating the frequency of conflagrations. After a terrible fire at Miako, a poet improvised these lines:—

"Kaze faya to
Kikoumo ouramesi
Teyono fi o."

[Whenever I hear a violent wind, I dread the breaking out of a fire while it blows.]*

To which one of his rhyming companions† immediately subjoined:—

"Simisoudani tote,
Yakemo no karesou."

[Were it even in a valley, watered by a running stream, everything would be consumed.]

---

* Among the Turks, in our time, it was a common police regulation n many of their towns, that blacksmiths should cease from their work, iand that all fires should be extinguished whenever a hurricane began to blow.

In a storm of this sort, some forty years ago, the wind blew the charcoal embers from a smith's shop to the shop of a carpenter, where the fire so took and spread that nearly the whole of the city of Brusa was burnt to the ground. In 1848, we saw some of the ancient stone buildings of that place still bearing on the blackened or almost calcined face of their walls, marks of this extensive combustion of the wooden houses of the Turks.

* It appears that improvisatori are common among the Japanese, and that, like the Italians, they can throw off, at their festive meetings, *brindisi*, or impromptu rhymed toasts.

According to M. Titsingh, there is in these two impromptus, as in very many of their longer and more studied productions, a double meaning, or a play upon words. The same writer, who lived long in Japan as chief agent to the Dutch East India Company, at Nagasaki, declares that the Japanese suffer no event at all worthy of notice to pass without making it a subject for exercising their passion for poetry. They have many historical ballads, which really appear to be not very unlike our Chevy Chase. M. Titsingh gives a version of a very curious old ballad on the death of Yamassiro, a councillor of state, who was assassinated and much regretted by the people. It runs thus: [We may dispense with the Japanese lines.]

"That the young councillor is cut off at the castle on the hill by a new guard, exciting a mob, I have just heard.

"Yamassiro's white robe being dyed with blood, every one sees in him the reddening councillor.

"Along the eastern way, through the village Sanno, the flowing waters rushed, burst the dyke of the swamp, and the mountain-castle fell.

"The precious trees planted in vases, the plum-trees and cherry-trees beautiful with their blossoms, who threw into the fire? It was Sanno that cut them down.

"A councillor, in madness, is cut down. We may say, if such things had ever before been heard of, this was a judgment of heaven."

In the Japanese original is one continued pun, or play upon the name of the hero of the ballad, Yamassiro. Yama means "mountain," and *siro*, "castle."

The Japanese have the counterpart of our very useful lines:—

"Thirty days have September,
April, June, and November,"

but they do not make up the months of the year as we do. Here is the curiosity:—

"Si yo daï mi o
Mou sio ni nikou mo ou,
Nanats ou bo si
I ma si kou si re ba
Si mo no si ya wa si."

These lines contain the names of all the Japanese months of thirty days, as well as of those that have but twenty-nine days. Yet the same verses, being read in their ballad sense, signify—

"All the grandees of the empire abhorred the bear (the arms of Yamassiro, which are seven stars); let it shine no more; it is a happy event even for the lowest servants."

They appear to have a great many of these aids to memory, some of their verses fixing the dates of historical events, like the late Dr. Valpy's chronology in rhyme, which we learned by heart in our schoolboy-days, and which still clings to our memory in spite of the mediocrity of its verse:—

"Through sixteen centuries the revolving sun,
And summers fifty-six his course had run,
When sinful man drew heaven's just vengeance down,
In one wide deluge the whole earth to drown," &c.

Some of the Japanese ballads seem to start off in the good old style of our nursery stories, "once upon a time," &c. M. Titsingh gives the following stanzas, which he informs us are set to the tune of an old and popular Japanese ballad.

"I de so no to ki ni	"In illo tempore
Fa si no gi va	Res magni momenti (evenit),
To no ma ya sanno ni	Tonoma a sanno.
Kira reta yo na	Prostratus cecidit.
Sono fin pa o	Prope regiam.
Kan no ni o-ota	Kanno et Oota
Yetchou ni Sakan ra da	Et Yetchou ab ostio postico (palatii).
O ote ni Sougi yama	Ad portam anteriorem Sougi-yama
Ava si te sanga	Simul pergebant
Sio no san ki son	Vulneratus est triplici loco.
Chi chi san sa ni	Pater ejus miser
Ita ron ura de	Factus est hoc (casu).
So o uro a ri so na	Sic profecto
Zi zito no sio	Ejus hora advenerat.
Tango in tori tsouki	Tango superbiens
Kago in no ri te zo ro	Ad currum eum duxit.

The lines may be thus Englished :—

"Once upon a time an event of great moment occurred. Tonoma was slain by Sanno near the palace: he was going with Kanno, Oota, Yetchou, and Sougiyama, from the back-door towards the front door. He was wounded in three places. His father was wretched on account of this deed. It was so decreed; his time was come. Tango proudly conducted him to his carriage."

Some of their poems seem to consist of religious dogmas or moral apothegms. The following might have been uttered by a pious Christian :—

"Kokoro da ni makoto,
No mitri ni kana fi naba
I! no ra tsoe to te mo kami,
Jamo mo ramoe."

"Upright in heart be thou and pure,
So shall the blessing of God

Through eternity be upon thee;
Clamorous prayers shall not avail,
But truly a clear conscience,
That worships and fears in silence."

Many of their proseta.es and romances appear to be exceedingly interesting, and far more imaginative, and at the same time more natural, than the general run of Oriental narrations.† We have given some short specimens, and more will be found in the works of Titsingh.

The dramas, which so attract and fascinate the Japanese, are said to admit, in one and the same piece, a Shaksperian mixture of the tragic and comic, and to bid a bold defiance to what classicists and the French of the old school call the "Unities." They think nothing of passing, in the twinkling of an eye, from one island to another, or from Japan to China or Corea, or from earth to heaven, or to the regions under the earth. We have already indicated the favorite staple materials of the plots of these plays.

They are generally founded on national history or tradition, presenting the exploits, loves and adventures of Japanese heroes and gods. Some of them may be called didactic, as they are designed to illustrate and enforce certain moral precepts. Their general tendency is said to be elevating, patriotic, and excellent, but they sometimes exhibit, in broad and revolting light, the unfavorable features of the national character, such as a demoniacal passion of

---

* We have mislaid our note on the subject, and have forgotten the authority, but we have somewhere seen it stated that the Japanese have a complete corpus poetarum, or collection of all their poets, with short memoirs to each.

† The monotony and unimaginativeness of *real* Eastern tales, almost force us to adopt the theory of the brilliant author of Eöthen—that the Arabian Nights' Entertainments had a Greek origin.

revenge, and a fondness for witnessing punishments and tortures. M. Fischer saw, on the stage, at Osacca, the representation of one of their punishments by torture, which he describes as astoundingly cruel.

It appears that more than twoactors are seldom, if ever, upon the stage at the same time.* The theatres are very large, and, to fill them with their voices, the actors have a sad habit of roaring and ranting. As, in the old times, in England and every other European country, the female parts are filled not by actresses, but by smooth-chinned boys. This we believe to arise, in Japan, from the excessive fatigue attendant on the profession, to which no woman's strength would be equal. The players begin business soon after the hour of noon, and seldom leave off until late at night. The actor is most esteemed who can most frequently change parts in the same piece, in the manner of Charles Matthews, of facetious and yet of mournful memory. The "stars," or very great favorites, are said to be enormously paid. But the profession is held in great contempt, the Japanese maintaining that the man who will give up his own character to assume that of another, for pay and profit, can have no sense of honor. As a natural consequence of their ban and proscription, the Japanese actors are the most immoral, licentious, and depraved people in the empire.

But the most singular point of all that has been told us about the Japanese stage, is the order of performance. Three long pieces are frequently represented on the same day; not, as with us, one after the other, in wholes, but in portions, namely, first, the first act of one, then the first act of a second, then the first act of a third; then, returning

---

* Thunberg.

to the first play, the second act of it, and, successively, the second acts of the second and third plays, and so on till all the three plays are played out. By this curious arrangement, any of the audience who wish only to see one of these pieces or who have not patience to sit out the whole, may withdraw to attend to business or to other diversion, or to smoke their pipes and drink rice-beer, whilst the dramas they have no wish to see take their turn on the stage; and they can then return, refreshed, to see and hear the next act of their favorite play. It is said, however, that the Japanese ladies seldom avail themselves of this facility, having no objection to sit out all the three intermingled pieces, and employing some of their time in changing their dresses in the manner already related. Little more is known of their theatres, except that, in general, the actors are magnificently attired, and change their dresses on the stage, still more frequently than the ladies change theirs in the boxes.

In science the Japanese have particularly cultivated medicine, astronomy, and mathematics. Unfortunately, their abhorrence of everything that is dead has prevented any proper study of anatomy by dissection. They cannot, therefore, be good surgeons. But as physicians, they very frequently give the best test of ability, for they cure their patients of alarming, and even dangerous diseases. Kämpfer, Thunberg, and nearly all the medical men who have ever travelled in the country, speak favorably both of their skill and of their ardent desire to acquire professional European knowledge.*

Acu-puncture and *moxa*-burning are both Japanese inventions. We believe that they are now almost entirely

* See particularly Dr. von Siebold's valuable work.

superseded among us by other processes, productive of the like effects; but they were brought from Japan into Europe, and were, during a very long series of years, adopted in the practice of every European country.

Of some of their medicinal preparations the most marvellous stories are related. The following is told by M. Titsingh, whose veracity has not been impeached, and who speaks from his own personal knowledge and experience.

"Instead of enclosing the bodies of the dead in coffins of a length and breadth proportionate to the stature and bulk of the deceased, they place the body in a tub, three feet high, two feet and a half in diameter at the top, and two feet at the bottom. It is difficult to conceive how the body of a grown person can be compressed into so small a space, when the limbs, rendered rigid by death, cannot be bent in any way.

"The Japanese to whom I made this observation told me that they produced the result by means of a particular powder called *Dosia*, which they introduce into the ears, nostrils, and mouth of the deceased, after which the limbs, all at once, acquire astonishing flexibility. As they promised to perform the experiment in my presence, I could not do otherwise than suspend my judgment, lest I should condemn as an absurd fiction a fact which, indeed, surpasses our conceptions, but may yet be susceptible of a plausible explanation, especially by galvanism, the recently discovered effects of which also appeared, at first, to exceed the bounds of credibility.

"The experiment accordingly took place in the month of October, 1783, when the cold was pretty severe. A young Dutchman having died in our factory at Desima, I directed the physician to cause the body to be washed, and left all night exposed to the air, on a table placed near an open window, in order that it might become completely stiff. Next morning several Japanese, some of the officers of our factory, and myself, went to examine the corpse, which was as hard as a piece of wood. One of the interpreters, named Zenby, drew from his bosom a *santock*, or pocket-book, and took out of it an oblong paper, filled with a coarse powder resembling sand. This was the famous *Dosia* powder. He put a pinch into the ears, another pinch into the nostrils, and a third into the mouth; and, presently, whether from the effect of this drug, or of some trick which I could not detect, the arms, which had before been crossed over the breast, dropped of themselves, and in less than twenty minutes, by the watch, the body recovered all its flexibility.

"I attributed this phenomenon to the action of some subtle poison, but was assured that the *Dosia* powder, so far from being poisonous, was a most excellent medicine, in child-bearing, for diseases of the eyes, and for other maladies. An infusion of this powder, taken even in perfect health, is said to have virtues which cause it to be in great request among the Japanese of all classes. It cheers the spirits and refreshes the body. It is carefully tied up in a piece of white cloth and dried, after being used, as it will serve a great number of times before losing its virtues.

"The same infusion is given to people of quality when at the point of death; if it does not prolong life, it prevents rigidity of the limbs; and the body is not exposed to the rude handling of professional persons—a circumstance of some consequence in a country where respect for the dead is carried to excess.

"I had the curiosity to procure some of this powder, for which I was obliged to send to Kidjo, or the nine provinces, to the temples of the Sintoos, which enjoy the exclusive sale of it, because they practise the doctrine of Kobou-Daysi, its inventor. It was after the death of Kobou-Daysi, in the second year of the *nengo-zio-wa* (A.D. 825), that this sand came into general use in Japan. The quantity obtained in consequence of my first application was very small, and even this was a special favor of the priests, who otherwise never part with more than a single pinch at a time.

"At my departure, in 1784, however, I carried with me a considerable quantity of the *Dosia* powder. Part was put up in lots of twenty small packets each, with the name written on the outside in red characters; the rest was in small bags; this was only a coarse powder, in which were to be seen here and there particles of gold, and which probably was not yet possessed of the requisite virtues. One small packet only had undergone the chemical operation which ensures its efficacy, and this was a powder as white as snow.

"The discovery of the *Dosia* powder is ascribed to a priest named Kobou-Daysi: he became acquainted with the properties of this wondrous mineral on the mountain of Kongosen or Kinbensen, in the province of Yamatto, where there are many mines of gold and silver, and he carried a considerable quantity of it to the temple to which he belonged, on the mountain of Kojas-an.

"The priests of this temple continue to chaunt hymns of thanksgiving to the gods who led Kobou-Daysi to the important discovery. When their stock is exhausted, they fetch a fresh supply from the mountain of Kongosen, and carry it away in varnished bowls. In all ages the common people are apt to attribute phenomena surpassing human comprehension to the agency of celestial spirits;

and, accordingly, the priests do not fail to pretend that the *Dosia* powder owes all its efficacy to the fervor of their prayers. As soon as the new supply arrives, it is put into a basin, varnished and gilt, and set before the image of the god Day-nitsi, or Biron-sanna. The priests, ranged in a circle before the altar, and turning between their fingers the beads of a kind of rosary, repeat, for seven times twenty-four hours, a hymn, called *Guomi-singo*, the words of which are:

"Ou o bokja Biron saunanomaka-godora mani
Fando ma, zimbara gara, garetaga won."

The priests assert that, after this long exercise, a kind of rustling is heard in the sand; all the impure particles fly out of the vessel of themselves, and nothing is left but the purified *Dosia* powder, which is then divided among all the temples of the Sintoos."*

Chemistry appears to be very imperfectly studied. Botany, on the other hand, is said to be diligently and successfully cultivated, at least as far as it is connected with the knowledge of simples. Some of the vegetable medicines are described as effective and excellent. The people, however, place their main dependence upon diet, and upon acu-puncture, and the *moxa*, which are still universally practised among them.

In astronomy, their proficiency really appears to be very considerable. They pursue this study with great ardor. Their best astronomers are said to be well acquainted with Lalande's Treatises, and other profound works which have been translated into Dutch. This surely disproves the assertion that they have only "some

* Titsingh. "Illustrations of Japan," &c.

little knowledge of mathematics." They have learned the use of most of our astronomical instruments. They have even taught Japanese artisans to imitate and reproduce them to perfection. They have excellent telescopes, chronometers, barometers, and thermometers of native workmanship; and they have learned to measure the height of mountains by the barometer. The courts of both the emperors are centres of science as well as of literature. Good almanacs, including the calculation of eclipses, are annually published by the colleges of Jeddo and Miako. From the few observations made by the officers of the "Samarang," we are disposed to believe that if we only knew more of them, the Japanese would be found to be in possession of far more scientific knowledge than the amount for which they have received credit.

It is quite clear that they are skilled in trigonometry, and in some of the best principles of civil engineering.

The mechanical arts, or all such portions of them as tend to abridge manual labor, and deprive people of the employments to which they have been bred, are discouraged, and, in fact, repressed by the government. The Ziogun would not accept, as a present, a European oil-mill: he said that it was very ingenious, but that if such a machine were generally adopted in the country, it would throw all the old Japanese oil-presses out of work and out of bread.

Although they are passionately fond of it, the national music—like that of all Oriental nations—appears to be utterly insupportable to European ears. Perhaps, however, this condemnation is too sweeping and general.

We have heard some of the music of the Japanese ladies highly commended by one who possessed a good musical ear. The *samsie*, or native guitar, is even more invariably

MUSICAL INSTRUMENTS.

a part of female education than is the pianoforte in England. Its touch is the signal for laying aside ceremony and constraint. The Japanese gentleman—truly a *gentleman* in this respect—has no notion of social enjoyment or conviviality without the company of the ladies. Every fair one takes with her to their parties her *samsie*, and they sing and play by turns, while the gentlemen smoke their pipes and take the cheering glass. At every feast it is the lady of the house that presides.

In the arts of design and painting they certainly possess both skill and taste, although they are somewhat negligent in the study of "the human form divine."

"This art," says M. Fischer, "appears to have developed itself, to a considerable degree, in very early times. Many screens and decorated walls in their temples have the stamp of a remote antiquity. Yet I never heard of a good portrait-painter in Japan, and am of opinion that a reluctance exists among their artists to devote themselves to this branch of their profession, founded on superstitious feelings. In all such works their attention is principally directed to accuracy in the details of costume and to the general air; the face is never a likeness."

It has been appositely remarked that "their Tartar brethren of St. Petersburgh, whose criticism on the portrait of Alexander, by Lawrence, was first directed to the great painter's delineation of his Imperial Majesty's epaulettes, crosses, and ribbons, displayed similar feelings with respect to the fine arts."*

It is curious to trace over the broad earth these Mongol affinities—these long lingering proofs of a common origin among so many and such distant nations. Those other

* "Quarterly Review," vol. lii.

brethren of the Japanese, the Osmanli Turks, would not, until quite a recent period, allow the human face or the human form to be depicted, or carved, or sculptured at all. It is true that the Koran prohibits all such representations; but we believe that the old Mongol antipathy had more to do with the interdict than any religious feeling or scruple, for we have seen Turks, who had no religious convictions whatever, express a strong dislike at the sight of a very agreeable English portrait.

The illustrations of M. Fischer's own book, all copied from the productions of Nagasaki artists, would, in themselves, be sufficient to prove that their painters have really very considerable skill, and can give to their works all that beauty of finish which we find in the illuminations of the best of our old missals. It is at least reasonable to suppose that the artists of Jeddo or Miako surpass those of the provinces, as our London painters and the other artists excel those of our provincial towns. Considering the interdict laid upon exportation, we may also imagine that the best specimens, the *capi d'opera*, of Japanese art have not yet reached Europe, or been seen and examined by competent European conoscenti.

The native delineations of flowers, fruits, and more especially of birds, are exquisitely beautiful. We have frequently had in our hands a small cup, or rather saucer, which is ornamented with the figures of two cranes. Nothing can be more perfect in drawing, more true in coloring, and more perfect in finish than this admirable miniature. The object is preserved in the Museum of the Royal Asiatic Society, New Burlington-street, and may be seen by any one, upon application to the Secretary, or to a member of the said Society.

Japanese artists produce beautiful maps of their own

country, which, by law, are not allowed to be exported, or even to be seen by foreigners. It was in procuring copies of the best of these maps of the empire that Dr. von Siebold became involved in very grievous troubles. An English officer—a very competent judge of such matters—to whom we have been indebted for some valuable assistance, saw these Japanese copies of the Imperial maps, three years ago, in von Siebold's own house at Leyden, and he assures us that they are most admirably executed.

If we had more good specimens before us we might, no doubt, have much more to say on the subject of the fine arts in Japan, but we trust that enough has been said to impress the reader with the belief that these people—super-refined Tartars—have, at least, artists of high taste and very extraordinary skill.

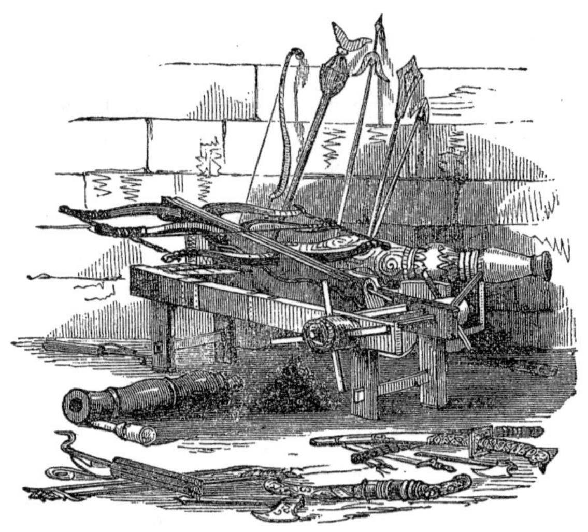

JAPANESE INSTRUMENTS OF WAR.

APPENDIX.

A.

EUROPEAN INTERCOURSE.

It has been made a matter of disputation whether Fernam Mendez Pinto was not really the first European, or in company with the first European party, that visited Japan.

In the year 1542, just half a century after the discovery of America by Columbus, two different parties of Portuguese were driven, by stress of weather, almost simultaneously, upon different islands of the Japanese Archipelago. One party consisted of Fernam Mendez Pinto, Diego Zeimoto and Christ. Borello; the other, of Antonio Mota, Francisco Zeimoto, and Antonio Pexota. Pinto gives an account of his visit, but is careless as regards dates, so that it is doubtful which of the two parties is entitled to the honor of the first arrival.

Pinto was then one of a party of desperadoes, who came to Ningpo, in China, and having, with his party, plundered the tombs of some Chinese kings, on a neighboring island, was afterwards captured, carried to Peking, and imprisoned. He was released from durance by the Tartars, who were then invading the country. After having spent some time in the service of his liberators, he returned to Ningpo, and, with his two companions, soon afterwards sailed from thence, or from Lampaçao, a Portuguese settlement near Macao, in a Chinese piratical junk, for Loo Choo.

Meeting with adverse winds, they were unable to reach those islands, and were finally compelled to make for the Japanese coast, where they landed upon the island of *Tansiximaa*, a dependency of the king of Bungo.

The strange vessel was hospitably received, and the governor of the island, having come on board, was much struck with the appearance of the Portuguese, and eagerly inquired of the captain what countrymen they were, and from whence he had brought them. The answers which he gave were satisfactory, and, on the third day, he and his passengers landed, and paid a visit to the governor. Here the Portuguese were objects of great curiosity, and were questioned as to the extent and riches of the kingdom of Portugal, and the greatness of its monarch. Pinto confesses that, in his answers, he had less regard for the truth, than for the necessity of inspiring the Japanese with great ideas respecting the grandeur and power of his nation and sovereign. Accordingly he vouched for the statements previously made by the Chinese, that Portugal was greater and richer than China—that his sovereign had conquered the greater portion of the earth; and upon being asked if it were true that his prince had 2,000 houses full of gold and silver, replied that he was not exactly informed as to the number of palaces in the possession of the king, because he had never thought it necessary to take an account of them. The strangers were treated with much hospitality, and an arquebuse which they had with them excited great curiosity and interest. Pinto presented it to the governor, and the ingenuity of the Japanese artisans enabled them, in a few days, to manufacture others from the pattern. After a stay of a month they were preparing to depart, when a message arrived from the prince of Bungo, inviting them to his court. Pinto accordingly proceeded to him at Usugui, or Vosugui, and having relieved the prince of a fit of the gout, was received into high favor. But soon afterwards he was very near losing it, together with his life, through an unfortunate accident which happened to the son of the prince. This young man, after much importunity, had been allowed to borrow the arquebuse, and, having overloaded it, the weapon burst in his hands, and wounded him severely. The accident was, by the populace, attributed to design on the part of the Portuguese, and they called loudly for vengeance; but the prince and his son shielded Pinto, and he successfully employed his knowledge of surgery to relieve the young man; so that he was retained in favor. After a short stay he returned to the port, and soon afterwards sailed with his companions, in the vessel which had brought them, for China.*

Of the adventures of the other party little more is recorded than the mere fact of their having been wrecked on the island of Kangusima,† in the kingdom of Satzuma, when on a voyage from China to

---

* F. M. Pinto's Adventures, &c.; French translation, edition of Paris, 1830; printed at the expense of the French government. Sir John F. Davis's admirable, unique work, "The Chinese," etc.

† "Asiatic Journal."

Macassar. This visit, however, seems to have attracted greater attention than that of Pinto, as the following curious note of it is found in the Japanese annals:—

"Under the Mikado Konaru, and the Ziogun Yosi-nao, in the twelfth year of the Nengo Tenbun, on the twenty-second day of the eighth month (October, 1543), a strange ship made the island Tanega-Sime,* near Koura, in the remote province Nisimura. The crew, about two hundred in number, had a singular appearance; their language was unintelligible—their native land unknown. On board was a Chinese, named Go-hou, who understood writing; from him it was gathered that this was a nan-ban ship (southern barbarian; in the Japanese form of the Chinese words nan-man). On the 26th this vessel was taken to Aku-oki harbor, on the north-west of the island; and Toki-taka, governor of Tanega-Sime, instituted a strict investigation concerning it, the Japanese bonze Tsynsynzu acting as interpreter, by means of Chinese characters. On board the nan-ban ship were two commanders, Mura-Syukya and Krista-Moota; they bring fire-arms, and first make the Japanese acquainted with shooting arms, and the preparation of shooting powder."

At this period the Japanese were a mercantile people, carrying on an active and lucrative commerce with, it is said, sixteen different countries. Their kindness to the strangers who had been wrecked upon their coasts, and the accounts given by them of their wealth and commercial character, soon brought many other traders and adventurers to the islands. All were kindly received, the new merchandise and wares which they brought found a ready market, and a steady intercourse arose between the western parts of Japan and the Portuguese settlement of Lampaçao. So ready were the natives to associate with the strangers, that they gave their daughters in marriage to some of those who settled among them.

The ever watchful activity of the Society of Jesus was soon attracted by the accounts given by the travellers of the extent and wealth of the islands, and the character and disposition of the inhabitants.

Accordingly, Xavier, with two other Jesuits, three converts, and some other Christians, sailed from India for Malacca, and from thence,

---

* It has been said that Zime means "island," whence it follows that Siebold's expression, "the island, Tanega-Zime," is tautological; but, in translating a language, and speaking of a country so little known, such tautology could hardly be avoided at a less sacrifice than that of perspicuity.

in a Chinese junk, to Japan. After a stormy passage of seven weeks, they landed at Kangasima on the 15th of August, 1549. Here they were very graciously received, the prince of Satzuma admitted Xavier to an audience, and gave him permission to teach and preach the Gospel.

At this period the Japanese empire was the scene of frequent commotion and internal strife. The different princes were almost independent sovereigns. Contending with the supreme government, and with each other, they eagerly embraced every opportunity for realizing the objects of their ambition. The few years of intercourse with the Portuguese had sufficed to enlighten them upon the advantages and profits to be gained from their trade. Every encouragement was consequently given to the traders and settlers, and every facility afforded them for carrying on their commercial concerns.

When Xavier arrived at Kangasima, the prince of Satzuma was not slow in observing the great respect and homage paid him by the merchants. To serve his own interests he, too, paid marked attention to Xavier, and endeavored by persuasion and kindness to retain him at his court; conceiving that if he could conciliate Xavier, and induce him to reside in his state, the commerce of the Portuguese would also find its seat there, and prove a source of great revenue to him.*

The following notices of visits to Japan are extracted from the *Chinese Repository*, printed at Canton in 1838–9, (pp. 221 and 538). The first is from the Journal of Captain Gordon (to which some allusion has been made), who sailed in a small brig, "*The Brothers*," from the Bay of Bengal for Okotsk in 1818, and on his way touched the Japan coast. His narrative thus commences:—

"On the 17th of June, 1818, we stood into the Bay of Yedo, and having joined with some junks which were apparently bound the same course as ourselves, were at sunset close in with the land, without having been recognized as a stranger, a circumstance which gave me much pleasure, as it was my wish to push directly for the capital, and I hoped, moreover, to be at the gate of the *Zeogun's* palace by daylight; but falling calm in the night, the vessel drifted near a rock, and we were obliged to anchor. At daylight we were visited by many boats, which came from several towns and villages about two

* Charlevoix. Von Siebold. "Chinese Repository." Klaproth.

miles off; and in the course of the morning many officers of government came on board, among whom were two of higher rank than the others, to whom great respect was paid by their attendants. I made known to this party my wish to proceed to Yédo, and acquainted them that the object of my visit was to obtain permission to return with a cargo for sale. As the wind and tide were against us, they advised us to remove the vessel into a neighboring bay, for shelter, and offered a pilot and two boats to assist, which I readily accepted, as I knew that we must wait an answer from the court, about sixty miles distant.* I was requested to allow the arms and ammunition to be landed, and subsequently to unship the rudder and send it ashore, with both of which I complied, knowing it was customary at Nagasaki; but I declined dismantling the vessel, on account of the loss of time it would occasion; the spare sails were, however, landed. The vessel was soon after encircled by twenty small boats, fastened to each other, at the distance of a few yards from us; and beyond this cordon lay about sixty larger boats and gun-boats, besides two or three junks, each equalling our own vessel in size, and mounting several small guns. Our floating-guard often amounted to a thousand men; and it was never less than half that number; it was incredible how good a look-out they kept, and how narrowly all our actions were watched; they noted every transaction, and made drawings of all the objects which attracted notice.

"At first our visitors were inconveniently numerous, and came on board continually, but after the first day the guard prohibited all strangers from approaching us. The shore was daily crowded with spectators, a very great majority of whom were females. On the fourth day of our stay in the bay, I was gratified by a visit from two interpreters, one of whom was a perfect master of the Dutch language, and the other was partially acquainted with the Russian. They could also both speak a little English, but all our communication was carried on in Dutch, and through this medium I was enabled to explain my motives for coming to Japan more fully than I had before been able to do, and to give an account of the vessel and crew. Captain Golownin's name being mentioned, they inquired very particularly if he was at Ochotsk. They also asked if the Dutch and English

---

* "We suppose the place whither Capt. Gordon removed his brig was the Bay of Shimoda, in the principality of Izu, on the western side of the entrance of the large estuary going up to the Bay of Yédo."

nations were at peace, and receiving an affirmative answer, the interpreter added, that he understood there had been peace throughout Europe during two years. When I remarked that I hoped permission would be granted for the vessel to return the next year, they replied that the laws of Japan were very hard, and that a similar request made thrice by Russia had been as often negatived. On taking leave, they said, that, if I would allow them, they would do themselves the pleasure of calling on board daily during our stay; to which I said, nothing could gratify me more than their doing so.

"The following day, about noon, we observed the arrival of a *norimor* at the governor's house, and imagined it contained an important personage, from the respect shown to it in passing. At two o'clock the interpreters favored us with a second visit, and inquired the place of birth of each person on board. They were particularly minute in their inquiries respecting my own family and its several members. On producing some vaccine scales, I was happy to find that the people of Japan were aware of the cow-pox, the advantages attending it having been made known by Captain Golowning, and its introduction was ardently desired. Nothing, however, could be done concerning a trial of the vaccine without advice from the superiors. Observing that one person was desirous of having a few grains of our paddy for the purpose of planting it, I brought forward a variety of garden seeds, and requested his acceptance of them; but they refused them, adding that the laws of Japan were so strict regarding intercourse with foreigners, that if we did not obtain permission to trade, they would not be allowed to accept anything from us. While on board, I took another opportunity of saying to them that, even if we were refused permission to return, I hoped we could leave the vaccine matter with them, together with the sheep, pigs, goats, and seeds, all of which had been taken on board for the express purpose of being left wherever they might be of use. I also said it would afford me pleasure to leave with them newspapers and other publications relating to the political state of Europe, as well as a few maps and books on geography, seeing they were particularly anxious to acquire information on these subjects, and moreover were able to understand English books by the aid of the Dutch-English dictionary, which was always brought on board with them.

"Our visitors asked the name of the king of Holland, as well as that of the family to which he belonged. In answer, I informed them that he was formerly prince of Orange, and had returned home after a residence of about twenty years in England. His age, and that of his son, were asked, which led to the mention of the marriage of the latter with a sister of the emperor of Russia. The name of the king of France, and the present abode of Napoleon, were inquired for, and if the English still kept possession of the Cape of Good Hope and of Java. I told them that we did not now own the island; and they wished to know if such had not been the case; to which I replied that we had occupied it and all the other Dutch settlements while the French overran Holland, but had restored them when the Dutch regained their independence. Reference having been made to the return of Napoleon, and to the battle of Waterloo, our visitors were much interested in the account of that engagement, and an enumeration of the different states who were then combined against France. The interpreters remarked that they had heard of the appointment of Captain Golownin to be Governor of Ochotsk this year, and wished to know if their information was correct. From the desire exhibited to ascertain this point, I am inclined to think the Japanese rather dread the neighborhood of one so intimately acquainted with their northern possessions, and natural character and resources. On entering the cabin, the interpreter asked if I had a barometer. I had not one on board to show him, but exhibited the instruments I had, and found them well acquainted with their names and uses. They observed that instruments were made much better in London than elsewhere.

"The next morning a supply of fresh water was brought alongside for the purpose of filling up our water casks, which I looked upon as an omen of our approaching departure. The casks had been gauged previously to this, and I imagined that the Japanese now wished to ascertain more correctly the number of days we had been at sea, particularly as the number of buckets handed on board was counted. Had it not been for this consideration, I would have declined the water, wishing it to be more clearly understood that my only object in visiting Japan was to obtain permission to trade. The persons who accompanied the water were more talkative than usual. They showed me a string of beads used like the rosary as a help to devotion, and read the Chinese characters on a tea-chest. They told me the Japanese names for many articles, and spoke much of the manufactures of London, which place they seemed to consider as the seat of the arts.

"About noon, the interpreters repaired on board, and, after the usual compliments, produced some papers, and said, in an official manner:—'You have applied for permission to trade to Japan; we are desired by the governor of this place to inform you that this permission cannot be granted, as the laws of Japan interdict all foreign intercourse, with the exception of that which exists already at Nagasaki with the Dutch and Chinese, and that the governor, consequently, desires you to sail the first fair wind.' After a little desultory conversation, they remarked, by way of explanation, from another paper, and in a demi-official manner, that in August, 1803, an American ship had arrived at Nagasaki,* and in the following November, an English ship from Calcutta had visited the same port, with views similar to our own; also that, in 1806, the Russian embassy [under Resanoff] had been at Nagasaki, since which time another ship of the same nation had visited that port. A third Russian vessel had also applied at Matsumai, in 1813, all of which had been dismissed, and we, too, could not be admitted; therefore, it was 'better not to return, as we could get nothing by it.' The bluntness of this caution would have displeased me, if I supposed they were aware it

---

* "We accidentally came across what may perhaps be another notice of this visit, in vol. xvi. of the 'Quarterly Review,' p. 71, in a review of the life of Archibald Campbell, a sailor on board the ship *Eclipse*, at Boston,—we say, 'perhaps,' because there is a discrepancy between the dates in the Review and Capt. Gordon. We give the account as we find it, not being aware that a full narrative of the voyage has ever been published:—'On the 16th of June they entered the Bay of Nagasaki, under Russian colors, and were towed to the anchorage by an immense number of boats. A Dutchman came on board, and advised them to haul down the colors, as the Japanese were much displeased with Russia, and it was thought prudent to keep the Russian supercargo out of sight. The American produced his trading articles, but the Japanese told him they wanted nothing from him; and desired to know what had brought him there? He replied, want of water, and fresh provisions; and to prove that this was the case, he ordered several butts to be started, and brought empty on deck! The next day a plentiful supply arrived of fish, hogs, and vegetables, and boats filled with water in large tubs, which the captain emptied on deck, stopping the scuppers, and allowing it to run off at night. For these supplies, thus fraudulently obtained, and wantonly wasted, he knew the Japanese would ask no payment. On the third day, when O'Kean found that nothing was to be gained by way of trade, he got under way; the ship was towed out of the bay by nearly a hundred boats; and, on parting, the Japanese cheered them, waving their hats and hands; but as they stood along the coast, the inhabitants made signs as if to invite them to land:'—the editor thinks, and we agree with him, that Campbell is here mistaken, and that these indications were meant to repel them, as Captain Saris was, with '*Core, core, Cocore, ware*,'—'Get along, you falsehearted fellows.'"

bore a threatening import; but, as it was, it only excited a smile. An offer was made of boats to tow us out of the bay, when ready for sea; and I was asked what flag I would hoist as a signal when ready. Having no other at hand than the ensign and jack, which I did not like to display, surrounded and guarded as we were, I said I would hoist a boat's sail instead of a flag; this appearing strange to them, they asked why I would not hoist the flag, to which I merely replied, that I could not as we were then situated. The name of the governor of Ochotsk was again asked; and so suspicious did the Japanese appear to be of the intention of Russia, respecting their detention of Captain Golownin, that were I to assign any specific cause for not being allowed to trade, independent of the national policy, it would be the wish on the part of the government not to give umbrage to Russia, by conceding to others a favor which had been denied to them; indeed, this was assigned as the true cause of our dismissal in a manner almost official. Expressing a hope that I would be allowed to leave some trifling remembrance with the interpreters, they answered that the laws of the empire were so strict, that they could not receive anything whatever.

"In the afternoon, our arms, ammunition, rudder, &c., were returned on board; and the following morning, having made the signal agreed upon, we were towed out of the bay by about thirty boats. As none of the gun-boats weighed, I hoisted the colors for the first time, as soon as clear of the bay, and when fairly out, dismissed the tow-boats, and our friends who had accompanied them, with three cheers. While leaving, the shore was not only thronged with spectators, but many hundreds came by water from the neighboring coasts, to gratify their curiosity by the sight of the strange vessel. We were scarcely quitted by the tow-boats, when some of these persons approached, and, at length, accepted an invitation to come on board, which they did in such multitudes that the deck was thronged to excess, and I was glad to see a guard-boat pull towards us for the purpose of dispersing the crowd. As soon as the people recognized the boat, they fled in every direction, but many of them quickly returned; and when we pointed out a guard-boat afterwards, some would merely laugh, and say they did not care for them, while others would quit, and give us to understand that they were afraid of being destroyed. In the course of that and the following day, there were not less than 2,000 persons on board, all of whom were eager to barter for trifles. I had the pleasure of obtaining, amongst other things, some little books, and other specimens of their language; and distributed two copies of the Chinese New Testament, together with some Chinese tracts. If inclined to set any value on ideas which can be formed concerning the hearts of men, especially of men accustomed to disguise their feelings, as we are informed the Japanese are, I would confidently say, that our dismissal was regretted by all: this opinion does not arise so much from anything which has been said, as from a remembrance of the eager satisfaction with which everybody used to examine the several articles of my dress, particularly such as were of a fine quality, and the desire very generally expressed of purchasing similar articles on our return.

"The next vessel on our list was an English colonial brig, called the *Cypress*, which sailed from England in August, 1829, for New South Wales, with thirty-two convicts on board, and a military guard, commanded by Lieutenant Carew, in the English navy. While the captain and some of the passengers and crew were ashore at Research Bay, in New Holland, the convicts rose upon the crew, and took possession of the vessel, which they carried to New Zealand, and there landed the soldiers, passengers, and such of the convicts as desired to be put on shore. The remainder, eighteen in number, sailed from thence to the Sandwich Islands, where nine more were left, and the other nine started for Japan. They were fired upon by the Japanese, and proceeded on to Canton, but at the 'Ten Thousand Islands,' four of the mutineers quitted her; and when off Formosa, she sank in consequence of making water, owing to the injury she had sustained from being fired upon by the Japanese, and the five remaining men reached Canton in the long-boat. They were here examined by the select committee in consequence of their extraordinary relations, and sent to England in one of the Company's ships, consigned to the care of the Admiralty Board, by whom they were tried and convicted. This is all we know of the visit of the *Cypress*, which is taken from the 'United Service Journal,' for November, 1830, and although bearing suspicious marks, and resting only upon the statements of mutineers and convicts, is still worthy of notice. The unexplained part of the story is, that we do not know any of the group called the 'Ten Thousand Islands.' We wish, however, that they had told us where they had been fired upon; for when the *Morrison* was in the Bay of Kagosima, the Japanese on board of her were told that, two or three years before, a vessel had touched at Tanega Isle, lying off the mouth of the bay, from which the foreigners had debarked, and violently carried off some cattle; and that these foreigners had been carried to Nagasaki; the people on the main land, too, supposed the *Morrison* to be that vessel returned. These may, from first to last, be idle stories; but some unknown transactions, it appears to us, of a flagrant nature, must have taken place on that coast, to have caused the Japanese to treat two vessels in a manner so diametrically opposite as they did the *Brothers* and the *Morrison*."

The reader who would further pursue this part of the subject may consult, with advantage, the account of Resanoff's Embassy to Japan, in 1804; Mr. Rundall's Memorials, and various articles in the "Naval Magazine," with others in the "Chinese Repository."

CHINESE INTERCOURSE AND TRADE.

The subjects of the Celestial Empire live in as prisoned a state as the Dutch. "The Chinese," says Thunberg, "have almost from time immemorial traded to Japan, and are the only people in Asia who have engaged in the trade, or are allowed to visit the empire. Formerly, they proceeded to Osacca harbor, although it is very dangerous, on account of rocks and shoals. The Portuguese showed them the way to Nagasaki. At first the annual number of their vessels amounted to upwards of one hundred. The liberty which they then enjoyed is at present greatly contracted, since they have been suspected by the Japanese of favoring the Catholic missionaries in China, and have made attempts to introduce into Japan Catholic books printed in China. They are therefore as much suspected and as hardly used as the Dutch. They are also shut up in a small island, and strictly searched whenever they go in or come out.

"When a vessel arrives from China, all the crew are brought on shore, and all charge of the vessel is taken from them till such time as everything is ready for their departure; consequently, the Japanese unload it entirely, and afterwards bring the vessel on shore, where, at low water, it is quite dry. The next year it is loaded with other goods.

"The Chinese are not suffered to go to the Imperial Court, which saves them considerable sums in presents and expenses. They are allowed to trade for twice as large a sum as that granted to the Dutch; but as their voyages are neither so long nor so dangerous, they are obliged to contribute more largely to the town of Nagasaki, and therefore pay more, as far even as sixty per cent. *fanndgin*, or flower-money.

"Their merchandise is sold at three different times in the year, and is brought in seventy junks. The first fair takes place in the spring, for the cargoes of twenty vessels; the second in the summer, for the cargoes of thirty vessels; and the third in autumn, for the cargoes of the remaining twenty. Should any more vessels arrive within the year, they are obliged to return without being allowed to unload the least article. Although their voyages are less expensive than the Dutch, and they are not under the necessity of sending an ambassador to the emperor, nor is any director put over their commerce, but interpreters, a guard, and supervisors are appointed to them, the same as the Dutch; yet, on account of the greater value per cent. deducted from their merchandise, their profits are less than those of the Dutch; and as they are no longer allowed to carry away any specie, they are obliged to purchase Japanese commodities for exportation, such as copper, lackered ware, etc., many of which are produced in their own country.

"When their vessels are loaded, and ready for sailing, they are conducted by a number of Japanese guard-ships, not only out of the harbor, but likewise a great way out to sea, in order to prevent their disposing to the smugglers of any of the unsold wares they may have been obliged to carry back."

Dr. Ainslie, who visited the port of Nagasaki in 1814, states, that the Chinese trade is limited to ten junks annually, which are fitted out from the province of Nankin, bringing principally sugar, with other trifling articles, and a large quantity of English woollens. In return, 1,000 peculs of bar copper are allotted to each junk; the remainder of the cargo consists of lackered ware, dried fish, whale-oil, etc. He adds, that the Chinese are treated in Japan with great indignity; and that their intercourse is tolerated chiefly on account of certain drugs which are produced in China, and to which the Japanese are attached.

B.

GEOGRAPHY.

One of the earliest attempts to describe in English the remote and very little known country was made by quaint old Peter Heylyn, who wrote in the time of James I., and dedicated his book to Charles Prince of Wales. I quote from the third edition, printed at Oxford in 1639.

"Japan, situated over against Canton in China, on the east, and the straights of Anian, south, is in length 600 miles; in breadth in some places 90; in others, 30 only. The soyle, and the people participate much of the nature of China, but that the Japonites are more superstitious; as washing their children as soone as borne, in rivers; putting off their shooes before they enter into the dining chamber. Perhaps these may be the Ilanders, who, in meere opposition to the Chinoys, put off their shooes in salutation; because they of China put off their hats. To whom our factious Puritans are fitly compared; who oppose themselves against the Papists in things decent and allowable, though this opposition be accompanied with many grosse and ridiculous absurdities.

"The chiefe cities of this island are—1, Okacaia; 2, Bunguin; 3, Fianocanca; 4, Meacum, which once contained in circuit twenty-one miles, though now not halfe so big; 5, Coia; 6, Bandum, which is said to be an University bigger than Paris. Here are in this island sixty-six kings, some of which are so rich, that their houses are covered with gold. The chiefest of these kingdomes is called the kingdome of Tenze, which of itselfe comprehendeth five of these petty realmes, all lying about Meacum, and doth now lord it over fifty of these sixty-six kingdomes; so that the K. of Tenza writeth himselfe Soveraigne Lord of Japan. This augmentation of the Tenzean kingdome came wholly by the valor of Faxiba, the father of Taicosama, now living; who, the better to assure himself of his new conquest, transported the vanquished kings from one country to another; to the end that being removed out of their commands, and placed among strange subjects, they should remaine weake, and without meanes to revolt against him; a politicke and mercifull course. What the revenues of this king are we cannot certainly tell; onely wee may guesse them to be very great, in that he hath two millions of gold for the yearely rent of that rice, which is gathered out of those possessions, which he hath reserved for his demeasnes. This Iland was discovered by Antonia Monta, a Portugal, & his fellowes, An. 1542. It is much frequented by the Jesuites, of whom 200 are said to live here; Xavier, one of Ignatius' first companions, leading the way."

The error of believing that the whole empire of Japan consisted of one great island appears to have been very commonly entertained for a great length of time.

The following quite recent geographical sketch is extracted from that valuable work the *Chinese Repository* published at Canton:

"Japan is a mountainous and hilly country, and its coasts are lined with steep rocks. Niphon is traversed, in its whole length, by a chain almost of uniform elevation, and in many places crowned with peaks covered with perpetual snow. This chain divides the streams which flow to the south and east, and which fall into the Pacific Ocean, from those which pursue a northerly course to the sea of Japan. Very many of the mountains of the country are volcanic. A full and, as far as we know, accurate account of these was published by Klaproth, in the 'Asiatic Journal,' for January, 1831. The volcanic chain, of which the first southern links are found in the island of Formosa, extends by the way of the Loo Choo islands to Japan, and thence along the Kurila Archipelago, as far as Kamtschatka. On the great island of Kewsew, in the department of Fiseu, and south-east from Nagasaki, is the Oün-zew-ga-da, or 'high mountain of warm springs,' which has several craters. In the early part of the year 1793, the summit of the mountain sunk entirely down; torrents of boiling water issued from all the parts of the deep cavity, which was thus formed, and the vapor arose like thick smoke. Three weeks afterwards there was an eruption of the volcano Bivo-no-kubi, about half a league from the summit; the flames rose to a vast height; the lava which flowed out extended itself with great rapidity, and, in a few days, the whole country was in flames for several miles around. A month after this there was a horrible earthquake throughout the whole island, which was principally felt in the district of Simabara; the shocks were repeated several times, and the whole ended by a terrible eruption of Miyiyama. In the interior of Figo is the volcano Aso, which emits stones and flames, the latter of a blue, yellow, and red color. Satsuma, which is the southernmost department of Kewsew, is entirely volcanic, and impregnated with sulphur. Eruptions there are frequent. In 764 of our era, three new islands arose out of the sea; they are now inhabited. At the southern extremity of Satsuma is Ivoc Sima, or 'Sulphur Island,' which burns incessantly.

"The most memorable volcanic phenomena, in Japan, occurred in the year 285, B. C., when an immense land-lapse formed, in a single night, the great lake Mitsu. At the very time when this took place, Foosi, the highest mountain in Japan, rose from the surface of the earth. Foosi is an enormous pyramid, covered with perpetual snow, situated in the department of Suruga, and near the borders of that of Kaï. It is the largest and most active volcano in Japan. There was an eruption of it in 799, A. D., which lasted thirty-four days; it was frightful; the ashes covered the whole base of the mountain, and the streams of water in the vicinity assumed a red hue. The eruption in the year 800 was without earthquakes, which preceded those in 863 and 864. The latter was most violent; on all sides of the mountain the flames rose high, and were accompanied with the most frightful reports of thunder. Three several shocks of earthquakes were felt, and the mountain was on fire for ten days, till at length its lower part burst; the explosion was tremendous; the devastation extended over a space of thirty leagues, and the lava ran to a distance of three or four leagues, principally towards the frontiers of Kaï.

"Again, 1707, on the night of the 23rd day of the 11th moon, two violent shocks of an earthquake were felt; Mount Foosi opened, vomited flames, and hurled cinders to the distance of ten leagues. Next day the eruption ceased, but it was revived with greater violence on the 25th and 26th. Enormous masses of rock, sand reddened by heat, and an immense quantity of ashes, covered all the neighboring plateau. The ashes were driven to a great distance, and fell several inches thick at Jeddo.

"Another volcano, called the Sirayama, 'white mountain,' and covered with perpetual snow, is situated in the department of Kaga, about a degree and a half north of Miyako. Its most remarkable eruptions took place in 1239 and 1554. Another, and a very active volcano, is Asama, which is situated in Sinano, near the centre of Niphon. It is very high, burning from midway to the crest, and throws out an extremely dense smoke. It vomits flames and stones, and frequently covers the neighboring country with ashes. One of its last eruptions was that of 1783, which was preceded by an alarming earthquake. A vast number of villages were swallowed up by the earth, or burnt and overwhelmed by the lava. The number of persons who perished by this disaster it is impossible to determine; the devastation was incalculable. Yake, in the department of Mooto, is the most northern volcano in Japan. The lofty mountains between Mooto and Dewa likewise contain several volcanoes.

"There are among the volcanic mountains of Japan a vast number of warm springs. Many of these springs are found in Sinano. In the department of Yetsingo, situated to the north of Sinano, there is, near the village of Nueru-gawaumra, a well abounding with naphtha, which the inhabitants burn in their lamps. In the district of Gazivara there is a spot, the stony soil of which exhales inflammable gas. The natives make use of this gas, by running a pipe into the earth, and lighting the end like a torch.

"Klaproth, in concluding his paper on the subject, remarks that six of the volcanoes of Japan, and four of the mountains from whence issue warm springs, are, according to the Japanese, the ten hells of the country. Of the rivers and lakes of Japan we can say but little. None are remarkable for their size. The rivers seem to be numerous, and most of them rapid in their course. The river of Yodo has already been sufficiently described. The Tenrio-gawa, or river of the heavenly dragon, takes its rise in Sinano, and passing through Tootami, disembogues itself by three mouths into the sea.

"The sources of the Ara are in the mountainous country between Kootsuke and Musai. It flows through the latter, and soon separates into two branches; the western, receiving the name of Toda, falls in the Gulf of Jeddo, to the eastward of the city of that name, which is watered by branches and canals from the Toda.

"Upon one of these canals is the celebrated *Niphon-bas*, or bridge of Japan, from whence distances are computed throughout the empire. Over some of the rivers bridges have been built; there are others which are passed by boats; others are forded. The lake Mistu, or Oïts, already noticed as the largest in the empire, is only about seventy English miles long, and twenty-two broad.

"The climate of Japan is healthful. In winter the north and north-west winds are exceedingly sharp, and bring with them an intense frost. The summer heat is frequently alleviated by sea breezes; and throughout the whole year it rains frequently: the most abundant rains are in June and July, and hence they are called the 'water months.' In winter, snow frequently falls, and sometimes lies several days, even in the southern part of the empire. Thunder is often heard during the hot season; and storms, hurricanes, and earthquakes are frequent. Golownin, who, it is true, never visited Niphon, gives Japan a gloomy aspect, and thinks it truly an empire of fogs. 'In the summer months,' he says, 'the fog often lasts three or four days without interruption, and there seldom passes a day in which it is not, for some hours, gloomy, rainy, or foggy. These fogs and this gloomy weather make the air cold and damp, and hinder the beams of the sun from producing so much effect as in other countries which enjoy a clear sky."

This information, added to that which has been given in the body of the book, will, we trust, enable the reader to form a tolerably clear notion of the country and climate.

C.

"On the first arrival of the Dutch, the Japanese were allowed to visit foreign countries. Their ships, though built on the plan of the Chinese junks, boldly defied the fury of tempests. Their merchants were scattered over the principal countries of India; they were not deficient either in expert mariners or adventurous traders. In a country where the lower classes cannot gain a subsistence but by assiduous labor, thousands of Japanese were disposed to seek their fortune abroad, not so much by the prospect of gain, as by the certainty of being enabled to gratify their curiosity with the sight of numberless objects that were wholly unknown to them.

"This state of things formed bold and experienced sailors, and at the same time soldiers, not surpassed in bravery by those of the most warlike nations of India.

"The Japanese, accustomed from their infancy to hear the accounts of the heroic achievements of their ancestors, to receive at that early age their first instruction in those books which record their exploits, and to imbibe, as it were, with their mother's milk, the intoxicating love of glory, made the art of war their favorite study. Such an education has, in all ages, trained up heroes: it excited in the Japanese that pride which is noticed by all the whole nation."*

"The Japanese have a cycle of sixty years like that of the Chinese, formed by a combination of words of two series. The series of ten is formed of the names of the elements, of which the Japanese reckon five, doubled by the addition of the masculine and feminine endings, *je* and *to*.

1. Kino-je, 2. Kino-to,	wood.	7. Kauno-je 8. Kauno-to,	metal.
3. Fino-je, 4. Fino-to,	fire.	9. Midsno-je, 10. Midsno-to,	water.
5. Tsutsno-je, 6. Tsutsno-to,	earth.		

The series of twelve is made up of the signs of the Zodiac.

---

* Titsingh.

1. Ne, rat	7. Ooura, horse.
2. Oos, ox.	8. Tsitsuse, sheep.
3. Torra, tiger.	9. Sar, ape.
4. Ov, hare.	10. Torri, hen.
5. Tats, dragon.	11. In, dog.
6. Mi, serpent.	12. Y, hog.*

"By substituting these words for the letters in the cycle, under the head of China, the Japanese names are found. Thus, the first year of a cycle is called *kino-je-ne*, the thirty-fifth, *tsutsno-je-in*, and so on. The cycles coincide with those of the Chinese; but a name is given to them instead of numbering them. Their years begin in February, and are luni-solar, of twelve and thirteen months, with the intercalation as before mentioned, under the head of China. The first cycle is said to begin 660 B. C.; but this cannot be correct, unless some alteration has taken place, as the Chinese cycle then began 657 B. C. We know, however, too little of Japan to pronounce positively respecting it, but thus far it is certain, that the cycle now coincides with that of the Chinese."

The valuable paper from which this extract is taken is the production of our valued friend, Edwin Norris, Esq., of the Foreign Office and Royal Asiatic Society. The paper appeared in Mr. Charles Knight's most useful publication, the "Companion to the Almanac," in the year 1830. As its learned author shuns celebrity with more care than that with which other men hunt after it, he put no name to his production, and never took any pains to claim it as his own. How frequently it has been used without any acknowledgment by other writers, or how many have claimed its substance as their own, we are not, at this moment, prepared to say. A curious controversy, in which our friend took no part, established the fact of his authorship good twenty years after the paper had been written. See the "Gentleman's Magazine," 1850.

The reader must look at the Chinese cycle, in order to understand the Japanese. But we would heartily recommend him to study the whole of Mr. Norris's very remarkable paper, the full title of which is, "The Eras of Ancient and Modern Times, and of various Countries, explained, with a view to the comparison of their respective dates."

The author of it has more varied knowledge and acquirements, and

* The Tartar names for these twelve signs are:—1. Mouse. 2. Ox. 3. Leopard. 4. Hare. 5. Crocodile. 6. Serpent. 7. Horse. 8. Sheep. 9. Ape. 10. Hen. 11. Dog. 12. Hog.

is more ready and liberal in imparting them to others, than any other man with whom it has ever been our lot to be acquainted with. As a philologist and etchnologist, his claims to eminence are now universally allowed. Yet we should hardly use the word "claims," for, in the modesty of his nature, he rarely *claims* anything.

FIRES.

M. Doweff thus describes the mighty conflagration he witnessed at the capital:—

"On April 22nd, 1806, at about ten in the morning, we heard that a fire had broken out about two leagues from our lodging. We paid little attention to the intelligence, the inhabitants of Jeddo being so well practised in the art of putting out fires. In fine weather there is generally a fire every night, and as this happens seldomer in rainy weather, it is usual with the citizens to wish one another joy of a good wet evening. In this instance, however, the fire made rapid approaches, and towards three in the afternoon the flames, excited by a strong breeze, broke out in four different places in our neighborhood. We had, since one o'clock, employed ourselves in packing up our effects, so that we were able to take immediate flight. The danger was pressing. On issuing into the street, we saw everything in a blaze. There was great danger in endeavoring to escape before the wind, and in the same direction with the fire; we therefore took a slanting direction through a street already burning, and thus succeeded, by following the flames, in gaining an open field. It was studded all over with the standards of princes, whose palaces had been destroyed, and whose wives and children had fled thither for refuge. We followed their example, and marked out a spot with our Dutch flags, which we had used on our journey. We had now a full view of the fire, and never have I seen anything so terrific. The terrors of this ocean of flame were enhanced by the heart-rending cries of the fugitive women and children."

This conflagration, after raging for twelve hours, was extinguished by rain. The number of houses consumed must have been enormous. Fifty-seven palaces of princes were destroyed, and 1,200 persons either burned to death or drowned. The Nipon Bas, a famous bridge, broke down under the weight of the flying multitude.

TEA.

"The poorer sort of people, particularly in the province of Narâ, sometimes boil their rice, which is the main sustenance of the natives, in the infusion or decoction of the tea, by which means they say it becomes more nourishing and filling, insomuch that one portion of rice thus prepared, will go as far with them as three portions if it were boiled only in common water. I must not forget to mention another external use of the tea, after it has grown too old and hath lost too much of its virtues, to be taken inwardly. It is then made use of for dyeing of silk-stuffs, to which it gives a brown or chesnut color. For this purpose vast quantities of the leaves are sent almost every year from China to Gusarattam (or Suratta)."

DOG SUPERSTITION.

A very curious specimen of this superstition has been traced in India among the Pársis, who are also of the Mongol race. With these people a dead body cannot be buried or removed, unless a dog be brought in to look upon it.

The "Sag-did," that is, *dog-gaze*, is the ceremony of bringing a dog to look upon the dead body; for, according to some superstitious notions of the Pársis, evil spirits are driven away by the presence of the dog, and the fate of the deceased's soul may be, they think, guessed at, by the manner in which he regards the corpse. This usage they do not willingly make known.*

CIVILIZATION.—VON SIEBOLD.

It is a fact, now universally acknowledged, that every nation that does not advance in civilization must inevitably retrocede. No people can be stationary. There is abundant evidence to prove this retrocession in the Chinese, who are very far from being so civilized now as they were in the thirteenth century, and the days of Marco Polo. Some writers have supposed that the Japanese also must have declined; but the hypothesis does not appear to be made out by the books and the other authorities which we have consulted.

A gentleman who has taken much interest in this work, and who is well acquainted with Von Siebold, assures us that the impression on that able writer's mind is that there has been rather progress than decline in the arts and civilization of Japan.

---

*"Illustrations of the Languages called Zend and Pahlavi," by John Romer, Esq., late Member of Council at Bombay, M.R.A.S.; Journal of the Royal Asiatic Socitey, vol. iv. p. 352.

It is with great pleasure that we avail ourselves of this opportunity of doing some little justice to a writer of great merit, who has been rather severely censured for the mournful consequences of his efforts to increase our knowledge of Japan. Von Siebold's behavior was most manly on that occasion, and admiration of his courage, and of his wish to take all the blame on himself, contributed, in a great degree, towards inducing the Japanese government to pardon the delinquents who supplied him with the duplicates of the government survey. It appears that one or two of his Japanese friends ripped themselves up when he (Von Siebold) was first imprisoned, but that afterwards nobody suffered death on his account.

We are indebted to the same kind informant for the two following facts:—

Dr. Von Siebold's private museum is much better worth seeing—for Japanese objects—than the public museum at the Hague.

His own villa, outside Leyden, is like a Japanese house, being made up of odds and ends brought from Japan, and the garden being full of Japanese shrubs and plants.

CHARACTER--STEEL.

The following is an extract from the old voyager Struys:—"The Japaneezes are in general a very hardy people, and can endure any extremity of heat or cold, hunger or thirst, to a miracle. This they seem to come to by a hardy usage when young; for they always bathe their infants in cold weather in rivers, and sometimes plunge them over head and ears in snow. They are excellent warriors, and are well acquainted with fire-arms; as also with the long-bow and javelin. They are grown famous in all the East, for expert armorers, and temper steel better than the Chineezes, which far exceed the Europeans. Their swords are so well tempered that I have struck with one through an iron pin, of half an inch thick, without the least token of damage to the edge. They follow hunting much, and prefer venison before any other dainty whatever. In their entertainments they are very open and liberal, and use tea for a caress, which is far better than that which is exported abroad, and prepared after a different manner; but they refuse to impart it to Christians, which I held somewhat strange, in regard that the more it is used in other countries, the greater is their advantage, seeing that they have better in this island than anywhere else in the world."

MILITARY.

In one of his letters, honest William Adams gives the following details. The place he speaks of is Fushini, a large city not far from Bosaca. "The nine-and-twentieth, at night, we found here a garrison of three thousand soldiers, maintained by the emperor, to keep Miaco and Ozaco in subjection. The garrison is shifted every three years, which change happened to be at our being there, so that we saw the old bands march away, and the new enter, in most soldier-like manner, marching five abreast, and to every ten files an officer which is called a captain of fifty, who kept them continually in very good order. First their shot, viz., calieners (for musket they had none, neither will they use any), then followed pikes, next swords, or cannons and targets, then bows and arrows, next those weapons resembling a Welsh hook, called *waggadashes*, then calieners again, and so as formerly, without any ensign or colors; neither had they any guns or musical instruments for war. The first file of the cannons and targets had silver scabbards to these cattans, and the last file, which was next to the captain, had their scabbards of gold. The companies consist of divers numbers, some five hundred, some three hundred, some one hundred and fifty men. In the midst of every company were three horses very richly trapped, and furnished with saddles, well set out, some covered with costly furs, some with velvet, some with stamped broad cloth; every horse had three slaves to attend him, led with silken halters, their eyes covered with leather covers. After every troop followed the captain on horseback; his bed and other necessaries were laid upon his own horse, equally peased [poised] on either side. Over the same was spread a covering of redde felt of China, whereupon the captain did sit cross-legged, as if he had sate betwixt a couple of panniers; and for those that were ancient or otherwise weak-back, they had a staff artificially fixed upon the pannel, that the rider might rest himself, and lean backward against it, as if he were sitting in a chair. The captain-general of this garrison we had met two days after we met his first troop, (having still in the meantime met with some of the companies as we passed along, sometimes one league, sometimes two leagues distant one from another). He marched in very great state, beyond that the others did (for the second troop was more richly set out in their arms than the first; and the third, than the second; and so still every one better than other, until it came unto this the last and best of all). He hunted and hawked all the way, having his own hounds and hawks along with him, the hawks being hooded and lured as ours are. His horses for his own sadle being six in number, richly trapped. Their horses are not tall, but of the size of our middling nags, short and well trust, small-headed and very full of mettle, in my opinion far excelling the Spanish jennet in pride and stomach. He had his own pallankin carried before him, the inside crimson velvet, and six men appointed to carry it, two at a time.

"Such good order was taken for the passing and providing for of these three thousand soldiers, that no man either travelling or inhabiting upon the way where they lodged, was any way injured by them, but chiefly entertained them as other their guests, because they paid for what they took, as all men did; every town and village upon the way being well fitted with cooks and victualling-houses, where they might at an instant have what they needed, and diet themselves from a penny English a meal, to two shillings a meal."

SLAVERY.

Slavery in the Empire of Japan is different from that prevailing in the western hemisphere. The person of a party, male or female, may be sold under certain circumstances, or a party may sell his or her service for a stipulated period for a sum of money which may be agreed on, and which must be paid down at once in the gross. On the expiration of the stipulated period, the party is free to dispose of his or her person again. Masters have power over the lives of their slaves, if they commit offences which by the law are punishable with death; but if a man should kill his slave for any cause that the law does not deem worthy of death, the offender is adjudged guilty of murder, and subjected to the penalty of the crime.*

DIFFUSION OF EDUCATION.

"The Japanese are extremely fond of reading; even the common soldiers when on duty are continually engaged with books. This passion for literature, however, proved somewhat inconvenient to us, as they always read aloud, in a tone of voice resembling singing; much in the same style in which the psalms are read at funerals in Russia. Before we became accustomed to this, we were unable to enjoy a moment's rest during the night. The history of their native country,

---

*"Memorials of the Empire of Japan." Edited, with notes, by Thomas Rundall. Published by the Hakluyt Society.

the contests which have arisen among themselves, and the wars in which they have been engaged with neighboring nations, form the subjects of their favorite books, which are all printed in Japan. They do not use metal types, but print with plates cut out of pieces of hard wood."*

CURRIERS.

In India, the arts of the currier, cordwainer, etc., are practised only by the despised aborigines—a large branch of the unhappy Pariahs. They are excluded from all towns and villages, and can keep only dogs and asses. Nearly every conceivable degradation is put upon these Indian aborigines; and yet, according to our friend General Briggs and other excellent authorities, they are the honestest fellows in the country, most faithful servants, and ready and brave soldiers. The best part of our native forces, in the campaign of Seringapatam, was composed of them. If the British government could only do away with those intolerable distinctions of "right and left hand castes," how great a blessing would be conferred on these ancient, primitive people? Since the commencement of the present century, many efforts have been made by English officers and administrators, but there yet remains much to be done.

VARNISH.

Captain Golownin gives the following short account:—

"The Japanese varnish is celebrated in Europe. The tree which produces this juice, grows in such abundance, that the Japanese lacker all their table utensils, boxes, saddles, bows, arrows, spears, sheaths, cartouch-boxes, tobacco-boxes; in their houses, the walls and screens, and in short, every trifle that they wish to ornament. We had the pleasure to see a master-piece in varnishing. It was a bottle-case belonging to the governor, who sent it for us to look at. The polish on it was so beautiful, that we could see our faces in it as in a mirror. The natural color of this juice is white, but it assumes any color by being mixed with it. The best varnish in Japan is usually black or red, and almost everything is so varnished; but we saw also green, yellow, blue, and other varnish. In varnishing, they also imitate marble. The juice, when fresh, is poisonous, and very injurious to those who collect it, for which reason they employ various precau-

* Golownin. "Memoirs of Captivity," etc.

tions; but after it has stood for some time in the open air, it loses its poisonous quality. The varnished utensils may be used without danger. The Japanese are so clever in varnishing, that you may pour hot water into a vessel, and drink it, without perceiving the slightest smell of the paint. This, however, is true only with respect to vessels of the best workmanship; in others, you smell the paint, even if warm water is poured into them."*

TOBACCO-SMOKING.

Golownin, though a Russian and a sailor, appears to have had no love for "the weed." Our sapient King James I. has hardly spoken more disparagingly of it.

"Tobacco is an article which is equally indispensable to the Japanese. The Catholic missionaries were the first who introduced this plant, and taught them its use. From them, too, the Japanese received its name, and still call it tobaco, or tobago. It is astonishing how the use of this *worthless herb* should have spread, in so short a time, over the whole earth, as it is entirely without taste, without any agreeable smell, without use to the health, and a mere amusement for idle people! Our interpreter Teske, one of the most sensible of our Japanese acquaintances, was himself a great smoker; but often said, that the Christian priests had not done the Japanese so much injury by the introduction of their faith, which only produced among them internal commotions and civil wars, as by the introduction of tobacco; for the former was a transitory, long forgotten evil, but the latter diverted, and probably would do for centuries to come, large tracts of land and a number of hands from the production of useful and necessary articles, which are now dear, but might otherwise be cheaper. Besides, the workmen could not then so often interrupt their labor, but now they were continually resting themselves in order to smoke their pipes.

"I do not know how many species of this plant there are in nature, nor how many of them the Japanese have; but I saw various kinds of prepared tobacco among them—from the most pleasant to the most disgusting. They cut both the good and the bad tobacco very small, as the Chinese do. In the manufacture of the better sort, they use sagi to moisten it, and sell it in papers which weigh about a Russian pound. The Japanese consider the tobacco from Sasma as the best, then that from Nagasaki, Sinday, &c. The worst comes from the

---

* Recollections of Japan.

province of Tgyngaru; it is strong, of a black color, and has a disgusting taste and smell. The tobacco from Sasma is, indeed, also strong, but it has an agreeable taste and smell, and is of a bright yellow color. The tobacco from Nagasaki is very weak in taste and smell, perhaps the best, and of a bright brown color. The tobacco from Sinday is very good, and was always given us to smoke. The Japanese manufacture tobacco so well, that though I was before no friend to smoking, and even when I was at Jamaica, could but seldom persuade myself to smoke an Havannah cigar, yet I smoked the Japanese tobacco very frequently, and with great pleasure. Snuff is not used in Japan. But enough of this plant. I could, indeed, for the pleasure of gentlemen who love smoking, write some sheets more on the article tobacco, for there was nothing concerning which we had such frequent opportunities to converse with the Japanese. The literati, the interpreters, and guards, all smoked; and used, too, different kinds of tobacco, according to their respective taste or ability. Out of politeness, they frequently offered us their tobacco, and mentioned its name. In this manner a conversation usually began upon tobacco, which often lasted for hours together. We often had an opportunity to speak of other more important things, and besides, the Japanese did not all like to converse upon them."*

But there is much worse smoking than tobacco-smoking. There is reason to fear that the Japanese are as much addicted to the opium pipe as either the Chinese or the Malays, the Siamese or the people of Annam. This vile habit is destructive of health, both mental and bodily.

COMMERCE.—MANNER IN WHICH THE DUTCH ARE TREATED.—SMUGGLING, ETC.

The following details, as given by Dr. Thunberg, will be found interesting, and may possibly be found useful at this moment, when efforts are making to open the trade with these extraordinary people. Though written so many years ago, there is reason to believe that the doctor's notes are still in the main correctly descriptive.

"On anchoring at the entrance of the harbor, all the prayer-books and bibles belonging to the sailors were collected, and put into a chest which was nailed down. This chest was afterwards left under the care of the Japanese till the time of our departure, when every one

* Recollections of Japan.

received his book again. This is done with a view to prevent the introduction of Christian or Roman Catholic books into the country.

"A muster-roll of the ship's company, consisting of about 110 men and 34 slaves, was made out, mentioning the age of every individual, which roll was given to the Japanese. The birth-place of each individual was not marked in the list, as they were all supposed to be Dutchmen, although many of them were Swedes, Danes, Germans, Portuguese, and Spaniards. According to this muster-roll, the whole ship's company is mustered immediately on the arrival of the Japanese, and afterwards every morning and evening of such days as the ship is either discharging or taking in her cargo, and when there is any intercourse between the ship and the factory. By these precautions the Japanese are assured that no one can either get away without their knowledge, or remain in the factory without their leave.

"As soon as we had anchored in the harbor, and saluted the town of Nagasaki, there came immediately on board two Japanese superior officers (banjoses), and some subaltern officers, as also the interpreters and their attendants. The business of these banjoses was, during the whole time of our ships lying in the road, to take care that all the wares, and the people that went on shore, or came on board, were strictly searched; to receive orders from the governor of the town; to sign all passports and papers which accompanied the merchandise, people, etc.

"After having several times fired our cannon, in saluting the imperial guards, and on the arrival and departure of the Dutch principal officers, we were obliged to commit to the care of the Japanese the remainder of our powder, as also our ball, our weapons, and the above-mentioned chest-full of books. For this purpose were delivered in a certain quantity of powder, six barrels full of ball, six muskets, and six bayonets, which we made them believe were all the ammunition we had remaining. All these articles are put into a storehouse, till the ship leaves the road, when they are faithfully restored by the Japanese. They have, of late years, had the sense to leave the rudders of our ships untouched, and the sails and cannon on board. They were, likewise, weary of the trouble with which the fetching them back was attended, and which was by no means inconsiderable.

"The Japanese having thus, as they suppose, entirely disarmed us, the next thing they have in hand is to muster the men, which is done every day on board, both morning and evening, when the vessel is discharging or taking in her lading. Each time the number of men that are gone on shore is set down very accurately, as well as the number of the sick, and the number of those that remain on board.

"On all those days, when anything is carried on board, or taken out of the ship, the banjoses, the interpreters, clerks, and searchers, are on board till the evening, when they all go on shore together, and leave the Europeans on board to themselves. On such occasions, the flag on board the ship is always hoisted, as well as that on the factory; and when two ships arrive here safe, business is transacted on board one or the other of them, by turns, every day. The ship's long-boat and pinnace were also taken into the care of the Japanese, from going to it, and trafficking, especially under cover of the night; and when no Japanese officers are on board, several large guard-vessels are placed round the ship, and at some distance from it; and besides this, there are several small boats ordered to row every hour in the night round the ship, and very near it.

"A great number of laborers were ordered to attend to the discharge and loading of the boats, and bringing them to and from the ship, others being set as inspectors over them. The Dutch formerly took the liberty to punish and correct with blows these day-laborers, who were of the lowest class of people; but, at present, this procedure is absolutely, and under the severest penalties, forbidden by the government, as bringing a disgrace upon the nation.

"When a European goes to or from the ship, either with or without any baggage, an officer is always attending with a permit, on which his name is written, his watch marked down, &c.

"On those days when there is nothing done towards discharging or loading a ship, no Japanese officers, nor any other Japanese, come on board, neither do any of the Dutch themselves go to or from the ship on such days. The gate of the island, also, towards the water side, is locked at this time. Should an urgent occasion require any of the officers to come on board of the ship, such as the captain or the surgeon—which is signified by the hoisting of a flag—in such case leave must be first obtained from the governor of the town; and should this be granted, still the gate towards the sea-shore is not opened, but the person to whom leave is granted, is conducted by interpreters and officers through a small part of the town to a little bridge, from which he is taken on board in a boat, after having gone through the strictest search. The banjoses and interpreters, who accompany him, do not, however, go on board the ship, but wait in their boats till he has transacted his business on board, from whence he is conducted back to the factory.

"Custom-houses are not known, either in the interior of the country or on its coasts, and no customs are demanded on imports or exports of goods, either from strangers or natives. But, that no prohibited goods may be smuggled into the country, so close a watch is kept, and all persons that arrive, as well as merchandise, are so strictly searched, that the hundred eyes of Argus might be said to be employed on this occasion. When any European goes ashore, he is first searched on board, and afterwards as soon as he comes on shore. Both these searchers are very strict; so that not only travellers' pockets are turned inside out, but the officers' hands pass along their bodies and thighs. All the Japanese that go on board of ship, are in like manner searched, excepting only the superior orders of banjoses. All articles exported or imported undergo a similar search, first on board the ship, and afterwards in the factory, except large chests, which are emptied in the factory, and are so narrowly examined, that they even sound the boards, suspecting them to be hollow. The beds are frequently ripped open, and the feathers turned over. Iron spikes are thrust into the butter-tubs and jars of sweetmeats. In the cheese a square hole is cut, in which part a thick-pointed wire is thrust into it towards every side. Nay, their suspicion went even so far as to induce them to take an egg or two from among those we had brought from Bavaria, and break them. The same severe conduct is observed when any goes from the factory to the ship, or into the town of Nagasaki, and from thence to the island of Dezima. Every one that passes must take his watch out of his pocket, and show it to the officers, who always mark it down whenever it is carried in or out. Sometimes, too, strangers are searched. Neither money nor coin must, by any means, be brought in by private persons; but they are laid by, and taken care of till the owner's departure. No letters to be sent to or from the ship sealed; and if they are, they are opened, and sometimes, as well as other manuscripts, must be read by the interpreters. Religious books, especially if they are adorned with cuts, are very dangerous to import; but the Europeans are otherwise suffered to carry in a great number of books for their own use; and the search was the less strict in this respect, as they looked into a few of them only. Latin, French, Swedish, and German books and manuscripts pass the more easily, as the interpreters do not understand them. Arms, it is true, are not allowed to be carried into the country; nevertheless, we are as yet suffered to take our swords with us.

"The Dutch themselves are the occasion of these over-rigorous searches, the strictness of which has been augmented on several different occasions, till it has arrived at its present height. Numerous artifices have been applied to the purpose of bringing goods into the factory by stealth; and the interpreters, who heretofore had never been searched, used to carry contraband goods by degrees, and in small parcels, to the town, where they sold for ready money. To this may be added, the pride which some of the weaker minded officers in the Dutch service very imprudently exhibited to the Japanese, by ill-timed contradictions, contemptuous behavior, scornful looks and laughter, which is greatly increased upon observing in how unfriendly and unmannerly a style they usually behave to each other, and the brutal treatment which the sailors under their command frequently experience from them, together with the oaths, curses, and blows with which the poor fellows are assailed by them. All these circumstances have induced the Japanese, from year to year, to curtail more and more the liberties of the Dutch merchants, and to search them more strictly than ever; so that now, with all their finesse and artifice, they are hardly able to throw dust in the eyes of so vigilant a nation as this.

"Within the water-gate of Dezima, when anything is to be exported or imported, are seated the head and under banjoses, and interpreters, before whose eyes the whole undergoes a strict search. And that the Europeans may not scrape an acquaintance with the searchers, they are changed so often that no opportunity is given them.

"This puts a stop to illicit commerce only, but not to private trade, as everybody is at liberty to carry in whatever he can dispose of, or there is a demand for, and even such articles as are not allowed to be uttered for sale, so that it be not done secretly. The camphire of Sumatra, and tortoise-shell, private persons are not permitted to deal in, because the company reserve that traffic to themselves. The reason why private persons prefer the smuggling of such articles as are forbidden to be disposed of by auction, do not receive ready money for them, but are obliged to take other articles in payment; but when the commodities can be disposed of underhand, they get gold coin, and are often paid twice as much as they would have had otherwise.

"Some years ago, when smuggling was still in a flourishing state, the greater part of the contraband wares was carried by the interpreters from the factory into the town; but sometimes they were thrown over the wall of Dezima, and received by boats ordered out for that purpose. Several of the interpreters, and other Japanese, have been caught at various times in the fact, and punished with death.

"Smuggling has always been attended with severe punishments; and even the Dutch have been very largely fined, which fine has of late been augmented; so that if any European is taken in the fact, he is obliged to pay 200 catties of copper, and is banished the country for ever. Besides this, a deduction of 10,000 catties of copper is made from the Company's account; and if the fraud is discovered after the ship has left the harbor, the chief and the captain are fined 200 catties each.

"The Company's wares do not undergo any search at all, but are directly carried to the storehouse, on which the Japanese fix their seal; where they are kept till they are sold and fetched away.

"The interpreters are natives of Japan, and speak with more or less accuracy the Dutch language. The government permits no foreigners to learn their language, in order that, by means of it, they may not pick up any knowledge of the country; but allow from forty to fifty interpreters, who are to serve the Dutch in their factory with respect to their commerce, and on other occasions. These interpreters are divided into three classes. The oldest, who speak the Dutch language best, are called head interpreters; those who are less perfect, under interpreters; and those who stand more in need of instruction, bear the denomination of apprentices or learners. Formerly the Japanese apprentices were instructed by the Dutch themselves in their language, but now they are taught by the elder interpreters. The apprentices had also, before this, liberty to come to the factory whenever they chose; but now they are only suffered to come when they are on actual service. The interpreters rise gradually and in rotation to preferments and emoluments, without being employed in any other department. Their duty and employment consist in being present—generally, one, or sometimes two of each class—when any affairs are transacted between the Japanese and Dutch, whether commercial or otherwise. They interpret either *vivâ voce*, or in writing. Whenever any matter is to be laid before the governor, the officers, or others, whether it be a complaint or request, they are obliged to be present at all searches, as well at those that are made on board ship as at those which take place at the factory, and likewise to attend in the journey to court. They were formerly allowed to go whenever they chose to the Dutchmen's apartments; but now this is prohibited, in order to prevent smuggling, excepting on certain occasions. They are always accompanied as well to the ships as to their college in the island of Dezima, by several clerks, who take an account of everything that is shipped or unloaded, write permits, and perform other offices of a similar nature.

"Kambang money, or the sums due for goods that are sold, is never paid in hard cash, as the carrying it out of the country is prohibited; but there is an assignment made on it, and bills are drawn for such a sum as will be requisite for the whole year's supply, as also for as much as will be wanted at the fair island. This kambang money is, in the common phrase of the country, very light, and less in value than specie, so that, with the money which is thus assigned over, one is obliged to pay nearly double for everything. All these kambang bills are paid at the Japanese new year only. Every man's account is made out before the ship sails, and is presented and accepted at the college of the interpreters, after which the books are closed. All that is wanted after the new year is taken up upon credit for the whole year ensuing. The 18th of February is, with the Japanese, the last day of the year. On this day all accounts between private persons are to be closed, and these, as well as all other debts, to be paid. Fresh credit is afterwards given till the month of June, when there must be a settlement again. Among the Japanese, as well as in China, in case of loans, very high interest is frequently paid, from eighteen to twenty per cent. I was informed that if a man did not take care to be paid before new year's-day, he had afterwards no right to demand payment on the new year.

"When the Dutch do not deal for ready money, their commerce can hardly be considered in any other light than that of barter. With this view, a fair is kept on the island, about a fortnight before the mustering of the ship, and its departure for Papenberg, a small island near the entrance of the harbor, when certain merchants, with the consent of the governor, and on paying a small duty, are allowed to carry their merchandise thither and expose it to sale in booths erected for that purpose.

"The copper, the principal article of export, was brought from the interior and distant parts of the country, and kept in a storehouse; and as soon as the ship was in part discharged, the loading it with the copper commenced. This latter was weighed, and put into long wooden boxes, a pecul in each, in presence of the Japanese officers and interpreters, and of the Dutch supercargoes and writers, and afterwards conveyed by the Japanese to the bridge, in order to be put on board. On such occasions a few sailors always attend, to watch that the laborers do not steal it, which they will do if possible, as they can sell it to the Chinese, who pay them well for it.

"When the ship is nearly laden, she is conducted to Papenberg, there to remain at anchor, and take in the residue of her cargo, and all the merchandise and other things belonging to the officers, the ship's provisions, etc. A few days after, when the ship has anchored in the harbor, the governor points out the day when she is to sail; and this command must be obeyed so implicitly, that, were the wind ever so contrary, or even if it blew a hard gale, the ship must depart without any excuse, or the least shadow of opposition. Before the ship leaves the harbor, the powder, arms, and the chest of books that were taken out, are returned; the sick from the hospital are put on board; and whilst she is sailing out, the guns are fired to salute the town and the factory, and afterwards the two principal guards at the entrance of the harbor."

It appears that the government allow the free importation of foreign books, provided only they have nothing to do with the Christian religion, and that scientific books from Europe are eagerly sought after by many.

LITERATURE.

We have seen the following curious books:—

I. "First Book for the Education of Youth," with explanations, for teaching Chinese as well as Japanese. This work was published in 1789, and, like most Japanese books, it is illustrated with woodcuts.

II. "The Nightingale resting on the Plum Tree." This is a curious collection of stories, legends, and wild traditions.

III. "The Casket of Jewels, being superior lessons for females."

IV. "Mirror of Female Education." This was published at Jeddo, and reprinted at Osacca in the year 1534. It contains pictures of female occupations and pastimes, pictures of young ladies at their toilette, and others showing how they ought to carry themselves in company.

V. "A Memoir on the Art of Smelting and Purifying Copper."

VI. "The Miriad of Flowers and the Hundred Men." This is a

collection of poetical pieces, said to have been writen by one hundred accomplished persons who had met casually at some pleasant spot. The volume, like so many others, is chiefly intended for female readers.

A friend has translated for us the preface to the "Tale of the Six Folding Screens," the work about which the learned Pfitzmaier has taken so much trouble. It is sufficiently quaint and curious.

The reader will find in this book nothing about fighting with enemies, or about conjurers or magical works, or fairy discourses, or jackalls, or wolves, or toads: nothing about pedigrees, or jewels, or any other lost property. Here are no stories of confusion between the names of father and son, or elder and younger brother; no sealed-up boxes, or hair pins, or mysterious revelations of the gods and Buddhas by means of dreams; no mortal swords pointed against each other; nothing which makes the blood run cold can at all be found in it. Convinced of the incorrectness of the adage, that "Men and folding screens cannot stand unless they be bent," we have here hastily put together, upon this perishable paper, covered with figures, the brief notes of good counsel, as a border or framė, to the tale of six such folding screens under the new forms of this transitory world, who have wholly disdained to bend; and we publish the same to the world.

The best short account of the Japanese language, and the different modes in which it is written, is given by Professor H. Brockhaus, in a review of Hoffmann and de Siebold's Bibliotheca Japonica (Gersdorff's Repertorium. Lpz. 1846, p. 372, ff.).

The first part of a great Japanese Dictionary, by Dr. Pfitzmaier, lately published at Vienna, has been already noticed. Several papers on Japanese dialects, grammar and poetry, by the same savant, have appeared in the report of the transactions of thė Imperial Académie des Sciences, Vienna, 1849 and 1850. A grammar was in course of preparation by the celebrated Chinese scholar, Professor Stephan Endlicher, of Vienna, but interrupted by his death.

Two recent works, by an Englishman, are said to be easy and useful.

An English and Japanese, and Japanese and English Vocabulary, by W. H. Medhurst, Batavia, 1830, and "Translation of a comparative Vocabulary of the Chinese, Corean, and Japanese Languages," by the same author, Batavia, 1835.

Brief as they are, these last notes may possibly be found of some service to such as think of commencing the study of the Japanese language, a knowledge of which will certainly be in great demand.

Some valuable remarks on the affinities of language and the connexion between the Japanese, Tartars, and other eastern peoples, will be found in two articles, "The Ethnology of Eastern Asia," and "The Ethnology of South-eastern Asia," in that valuable publication, the "Journal of the Indian Archipelago and Eastern Asia," vol. iv. Singapore, 1850. Both these papers are written by the editor, J. R. Logan, Esq., Member of the Asiatic Society, etc.

THE END.

www.ingramcontent.com/pod-product-compliance
Lightning Source LLC
LaVergne TN
LVHW020112110826
845151LV00001B/139

9781425543495